ROCK BOTTOM

An American Heartland Farm-Town and Family From Settlement Through the Great Depression

By

JOHN M. WILKINSON

970453

1993
Lexington, Massachusetts

ROCK BOTTOM
An American Heartland Farm-Town and Family
From Settlement Through the Great Depression

By John M. Wilkinson

Copyright © 1993 by John M. Wilkinson

Published by John M. Wilkinson

Printed in the United States of America

Library of Congress Catalog Card number: 93-93935

ISBN 0-9637091-0-0

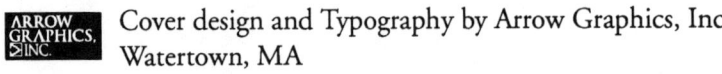 Cover design and Typography by Arrow Graphics, Inc.
Watertown, MA

FOR BUNTY
THE STEADY HAND

&

CHRISTINE AND SYDNEY
THE BELOVED BLIGHTERS

ACKNOWLEDGEMENTS

      I am especially grateful to Mrs. Donald (Novella Wyborny) White and the late Ms. Merle White, former members of the Book Committee of the Rock Falls Bi-Centennial Community Committee, for so generously making available to me their complete files of research notes and working papers, which they had assembled for preparing the <u>Rock Falls Historical Book</u> (1977), a publicly sponsored project for the Bi-Centennial Year observance. Their material assisted me greatly in tracing the history of the Town of Rock Falls, Iowa, from its founding in 1855 to 1920 (my Chapters II, III, and IV) at a great saving of time and effort for me. I also wish to achnowledge with special thanks the careful review and editing of an early draft by Andrew Schrank, at that time a Professor of History, University of Southern California, Los Angeles. My sister, Mrs. Kenneth Hoffman, Hudson, Iowa, and my cousins Ms. Jessie Bliem and Ms. Mary Jane (Bliem) Maxon, were helpful in refreshing my memory on a few occurences in town and family history during the 1920s and 1930s. Finally, I am forever grateful to Bunty, my wife, for generous, continuing professional review, editorial assistance, and patience during the more than four years that I have devoted to writing this history, most of which was spent at the typewriter down here in the cellar.

CONTENTS

PREFACE

CHAPTER I
SETTLING THE HEARTLAND   1

CHAPTER II
THE GOOD OLD DAYS   21

CHAPTER III
THE NOT-SO-GOOD OLD DAYS   46

CHAPTER IV
THE GATHERING STORM   60

CHAPTER V
ROCK FALLS IN THE TWENTIES ... WHAT IT WAS   82

CHAPTER VI
ROCK FALLS IN THE TWENTIES ... HOW IT WAS   92
Peace, Politics, and Prosperity
R.V. and Family
The Seasons
Major Events

CHAPTER VII
ROCK FALLS IN THE THIRTIES ... COPING   127
The Storm Breaks
Crisis Politics
The Local Economy
School Days, School Days
Entertainment

CHAPTER VIII
ROCK FALLS IN THE THIRTIES... HOPING   163
More Politics... Local and Global
Iowa's Skies Brighten... Briefly
Transition
Odette

CHAPTER IX
ANOTHER STORM, ANOTHER WORLD, A FINAL SUMMER   188
Bright Lights
Decisions, Decisions
The Distant Thunder
R. V. at His Best
Indian Summer

POSTSCRIPT — ONE MORE TIME!   210

NOTES

SELECTED BIBLIOGRAPHY

PREFACE

In the 1991 Rand McNally, Commercial Marketing Guide (122nd Edition), a listing of cities, towns, and villages by States, I counted 9,483 place-names with 1980 populations between 25 and 250 inhabitants in 13 midwest States which roughly define America's heartland area. Of these small towns, most are dying. About as many with some 250 to 500 inhabitants are struggling to stay alive. Another 780 hamlets -- no longer towns, each with some 25 people, are dead. Many of these nearly 20,000 small settlements are quiet, clean, friendly, peaceful, crime-free, closely knit communities, many of whose residents wouldn't desire to live anywhere else. But far too many do not enjoy so happy and tranquil a situation. Rather, they are pockets of poverty for the elderly. They are weathered, littered and unsafe, deprived of minimum basic health, transportation, medical, water supply and waste disposal services, police and fire protection, and parks, playgrounds, small libraries, and other public amenities.

What happened? Why should this be? What brought on what is called America's "rural crisis"? How can our nation lavish money on huge urban areas, big corporate farm businesses, frightful military programs, esoteric probes into space, often wasteful foreign aid, and not to mention disgracefully expensive political campaigns, at the same time leaving behind, neglected and forgotten, about two to three millions of mostly needy and elderly persons in our once proud and flourishing farm-town communities?

In writing from first-hand knowledge about just one of these communities, typical of most others, I attempted to reveal the root causes of what has happened and what is still happening throughout the midwestern heartland. The original purpose of my chronicle was to tell my daughters (the two blighters), who grew up in the 1960s and 1970s in a prosperous New England suburb, about life and hard times in the 1920s and 1930s in an impoverished village in Iowa. Those cataclysmic decades marked the beginnings of the end for much of small-town America.

During my working years in New England, I had to fly around the country a lot, frequently to Colorado. Before take-offs on the nonstop Boston-Denver flights, the pilot would routinely inform us "....today's flight will take us over Albany and Buffalo, with a view of the Niagara Falls on your right, then over Lake Michigan, then on over Mason City, Iowa, Grand Island, Nebraska, into Denver." My routime was to work during those long rides, but sight of the magnificent Mississippi River on its winding course across the nation's agricultural heartland demanded my attention. It signaled the flight's major event. When the captain announced our approach above Mason City, it was time for me to peer out, searching for the cluster of small squares on the landscape which defined that prairie metropolis seven miles below. Then I would find the faint features of the Shell Rock River to the northeast of Mason City, a bridge over the river, then a few nearby rooftops. For the rest of the flight over the great colorless Plains to the west, I would think about the little place along the Shell Rock, where the bridge crosses into town, that town beyond whose boundaries I had scarcely ventured for the first 18 years of my life. I would remember Rock Falls as I knew it back then, in the 1920s and 1930s.

During World War II, verbal exchanges among strangers about their origins were means for soldiers to become acquainted. When first meeting a fellow officer in 1942, I described Rock Falls during the recent Great Depression. He responded: "Rock Falls? I'd call it Rock Bottom." So it was in those days, and an apt title for my tale of good times and hard times in a small farm-town community from its settlement in 1855 until the end of the Great Depression and the coming of war in 1940. Framed by larger historical events that surrounded it and thousands of similar small communities in the heartland, my history is also one of political, economic, and social forces that have shaped the nation. Whenever ominous storm clouds again threaten across America, the official counsel is, "Don't worry, it can't happen again." I say, "Don't bet the farm on that."

Lexington, Massachusetts   John M. Wilkinson
March 1993

CHAPTER I

SETTLING THE HEARTLAND

Elijah Wiltfong had to be among the most adventurous young men of his time. On a spring day in 1853, alone astride his horse, he penetrated the uncharted wilderness beyond the fringes of the western frontier, well beyond the chain of small military forts manned by a few federal troops in still hostile and remote Indian country in the recently created State of Iowa. Several days earlier, he had left the family farm in Indiana, and after ferrying across the Mississippi River near the river-town settlement of Davenport, he struck an overland route to a large tributary river. He rode upstream along its banks to a small tributary stream whose course took him still deeper into the rolling prairie grassland. He finally came upon a waterfall, a modest fall of three or four feet over a ledge of shell rock spanning the stream, and it was what he had been seeking. With a small dam raised across this stream, both to heighten the waterfall and to store some of the stream's flow, the prospect was there for a water-powered mill for grinding grains into flour and meal and to saw logs into lumber. For Elijah, this was the place.

Elijah was well-traveled for his 37 years. Born in 1816 in Drake County, Ohio, his parents were of English descent who had been colonial farmers in Vermont before joining a tidal wave of migration to the American heartland in quest of cheaper -- and in the family's hopes, a more fertile and less rocky -- soil than it could find in Vermont. As a young man, Elijah had moved to a farm in Marshall County, Indiana, then to a farm in Laporte, Indiana, on the south shore of Lake Michigan. A seemingly restless fellow, he had taken the long overland routes to California to become a Forty-niner in the gold rush of that year. Soon he returned to the midwest, in 1850, and "by water," it is said. If by water, the journey had to be southward off the Pacific Coast and around Cape Horn, northward off the Atlantic Coast to the St. Lawrence Bay, inland on the river and over a portage to the Great Lakes, and on to Laporte County. Some journey.

Surrounding the banks and waterfalls of what came to be named the Shell Rock River, Elijah quickly staked out a claim to this promising, scenic land. He was in a hurry. Other land-hungry migrants had already beaten him to better sites down-river, hundreds more were on their way, and thousands more were to follow very soon. If a Winnebago tribesman, had been watching from the underbrush by the Shell Rock, as is likely, he would have seen Elijah driving a stake or two in the ground at intervals over a considerable spread of grassland and river-valley woodland before mounting his horse and disappearing into the tall prairie grass. Elijah would seek out a State Land Office where a claim could be recorded based upon the government survey -- if such there existed for this virgin expanse of territory at the time.

He was in a hurry for another important reason. He needed to ride his horse a full 350 miles eastward to Laporte, Indiana, sell the home place and assemble the minimum of transportable provisions, and bring his wife Elizabeth and their three children to the new land in Iowa before the pleasant autumn turned into one of those vicious prairie winters. He must have known that he was in Cerro Gordo County, Iowa from maps or by word of mouth, and he may have known that a county seat of government had yet to be established for that county. The pathes of settlement had fanned out in a rush from the point of entry at Davenport when the State opened land to the settlers. While the State had managed to keep ahead of waves of immigrants with its land survey task, Cerro Gordo County was on the western edge of the frontier. Such few services that could be expected of county government, and particularly those meticulous land recordings, were being handled for Cerro Gordo County by a more settled neighbor, Floyd County, to the east. Its seat was in Charles City, on the Cedar River some 30 miles to the southeast of the Wiltfong claim.

Map I shows the State of Iowa, how it was laid out from the 5th Principal Meridian (the single line superimposed on the map by the State's eastern boundary), and the names of counties and each county seat town. Elijah returned to Indiana by way of Charles City, recording his land claim. It would be known forever more -- for reasons soon to be described herein -- as "the north one-half of Section 21, Township 97 North, Range 19 West, of the 5th

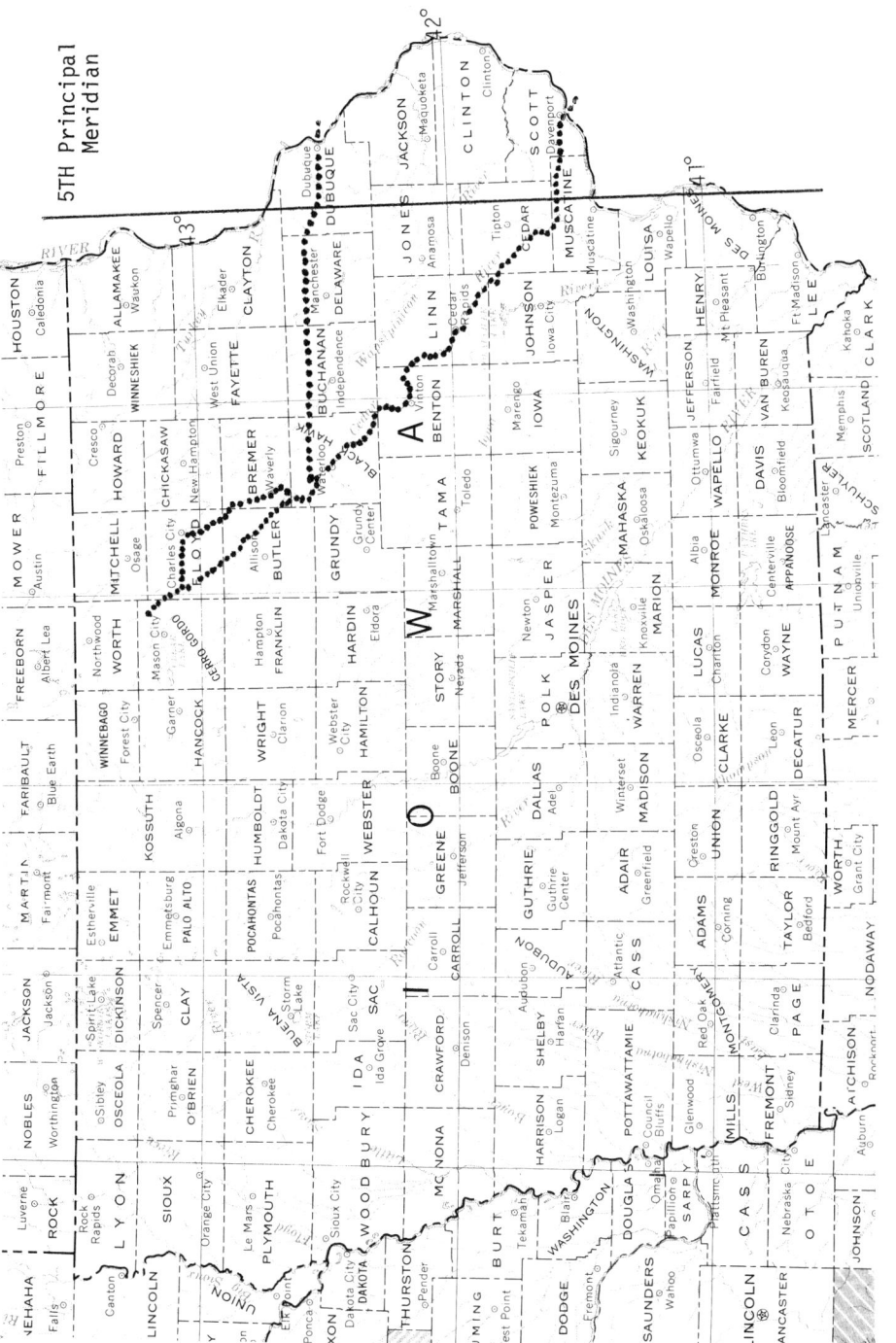

MAP I

STATE OF IOWA, COUNTIES, AND COUNTY-SEAT TOWNS

Principal Meridian, County of Cerro Gordo, State of Iowa." Elijah would then follow the Cedar River downstream to the Cedar Falls, from which he would take a more direct overland route to Dubuque, the earliest of Iowa's river port settlements, and to a ferry across the river to Illinois. There he would follow a wagon trail back to the old family farm in Laporte. His approximate route for the initial round-trip horseback ride is marked by the dotted lines on the accompanying map (page 3).

The family farm was sold quickly, and soon Elijah and his wife and three children headed west to settle the new claim. They ferried the Mississippi at Dubuque, driving two covered wagons pulled by oxen, an oil-cloth covered light wagon pulled by a span of horses, and a small herd of milk cows. The trip was made in the blistering heat of mid-summer. With a good supply of groceries, a stove and a few utensils, they made it all the way to Rock Grove, a small settlement on the Shell Rock River about ten miles downstream from their claim, stopping only as darkness set in each day. Finally in Rock Grove, they rested for a few days with old friends in the home of the J. M. Hunt family then pushed on upstream to their land claim, becoming the very first settlers in Falls Township. A written account that survives called it "an uneventful trip."

The five Wiltfongs lived in a tent on their claim on the north bank of the river until logs could be cut and a one-room cabin was built, with stone fireplace but not any flooring. The family moved into their cabin before winter set in. They ate abundantly, if not well, on deer, elk, bear, buffalo, prairie chickens, and pheasants. There was an abundance of wild fruit and berries in the autumn, such as plums and crabapples, blackberries, raspberries, and strawberries. The river provided a plentiful supply of fish to add to the variety of their diet. There certainly was plenty of wood for the cook stove and the fireplace. A small boat of walnut wood was given to the Wiltfongs by their Rock Grove friends, so that the frequent crossing of the Shell Rock was made easier, and the two daughters were said to have become adept with the pole and paddle. There is no record of their names but the oldest child was a boy named Enoch. The children were of school age, and having been taken from the schools in Indiana, they pursued their studies diligently (so it was said) in their new cabin under the close supervision of their parents. Their first winter was a mercifully mild one but the next several were severe. Nothing is said of what provisions were made for shelter for oxen, horses, and milk cows. Some protection must surely have been provided for them against the winds and snow, as they could not have survived the Iowa winters without it.

Knowing of the flow of immigrants pressing relentlessly westward as the wilderness rapidly came under territorial direction and then statehood, the enterprising Elijah Wiltfong would quickly build his mill dam and saw mill and as hurriedly would have a portion of his section of land on both sides of the river platted to be a town site. In the spring of 1855, he officially founded and named a town called Shell Rock Falls.

Where in the world was this place? What kind of an environment had this young family chosen for its home? To gain some perspective, think of continental America's two great mountain ranges, the Appalachians in the east, the Rockies in the west. Between these mountains is the vast American heartland, shaped like a huge, shallow saucer tilted slightly to the south. This tilt allows the Mississippi River and its many tributaries to drain the water from 1,243,700 square miles of the heartland, an eighth of the continent, into the Gulf of Mexico.

Imagine a line drawn along the 43rd degree north parallel, a line starting near Olean, New York, in view of the Appalachians to the east, and ending near Dubois, Wyoming, in view of the Grand Tetons to the west. Imagine a line also drawn along the 93rd meridian west, starting at Hibbing, Minnesota, to the north, and ending on the Gulf of Mexico near Lake Charles, Louisiana, to the south. The parallel of latitude would be 1,700 miles long, the meridian of longitude 1,250 miles long. Those lines, spanning the widest dimensions, east to west and north to south in the Mississippi drainage basin, would intersect within a stone's throw of the original Wiltfong town site, the very heart of America's heartland.

This huge river system emerges from the springs, the marshes, and the ponds of 28 States and the Canadian Provinces of Alberta and Saskatachewan. Flowing off mountain slopes, a thousand brooks and stream channels take the waters quickly toward the saucer's center and three great rivers form, the Ohio, the Missouri, and the upper Mississippi. They converge near St. Louis to form a giant watercourse that meanders slowly southward to the ocean. The flatness of the heartland is such that, from St. Louis to the river's mouth where freshwater joins saltwater, the Mississippi falls a slight 400 feet, less than six inches per mile. Most of the basin's land surface is less than 1,000 feet above sea level.

Here, in the beginning, were the once vast grasslands which a physiographer of the 19th century named the Rolling Prairies and Great Plains Provinces, now variously called the grain belt, corn belt, heartland, and American breadbasket. In the prairies and central plains, perennial grasses once grew six or eight feet tall in a year; in the semi-arid high plains to the west, four to five feet tall. Bison and pronghorn antelope grazed in this habitat while beaver, quail, and dozens of other fish and wildlife kinds thrived in the lakes, streams, and bordering woodlands. The grazing species would be pushed into the western high plains with the coming of settlement in the Rolling Prairies. In the midwest, deep and fertile soils and abundant rainfall favored more productive uses than grazing. Thus, only few vestiges remain of the original grasslands. This vast undulating prairieland is often monotonous, sometimes beautiful, almost always frightening, a land of grass and underbrush and woodlot under an endless sky. It is a land devoid of mountains, hills, or a visible landmark to give one his bearings, a land baked in the heat of the summer's sun, frozen in the cold of winter's darkness, lashed and drenched and parched in the continental winds, rain, snow, sleet, hail, and dust.

In the very beginning, there was another of nature's species, the North American Indian -- savages and redskins as names they were given. Their ancestors were the mound builders, identified as "slant-eyed, copper-skinned," who migrated from Asia, across the Bering Straits to Alaska and on southward to temperate zones. Some 10,000 or more burial mounds found throughout Iowa, many in village-type clusters, reveal a crude agriculture supported by hunting and fishing. Their artisans produced implements of stone, flint, and wood, made pottery, and carved wood. When the first European began probing inland following 15th century sea voyages of discovery across the North Atlantic ocean, some eight million Indians inhabited the continental landmass north of Mexico. They spoke 275 languages. Well defined cultures had been established.

Before they met their various fates -- uprooting, deportation, resettlement, or annihilation between 1500 and 1850, these earliest Americans were distinguishable by the cultural groups: Plains Farmers and Hunters who inhabited the prairies surrounding the Missouri and lower Mississippi Rivers were the Sioux, Yankton, Santee, Omaha, Ioway, Pawnee, Oto, Kansa, and Missouri; and Northeast Hunters and Fishermen who lived in forested lands of the Mississippi and Ohio River basins were the Chippewa, Sauk, Fox, Kickapoo, Potowatamie, Winnebago, Miami, Illinois, Shawnee and Chickasaw.

The prairie tribes were content to live peaceably when times were good, when the hunting, fishing, and farming provided a needed sustenance. They cultivated maize, squash, and sunflowers on the riverside farms. When times were not that good, nasty encounters over turf occurred. The Northeast tribes were traditionally warlike because of their greater dependence on fish and game from forests and lakes. This led to persistent rivalries over hunting and fishing ground, in good times and bad. The Ioway, meaning "dustyface" in the Sioux dialect, were inclined to a domestic life or to agriculture. They were continally harassed by the warlike Sauk and Fox from the east, who coveted the abundant prairie hunting grounds with their enormous buffalo herds. Long before the white man intruded, this cultural interface made a battleground of the area between the upper Mississippi and lower Missouri Rivers, the area that was made the United States Territory of Iowa in 1838 and was granted statehood by the U. S. Congress in 1846. Still, in a bountiful land, natives probably lived as much in harmony as in conflict.

It was into this sometimes peaceful, often war-torn and always volatile environment that Elijah Wiltfong intruded on that spring day in 1853. By penetrating so far into unmapped wilderness, he was extending the far-western frontier well beyond the ragged edge of safety. The nearest permanent white habitations were several miles to the east. Two other brave, young and land-hungry adventurers, John Long and John McMillan, were thought to have camped along the Winnebago River some ten miles southwest of the shell rock falls in that same year, but nothing suggests that they established contact with Wiltfong. It was also discovered later in that year that several Freemasons had clustered on the banks of the Winnebago River, giving to their embryonic settlement the name Masonic Grove, and at an encampment ten miles west of the Winnebago, a group of families had gathered on the shore of a "clear lake." The seeds of Mason City and Clear Lake, Iowa, were sown.

The sudden influx of foreign migrants to the eastern ports of entry, New York, Boston, Baltimore, and Philadelphia, must have caused immigration officials to wonder at it all. Where were they coming from, why were they coming, where were they going? Answers to these questions can help us to understand the character of the town that grew, prospered, and nearly died along the river with the shell rock and the waterfall. Also, to read again how the young nation acquired immense tracts of land and then disposed of them in small parcels to the flood of immigrants sheds further light on the character of this prairie hamlet.

Three hundred and fifty years earlier, seafaring mariners in the hire of Britain, France, and Spain discovered and mapped most of the eastern shore of the North American continent. The explorers followed, penetrating deep into its interior regions along major water routes -- the St. Lawrence, Hudson, and Mississippi Rivers and the chain of Great Lakes. They were followed in turn by British colonizers, French missionaries and fur traders, and Spanish gold-seekers. In less than one hundred years, the three empire builders from Europe -- England, France, and Spain, had laid their claims and counter-claims to virtually all of the North American landmass. Vast areas were named New England, New France, and New Spain.

Sovereignty over the interior was bitterly contested for the next 200 years, as each power sought to extend its empire into the new world. As the conflict over territory dragged on, there were no clear winners, but the Indians were always the losers, no matter when, where, or whether they allied themselves with the British, French, or Spanish. Then, in rapid succession, three consequential events at 20-year intervals settled for all time (we must assume) the sovereignty issues and the subsequent course of empire on the entire North American continent.

First, in February, 1763, was the signing of a peace treaty in Paris. It ended the Seven Years War, a slaughter that had raged in Europe among the six major powers - France, Spain, Austria, Russia, Prussia, and Britain. Of the adversaries, France lost the most as Britain gained the most. As part of the settlement, treaty provisions also ended the nine-year-old French and Indian War over North America between France and Britain. While scarcely changing political maps of Europe, the Treaty of Paris was of profound significance to America. France gave up all of Canada and the strategically valuable trans-Appalachian Plateau to the British. This plateau constituted all lands drained by the Ohio and Tennessee Rivers from the boundaries of the British seaboard colonies in the Appalachian Mountains west to the Mississippi River, plus land from the Ohio valley north to the Great Lakes. And France gave up to Spain the rich and extensive Louisiana Territory, spreading from the Gulf of Mexico to Canada, from the Mississippi to the western continental divide. Spain ceded all of Florida to the British. By the treaty terms, Britain ruled all of North American land east of the Mississippi, Spain ruled all lands to the west of the river and Mexico, and France lost everything in the new world except minor Caribbean Islands. About all that remained to recall her once powerful presence were place names such as Detroit, St. Louis, St. Paul, New Orleans, Louisville, Dubuque, Champagne, Pierre, La Cross, Lafayette, and dozens more within the great American heartland.

The second momentous event was the signing of still another treaty of peace in Paris, this one in September, 1783, ending the war of the American Revolution. By the treaty terms, Britain gave up all colonial land along the eastern seaboard and extending westward into the Appalachian Mountains. Much more than that, Britain gave to the 13 new American States all of their elongated territorial claims westward to the Mississippi, the valuable Plateau so recently acquired from the French, and a large region east of the Mississippi from the Ohio valley to the shores of the Great Lakes.

The third event occurred on December 20, 1803, when the United States took possession of Louisiana Territory, purchased from Napoleon's France for only 15 million dollars. The severely battered France of 1763 had regained impressive status as a world power following the French Revolution of 1789 and the rise of Emperor Napoleon Bonaparte. He had pressured a weaker Spain to retrocede the vast Territory of Louisiana, ceded by France to Spain in 1763. However, Napoleon too came upon trying times. His European conquests had cost France dearly in men and material; a huge burden of debt had brought the French Treasury to virtual bankrupcy. He was unable to defend far-off Louisiana any longer. U. S. President Thomas Jefferson seized the opportunity, effecting the greatest real estate deal ever conceived -- 828,000 square miles, 531,000,000 acres, at less than three cents per acre, a land immensely rich in oil, natural gas, coal, copper, gold, silver, sulphur, uranium, timber, and some of the finest farmland in the world. Comprising all lands drained by the Missouri and Arkansas Rivers, it extended the public domain of the United States west to the Continental Divide. This famous purchase included Ioway country and the little stream that tumbled across the ledge of shell rock, the waterfall that had attracted the attention of Elijah Wiltfong.

From the beginning of their new-found freedom, the independent but united States faced enormous problems associated with the land claims of settlers. There were only 13 States, and they had settled a mere 4.5 percent of the land from the east coast to the Continental Divide. Seven States claimed not just their colonial lands but all lands due west of them to the Mississippi, those which had been given up by the defeated British. And six States had no claims to this trans-Appalachian Plateau; still, they had fought just as hard for independence as had all the other seven. They felt that all newly acquired lands should be ceded to the <u>national</u> government for later distribution as public domain to additional States to be formed as the westward migration populated the interior heartland.

The situation in the Plateau lands had become rather chaotic. The question of ownership in the sense of <u>sovereignty</u> was settled by simple transfer by the peace treaty. The same question about Louisiana Territory was settled by the purchase from Napoleon's France. But these transfers by no means settled, nor could they even address, the far more complex question of individual ownership of specific parcels. There were more than enough contending parties -- land speculators, colonial land companies, war veterans and charter grantees, settlers, Indians -- for parcels of land. In the absence of any surveys, there was no descriptor or measurement of disputed parcels, quite apart from the legalities of claims, except for such markers as river bends, rock piles, and hatchet marks in a tree's trunk, to define alleged ownership. With only 30,000 settlers west of the Appalachians and perhaps half a million Indians, it was clear that the new nation needed to people its western lands quickly or risk losing them, either back to the Indians, the French, the Spaniards, or the British. But concerted inducements to settle the heartland had to await a desperately needed land ownership policy.

Twenty-five years elapsed before the United States could manage to resolve the State claims. Georgia was the last to cede its land to the national government, in 1802, marking the end of a dispute, the outcome of which was of far-reaching significance. In all, some 200 million acres were passed by eastern seaboard States to the Congress of the United States as public domain for territorial, and ultimately new State, administration.

The source of conflict over individual ownership remained, and it was a vexing problem. How to define the entirety of the wilderness, simply and uniformly, such that the federal government could proceed to dispose of it to settlers with assurance that their purchases would give them firm, precise, and lasting title? Without a definition, settlements would be impeded by land title litigation, boundary disputes, overlapping claims, faulty survey and confusing records, a veritable gold mine for frontier lawyers! Fortunately, farsighted statesmanship prevailed over greed in legislation passed to deal with the problem. This landmark legislation, the Land Ordinance Act of 1785, was among the most important and admirable -- if historically most often overlooked -- measures ever enacted by an American legislature. Actually, it was the work of the Continental Congress under the Confederation of States, adopted while disputes over State's cessions of Plateau lands were still unresolved. Full implementation was delayed for a quarter of a century by political maneuverings and by lack of a federal means to pay for implementation costs, and by the persistent Indian hostilities that hindered field survey work.

The Ordinance established principles for disposing of the public domain to settlers. These principles came to be extended to all western lands coming into federal possesion, and they were even adopted by Canada, Australia, and New Zealand. First, there was the principle that a proper land survey must precede a sale of land. The survey was to be based upon a pattern of east-west (baseline) and north-south (prime meridian) alignments, the socalled rectangular survey. Its starting point, or first intersection of alignments was the point where the Ohio River crossed the western boundary of the State of Pennsylvania. Clearly, the survey could apply only to lands to the west, not a seaboard State in which a hodge-podge of ownerships had been defined by the colonists since 1620. As settlement moved westward, more meridians and baselines would be started when, where, and if needed. Thus, the new system would not disturb ownerships in former colonies, but it would profoundly influence the landscape of the heartland.

Please see drawings that describe this system on page 12.

From the fixed starting point, a baseline would be drawn due west across which rangelines would be drawn at right angles (north-south) at six-mile intervals from the first principal meridian (of many to follow). Parallel baselines (east-west) would also be drawn at six-mile intervals. Within this grid of lines, each six square miles would be a "township," each numbered in ascending order eastward and westward from the principal meridian and northward and southward from the baseline (Drawing #1). Each township would be further cross-hatched into 36 "Sections," such that a section would comprise a square mile of 640 acres, each numbered in zigzag fashion toward the west and then toward the east within the township starting with number one in the northeast corner of the townships (Drawing #2). This checkerboard pattern became the universal delineation of all lands. It was particularly important for later homesteading on the 160 acres quarter section typical of the socalled family farm and subdividing into smaller farms (Drawing #3). Its creation was the stroke of genius as it offered a solution to massive problems of the settlement era. Henceforth, any recording of title on original purchase from the government or subsequent sale between any settlers and farmers or developers would be by a township and a range number as descriptors rather than by the tree notches and the rock piles.

A second principle of the Ordinance was a consistent reservation of land for educational purposes. Every township in the heartland was to reserve Section 16 of its 36 sections for "school land." This reservation, a carryover from the New England town system, was intended to disperse thousands of one-room country schoolhouses more or less evenly throughout rural America. They became "one-room" because the original concept of the 16th section for the Township center of education had to be abandoned in favor of a larger number, usually eight or ten, ten-acre tracts for schoolhouses spread around each township for better service to farmsteads within walking distance. Educational efficiency and economy were sacrificed for convenience to the farmers and their child laborers. These schoolhouses, meager as they were, would become prairie landmarks -- havens for winter travelers caught in the sudden blizzard, centers of box socials and country dances, meeting places for neighborhood clubs and boards, launching pads for careers of many notables in American history.

A third principle dealt with financial matters. This required competitive bidding at public auction for a land parcel. The lowest bid permitted would be two dollars per acre. Once offered at auction but not bought, lands could then be bought at the minimum price without bidding. Payment was to be by cash on the barrel-head, no credit to

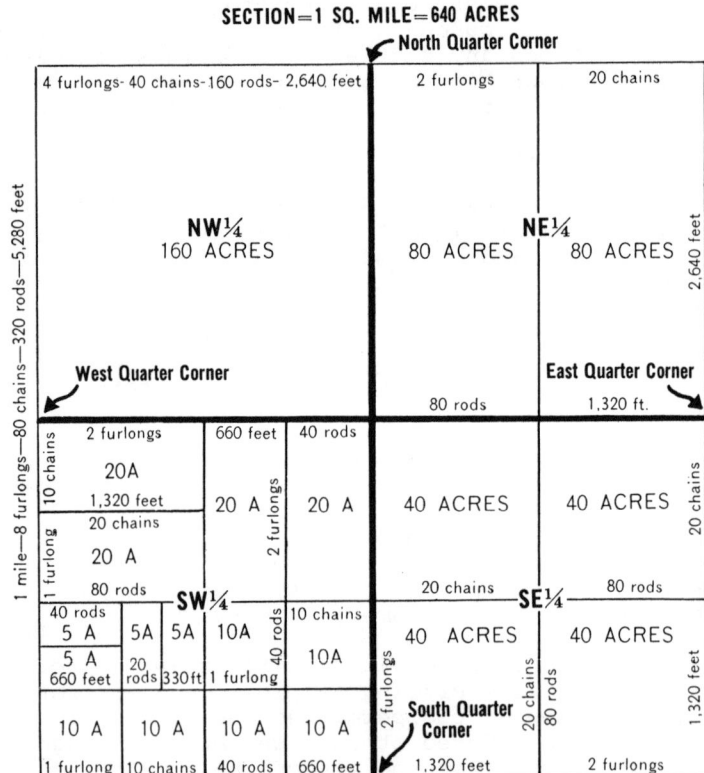

DRAWING #1 — Dividing an area into townships.

DRAWING #2 — A townships divided into sections. Section 1 through 6 on the north side and 7, 18, 19, 30, and 31 on the west side are fractional sections.

DRAWING #3 — Section of land showing acreage and distances.

Source:
U.S. Department of Agriculture Yearbook 1958

be given, no mortgages. These were very harsh terms for the times, but necessitated by the weak fiscal condition of the new government in Washington and its need for funds to pay for survey costs.

The Ordinance also provided for delineating immense land areas as "territories" pending growth in population. So long as the territories had few settlers widely dispersed, they would have only a territorial Governor, one Secretary, and three judges each, appointed by the Congress. When populations rose to 5,000 male adults, an elected assembly was permitted. Then, with 60,000 or more inhabitants, right of statehood was assured in the federal Union on a basis of equality with the original founding States. This system of gradually increasing autonomy was intended to prepare each future State to assume its position of equality, partnership, and responsibilities with all of the others. Finally, the Ordinance guaranteed religious freedom to every citizen, the right of habeas corpus, the right of trial by jury, and other freedoms now taken for granted, but at the time beyond the wildest dreams of oppressed peoples everywhere. It also declared against slavery or other involuntary servitudes within any State, a matter sure to cause conflicts as "border" States -- partly northern, partly southern -- sought admission to the Union.

Thus, settlement was vastly facilitated and emigration to America was accelerated. As the survey came to be adequately funded, the disposal of public domain proceeded "with bewildering rapidity," as one historian wrote. Slowly at first, this great historical folk migration ultimately became a tidal wave.

When the Declaration of Independence was being drafted in 1775, British colonists numbered about 2,500,000, of which some 500,000 were negro slaves imported from Africa, primarily to the five southernmost colonies. Fifteen years later and after the war, the first U. S. Census, of 1790, counted just under 4,000,000 Americans. During these 15 years, few immigrants could get to America due to war in the colonies, a war-ravaged Europe, and consequent lack of ships. The immigration statistics were not compiled until 1820, but estimates of arrivals in America during those 30 years, 1790 to 1820, were only 7,800 on average annually, 234,000 all together. During the next 40 years, more than 5,400,000 "passengers of foreign birth" arrived, 125,000 a year. These numbers, plus the movement westward by colonial Americans from "back east," were more than enough to transform the wilderness to territorial status, then to statehood, in a rapid succession of entrants to the Union.

The surge westward began through the Cumberland Gap, discovered in 1750 by the trapper Thomas Walker nearby the far southwest corner of Virginia. This Gap, one of a few easy overland passageways through the Appalachians, giving Kentucky and Tennessee Territories early statehood in 1792 and 1796, respectively. The next was Ohio, in 1803, after three years of territorial status. It was just down river from Pennsylvania and closest along the Indian trails that lead westward out of New York State. Louisiana was next, in 1812. The Great Lakes offered an excellent water route access to Indiana and Illinois territories, so they were next, in 1816 and 1818, respectively.

Missouri Territory was established in 1805 but statehood was delayed by bitter controversy until 1821, due to Missourians wanting slavery despite the 1785 Ordinance prohibition. Finally, the Congress reached the famous Missouri Compromise, allowing Missouri to enter as a slave State, with Maine, created out of Massachusetts colonial lands, admitted as an offsetting free State, so preserving a delicate political balance. The Compromise further banned slavery in future States north of Missouri's southern border, about longitude 30 degrees. Wisconsin and Michigan became States in 1836 and 1837, respectively. Then slave States of Alabama and Mississippi, originally in colonial Georgia territory, entered in 1817. Arkansas entered the Union in 1836.

That is how matters stood a third of the way into the new century -- 13 original States, 13 added to the young nation with lands four times the size of colonial America spreading from the Atlantic to the Mississippi and on into the High Plains. It had all happened so fast. Total population had more than quadrupled to about 20,000,000 inhabitants, overtaking those in Britain, or France, or the German States of Prussia, and Bavaria. Incredibly, millions would uproot themselves, striking out on a fantastic point-of-no-return venture into the dangerous American unknown. Who were they, where were they from, why did they do it, knowing that the journey meant hardships by land, unbelievable dangers, disease, and filth during the sea passage, then humiliations, fraud, and thefts by unscrupulous "helpers" at points of entry to the new world?

A clue to national origins of the four million colonials is found in the official Census of 1790. The immediate post-revolutionary war residents were largely Anglo-Saxon. The white population was 60.9 percent English, 9.7 percent Irish, 8.3 percent Scot, 8.7 percent German, and the remaining 12.4 percent a mix of Dutch, French, Swedish, Italian, and Norwegian. They were the immigrants and descendants of immigrants who colonized the eastern seaboard. While generally of a rural caste, they brought a variety of occupational skills, including artisans in the building trades, millers, weavers, shopkeepers, factory workers, preachers, and teachers. Together, these "urban" groups probably outnumbered colonial farmers. The variety is explained by a diversity of reasons -- political, social, religious, economic -- for taking the great plunge into the new world. Others had not actually taken this plunge; some 50,000 were criminals and felons, shipped out by the British government, never a well-publicized fact.

As political unrest and religious intolerance diminished in Europe and as social improvements were grudgingly offered by the aristocracy and clergy, the rationale for emigrating changed markedly. Cheap land and superior economic opportunities in America as perceived by the still hopelessly disadvantaged and landless peasantry of continental Europe provided the motivation. Vestiges of feudalism persisted, with great numbers in bondage to baronial estates, disproportionately taxes, required to share the fruits of their exhausting labors with lords of the manor, doomed to a lifetime of grinding toil. These conditions served to swell the ranks of immigrants from central Europe. For Britains and Scots, sordid conditions for the factory workers -- 12-hour days, six days a week for all ages, at unsafe machines, in smoke-clogged and soot-laden mill towns -- assured a continuing tide of emigrants, as did the disastrous potato famines in Ireland.

A third factor in the 1800s for the 20 million or more who came shortly after the colonies became States was the promotional pitch of the new "developer" class in America which arose following resolution of the land policy questions by the 1785 Ordinance. This new breed of speculators touted cheap American land in the European presses and by the pamphlets and handbills circulated throughout the old world. They and their counterparts in foreign syndications, as well as back-east Yankee promoters, put together land companies and purchased extensive tracts of farmlands for resale at handsome profits. Territorial governments, seeking early statehood, also touted their wares.

Liberal as the Ordinance was, legislation became more so by the 1820s. The U. S. Congress made land purchasing terms easier by reducing the minimum $2.00 per acre purchase price, then the all-cash payments terms, then the minimum 640-acre purchase required by the Ordinance. In 1796, one-half of the payment could be in cash, one-half on credit. In 1800, the minimum purchase could be but 320 acres, a half section. In 1804, it could be 160 acres, the family farm concept. In 1820, only an 80-acre minimum purchase was allowed and a $1.25 per acre price. In 1832, 40 acres was purchasable at $1.25 per acre. In all, the attractions were irresistible and the Ordinance principle effectively demolished.

The remarkable influx of more than 33 million Europeans in a century's time, 1820 to 1920, was only 14,000 per year in the 1820s, then rose rapidly until 1837, primarily from the United Kingdom. Thereafter, arrivals surged to 427,000 in 1854, mostly Germans. The average in the 1850s was nearly 260,000, largely due to the Irish famines and to central European political upheavals and agricultural depressions. A new surge occurred from 1900 to the start of World War I in Europe, but the countries of origin had changed. No longer were there so many from the United Kingdom and Germany; great numbers were from Italy, Austria-Hungary, and Russia. Few of the latter were destined for the heartland, rather populating the fast urbanizing east coast region. The 100-year totals were:

United Kingdom	8.1 million
Germany	5.6
Italy	4.1
Austria-Hungary	4.0
Russia	3.2
Scandinavia	2.1
Canada	1.0
France	0.6
All others	4.6
Total	33.3 million

But why did it take so long to settle Iowa country so that it could gain statehood? There are two good reasons: geography and Indians. First, getting to the heart of the heartland was not so easy in those days. Generally, early settlement followed watercourses; upstream along the St. Lawrence and Mississippi, downstream on the Ohio and then through the Great Lakes. The Erie Canal, connecting the Hudson River with Lake Erie at Buffalo, was not opened until 1825. The Great Lakes added unexcelled flatwater navigation routes to the interior, but none offered a direct and quick access. Besides, with attractive land available along the pathways to Iowa country, and at $1,25 per acre, why venture further inland than necessary?

Robert Fulton proved in 1817 that a steamboat could go from New Orleans up-river to St. Louis in 36 days, back in 12 days. By 1831 the return trip was only seven days. By 1834, the number of steamboats using the Mississippi, Missouri, and Ohio rivers as transportation arteries rose to 230. Still, most immigrants arrived at Atlantic ports, the shortest distance from Europe. From 1821 to 1860, only ten percent came to the Port of New Orleans, the rest to east coast ports, mostly New York. How extraordinarily difficult it was in the early years of this huge new nation to get from one place to another. There were only crude wagon trails and the rivers as "roadbeds." Not until 1826 did "rail" roads, horsedrawn or stationery, come into use, and steam-driven railroads traversed only 23 miles in 1830.

Geography was a hindrance, all right but relations with the Indians, initially favorable and accomodating on both sides, would soon worsen. The usual problems were made worse by rapid settlement in surrounding States to the east and south of Iowa -- in Wisconsin, Illinois, and Missouri. Whether by phony treaties, persuasion, the lure of cheap whiskey, or outright warfare, the Indian nations were being pushed westward with unrelenting pressure along a broad front.

Settlement near the Mississippi River above St. Louis came in 1788 when the Fox Indians granted Julian Dubuque rights to mine extensive lead deposits. This region was fabulously rich in fur-bearing animals, so trading posts were soon established where Indians brought pelts to exchange for guns, blankets, ornaments, and whiskey. The American Fur Company had river posts at Keokuk, Eddyville, Muscatine, Sioux City, and Council Bluffs. George Davenport, a U.S. soldier, traded furs near the river city that now bears his name. Maurice Blondeau, a French trapper, traded furs on the Des Moines River for John Jacob Astor to sell in Paris and London fashion shops. Many trappers and soldiers married Indians. In 1824, a small settlement below Keokuk was established called Half-Breed Tract, where Indians and whites intermingled peacefully. Later, it was left for the children of these "marriages."

The peaceful times soon ended. Iowa land was part of Missouri Territory in 1812, reverting to unorganized public domain when Missouri gained statehood in 1821. Inadequate federal laws governing the public domain caused relations with the Indians to deteriorate rapidly. Relentless settlement pressures on the Sauk and Fox tribes led to vicious, brutal, and prolonged engagements throughout 1832. Battles of the Black Hawk War, named after a Sauk chieftain, were especially savage. By the punitive treaty following capture of this chief, tribal lands in eastern Iowa country for 50 miles to the west of the river were ceded to the United States. Called the Black Hawk "Purchase" only because a 30-year, $20,000 annuity sum was granted as a gesture to the friendly Keokuk faction, this immensely rich region was surrendered to the whites, except for a 400-square-mile reservation, and even that was surrendered in 1836, as the tribes were pushed westward into Kansas Territory with the false assurance that a similar reservation awaited them in that semi-arid, barren, and desolate land.

Iowa lands were made a part of Michigan Territory in 1834 and, when Michigan gained statehood, were transferred to Wisconsin Territory. By this time, some half a million impatient immigrants, camped in nearby Missouri and Illinois, became insistent in demands that the United States should open Iowa to settlement. Finally, on June 1, 1838, the Territory of Iowa was officially approved, providing badly needed courts of law and administration. The Black Hawk Purchase lands were thrown open for settlement.

The rush was on. Land hungry pioneers jammed all the trails leading to the Mississippi crossings, waiting for days during that summer before rowing across, then spreading like wildfire across Iowa's prairie. The ones in front staked out farm lands in the rich, tree-lined river bottom soils, later ones grabbed for the higher, treeless rolling prairies where grass grew shoulder high, still later ones settled in towns along the big river -- Dubuque, Davenport Burlington, and Keokuk. About 50 persons had lived on the river's west side in 1832; within eight years, more than 43,000 had settled there. The point of entry, the ferry crossing near Davenport, was kept busy night and day, for the rest of the decade.

The first Territorial Legislature for Iowa met in November 1838 in a Methodist church in Burlington on the Mississippi River bank. Government land surveys were soon initiated and land offices opened from east to west as the needs dictated. A fixed price of $1,25 per acre was set and protection of settlers' claims against speculators was provided. The Legislature also authorized the building of roads and schools. The frontier moved westward quickly to 90 miles west of the river by 1845. Following the frontier for protection, Fort Des Moines, Camp Kearny, Fort Atkinson, Fort Groghan, and Fort Sanford were built and manned by the U. S. Army. By 1837, a million and a quarter acres in eastern Iowa Territory had been given up by the Sauk and Fox Indians. In 1842, the Potowatamis of southwestern territorial lands were moved into Minnesota Territory, but the troublesome Sioux of the north remained to be dealt with. Soon even they would be west of the Missouri River, far from their porductive hunting grounds, onto the barren plains of Kansas and the Dakotas. It was a harsh settlement for the Indian nations.

Farming was no picnic in those early years. The hard prairie sod didn't give up easily. It had to be broken with a horsedrawn, wooden-bladed plow with a metal strip at the share, guided from behind by the walking farmer. For the first year's planting, a few kernels of seed corn were poked into the overturned sod. This yielded less than a half a crop, but it broke up the soil, making the second year's work easier. Markets were distant, so grains and hogs were consumed on the farm. Hard-up Territorials were in no hurry for statehood under early conditions, as the "feds" paid administrative costs under territorial status, hence no State taxes.

However, the politicians could smell a good thing for themselves in statehood. They promoted a vote in 1844 for a constitution. This fixed the boundaries to be defined, come statehood, to include all land between the big rivers north of Missouri and south of the new Northwest Territory (later Minnesota). A second convention in May 1846, obtained settler approval of a revised constitution in August, pushed the statehood application through the U. S. Congress, and had it signed by President James Polk on December 28 of that year. The process was speeded to completion by larger political maneuvers. Territorial Florida had sought admission as a slave State since 1838, and Iowa now provided the opportunity for a "pair" with Florida to preserve the north-south political balance.

The region north of the Iowa border to the southern border of Canada remained Northwest Territory, acquired as part of the Louisiana Purchase. Pressure mounted for settlement and public administration. In 1849, a bill organizing the Territory of Minnesota for its 6,077 settlers passed the U. S. Congress. With the State constitutional convention in July 1857, a special census showed 150,037 settlers in the territory, more than enough to permit the statehood status. This was achieved quickly; on May 11, 1858, Minnesota was admitted to the Union.

To the west vast tracts of the Louisiana Purchase remained as Nebraska Territory and Kansas Territory, both organized in 1854. These lands, situated north of line 36 degrees, 30 minutes, and extending to the Canadian border, were "free" -- not slave -- lands by the Missouri Compromise of 1820. The Kansas-Nebraska bill and Act of May 30, 1854, creating these two territories was hotly contested because, by not excluding slavery, the Compromise was effectively repealed. The consequence was to revive all of the old animosities over slavery. A bloody tug-of-war in Kansas Territory over the slavery issue ended in victory for the "Jayhawkers" who brought Kansas into the federal Union as a free State in 1861. A much more peaceful passage into statehood for Nebraska would be delayed by the Civil War until 1867, but it excluded public domain north of the 43d parallel. This remained Dakota Territory, basically a huge Indian reservation, for another two decades. Finally, the insatiable hunger for land by the continuing tidal wave of settlers saw North Dakota and South Dakota into the Union in 1889. So much for political subdivision of the American heartland.

So there you have it -- my elementary historical perspective for a century, more or less, as the forerunner to my tale of a prairie town on the banks of the Shell Rock. Iowa was now four years into statehood, its population going from zero in 1800 to 192,214 in 1850. It would grow to 1,194,200 by 1870, more than 60,000 a year on average. Land and freedom were indeed irresistible. The uncertain and dangerous years were passing, a bridgehead across the Mississippi was firmly established. Now would be a time to build. Still, to Elijah Wiltfong in 1853, there remained more uncertainty and danger than was to his liking as he ferried the river and disappeared into the tall grasses. Like the thousands who joined the trek to Iowa, he had to be young, rugged, tough, and brave, or he would not have been there looking for land and a mill-dam site. For all of them, it was well worth the chances taken.

This phenomenal growth phase would mean exciting and busy times, as the prairie came under the plow, as industries formed and flourished, and as communities were laid out and built up. The development of Rock Falls as a community of farmers and townspeople was representative of thousands more larger -- but few smaller -- communities throughout the heartland. The same kinds of things were happening, the same events, problems, successes, and failures were being experienced everywhere.

So much for background. My tale has taken us a long way into new territory and into the 19th century. Now let us have a look at the Township of Falls, 97 North Range, 19 West of the 5th Principal Meridian, the County of Cerro Gordo, State of Iowa.

CHAPTER II

THE GOOD OLD DAYS

Actually, a great many of them were not good old days in the least; there was unremitting disappointment, hardship, and tragedy for far too many of those venturesome pioneers. What made them seem good in the memories of the settlers and their descendants was largely relative -- relative to what many of them and their sons and daughters came to experience in the devastating years of the 1920s and 1930s. They were also good new days compared with the earlier days of peasantry and servitude in central Europe, of drudgery and toil in industrial Britain, of poverty and famine in Ireland. While the midwestern prairies and the Great Plains to the west came to be alluded to as "next-year country," as there was always hope after a year of crop failures that next year would see better crops, still for most of those who had emigrated to America every year was better than the year before.

Ancestors of 19th century midwesterners called them the good old days because they heard their forbears talk about the happy times more than about the grim times. This was a reflection of the irrepressible optimism of those people and that age. They remembered the family life, the struggles, the children growing up, the church and school picnics and parties, the sleigh rides, the quilting bees, threshing seasons, husking bees, box socials, shivarees, and the Fourth of July celebrations. They remembered the farm-town's community of spirit, strong feelings that they were all in this risky venture together and would stick together -- for protection against Indians, speculators, patent medicine men, and assorted "out-of-town jaspers." They remembered the neighborly readiness with never a moment's hesitation to assist in times of sickness and injury when there wasn't a doctor within a two days' buggy ride away, to help in the plantings and harvestings to beat the threatening weather, to share when one or more among them was wiped out by hail or tornado. These were what made it the good old days. Moreover, despite incredible uncertainties and hazards, there was a certain predictability to events, year in and year out, in the insulation and isolation of small rural settlements, a predictability that was not to survive complexities to come in the 20th century.

The United States Army had not been altogether successful in Indian removals and for securing the frontier to the extent that settlers had generally been led to expect from government forces. There was the ever present threat of brief but often savage skirmishes with the withdrawing tribes. It was a shameful, degrading period in American history, a period rarely told of, talked about, documented in its full ugliness and savagery. Who were the savages, who the savaged? Who were the civilized, who the uncivilized? The Spirit Lake Massacre in Dickinson County, on the Minnesota border, is used in history books to portray the brutal redskins; rare are the accounts of brutal whites at their cruelist. Many were the years of rough times before the good times came.

The first Indian scare for the Wiltfongs came in the summer of 1854 when Elizabeth and the children were alone in their cabin. Elijah was back in Indiana obtaining more provisions. From an encampment of Sioux Indians on the banks of the Shell Rock a few miles upstream, two armed "braves" came to the cabin, asked for food, were given some, and left quietly. But soon the word was abroad of potential Indian troubles, so the Wiltfongs returned to friends in Rock Grove to await Elijah's return. Fortunately, the Indian uprising called the Grindstone War, 20 miles west at Clear Lake, on July 4, did not spread to the Shell Rock River valley.

It would be another summer before a group of bold but foolish men and their families penetrated far beyond the frontier line of populated settlements, there to trigger Iowa's best-known and most tragic events of the period -- the Spirit Lake Massacre. Rowland Gardner and Harvey Luce and their wives and children virtually invited this incident by needlessly venturing so far into unknown territory, miles to the west of Wiltgong's claims and without hope of protection from the U. S. Army. They were soon joined by Dr. Isaac Herriott, Alvin Noble, J. M. Thatcher, and William Marble and their families in a settlement of crude huts and cabins on the shores of West Okoboji Lake, 119 miles west of Falls Township. This band of 36 whites in a world of redskins barely survived the cold winter of 1857.

In the spring, a few hungry Wahpeton Sioux, a fierce

and warring tribe, led by their outlaw chieftain, Inkpaduta, swarmed about the cluster of cabins demanding food. As the meager food supplies were being divided and shared, the Indians began killing the families. When it was over, 32 whites had been brutally massacred. Of four briefly spared women, Mrs. Thatcher was pushed into the lake and drowned, Mrs. Noble was beaten to death, and Mrs. Marble and Abigail Gardner were ransomed and set free. Only Miss Gardner lived to give a first-hand account of the murderous assault by the "repulsive, pock-marked Inkpaduta" and his bloodthirsty Sioux companions, none of whom was later apprehended.

This tragic incident was but one of many brutal massacres inflicted by each side against the other, as the white man pushed the red man inexorably westward onto less fertile land and less productive hunting grounds. These brutalities were an outgrowth of disappointments, leading to bad feelings, then to anger, and finally to savage retaliations by Indians on defenseless whites, scalping and raping, stealing and beating, drowning and butchering. But similar raids had long been inflicted upon helpless Indians by savage white men. Another nearby massacre of hundreds of white settlers centering around New Ulm, Minnesota Territory, 105 miles northwest of Shell Rock Falls, would soon prompt a call to the U. S. Army in Washington from the territorial governments for more troops and more forts along the frontier. Small wonder that the Elijah Wiltfong family lived in terror that first summer of 1854 on their claims. It might have been said of them too that they were foolhardy to have probed so deeply into the vast wilderness.

During the next spring, in 1855, Elijah built a small dam just upstream from his claims, near "the mouth of the creek," as it is known to this day, where a small tributary flows into the Shell Rock from the northeast, but the dam was washed out in the spring floods. Later he built a water-powered saw and grist mill on his claims, diverting some of the river's flow into a flume leading to the mill wheel. He soon turned the operation over to his son Enoch and took up blacksmithing. Elizabeth died in 1861 of a long illness and what must have been a terribly hard life. In 1862, Elijah remarried and in 1863 sold his properties and moved with his new wife to the west coast. Nothing more was heard of the original pioneer founder of the town of Shell Rock Falls.

Other settlers appeared in Falls Township singly or in groups of families during 1854 and 1855 (see Map II, circa 1895, on page 24), among them James and Clarissa Wright (Section 16), Robert and Amanda Campbell (Section 16), Richard and Fannie Morris (Section 22), Thomas Perrett (Section 16), J. C. Perrett (Section 17), Joseph Perrett (Section 17), Charley Johnson (Section 17), Horace

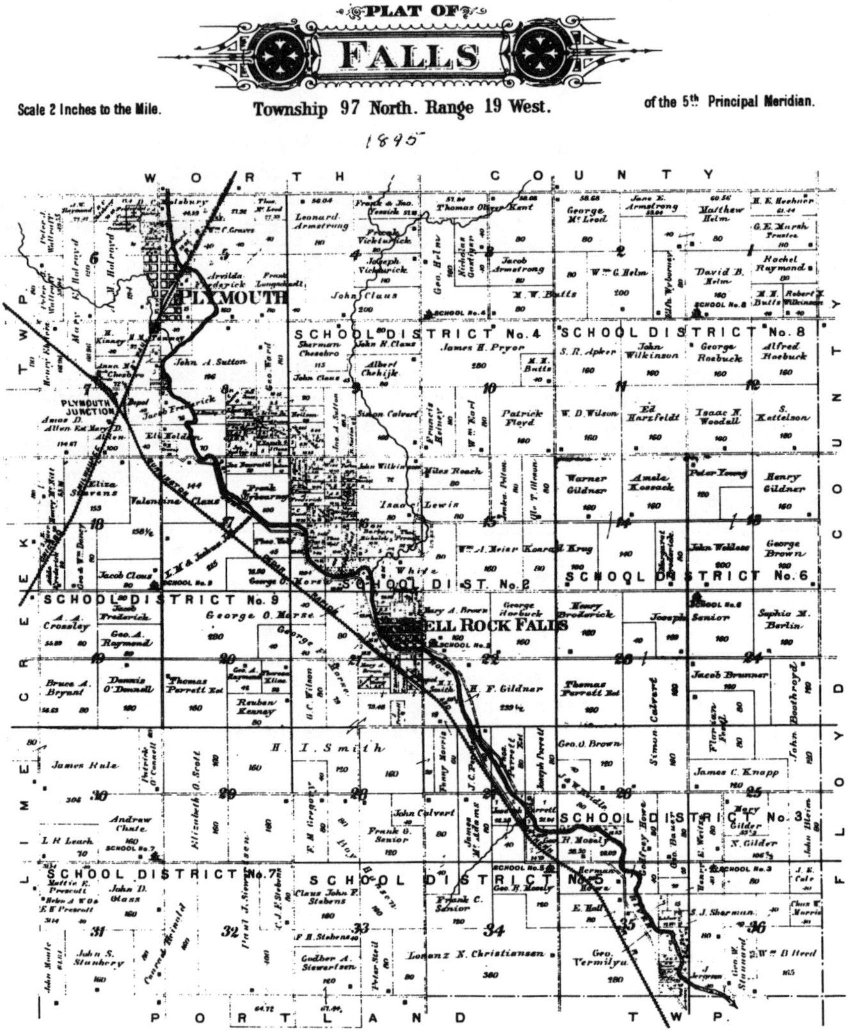

Scale 2 Inches to the Mile.   Township 97 North. Range 19 West.   of the 5th Principal Meridian.

1895

MAP II

(Source: Rock Falls Historical Book, 1977)

and Sally Gregory (Section 17), Ira Williams (Section 17), George and Helen Vermilya (Section 35), Henry and Mary Senior (Section 15), and John and Hannah Brown (Section 20). As the names suggest, these earliest of families to make their homes in Falls Township were of Scotch-Irish and English origins. Most of them stayed to become farmers, millers, hired hands, or merchants and to raise large families, but there is a story of one family not so lucky.

Mr. and Mrs. Rolfe and their five children arrived in Falls Township and staked a claim to land near the Worth County line in the winter of 1855. One day, the parents went to the little settlement of Nora Springs, just seven miles downstream on the Shell Rock River, for provisions. They stayed at the James Wrights for two nights in nearby Rock Grove, then began the return to their home north of the Shell Rock Falls town site. They traveled by sled pulled by two yoke of oxen. They were caught in a blizzard, a common predicament for farm families for a century or more in the northern prairies and plains. That night a pair of their oxen appeared back at the Wright's place, a forewarning of trouble. The next morning, Charley Johnson found Mr. Rolfe's frozen body in the sled, and his wife's frozen body was later found three miles away. Apparently she had gone in search of help or shelter. Their bodies were taken to the Wiltfong place to be buried in a single coffin in a grove behind the house near an old trail along the river. The children were taken back east by friends.

Shell Rock Falls (later shortened to Rock Falls at the insistence of the railroad company to avoid confusion with another town named Shell Rock, downstream) was officially founded in the spring of 1855. The Town land, part of the original 320-acre Wiltfong claims which had been deeded to Andrew J. Glover, a merchant and land speculator, included all of Section 21 north and east of the river and the parcel earlier deeded by Wiltfong to Glover south and west of the river. These lands were surveyed on April 25 and 26 and laid out in blocks, streets, and alleys (see Map III, page 26). Other residents at the time of founding were recorded as David Johnson who ran a public house or two-room hotel, Jesse Clausen, a blacksmith, George Bruce, Joseph Wolesberry, Enoch Wiltfong, and T. W. Lane. Mr. Glover sold most of his lots to eastern land agents, keeping some choice lots along the river, and he built a store and post office on Main Street. This first store in town was purchased the following year and expanded into a fine general store by L. E. Eager. As nearly as can be estimated, some 20 adults and 30 or 40 children resided within the town's boundaries or just outside at the founding, and there were perhaps 15 structures of one kind or another in town.

Unlike some Counties of odd shapes and sizes reflecting in part how States were carved out of territorial land areas, Cerro Gordo County, Iowa, was a classic square, 24

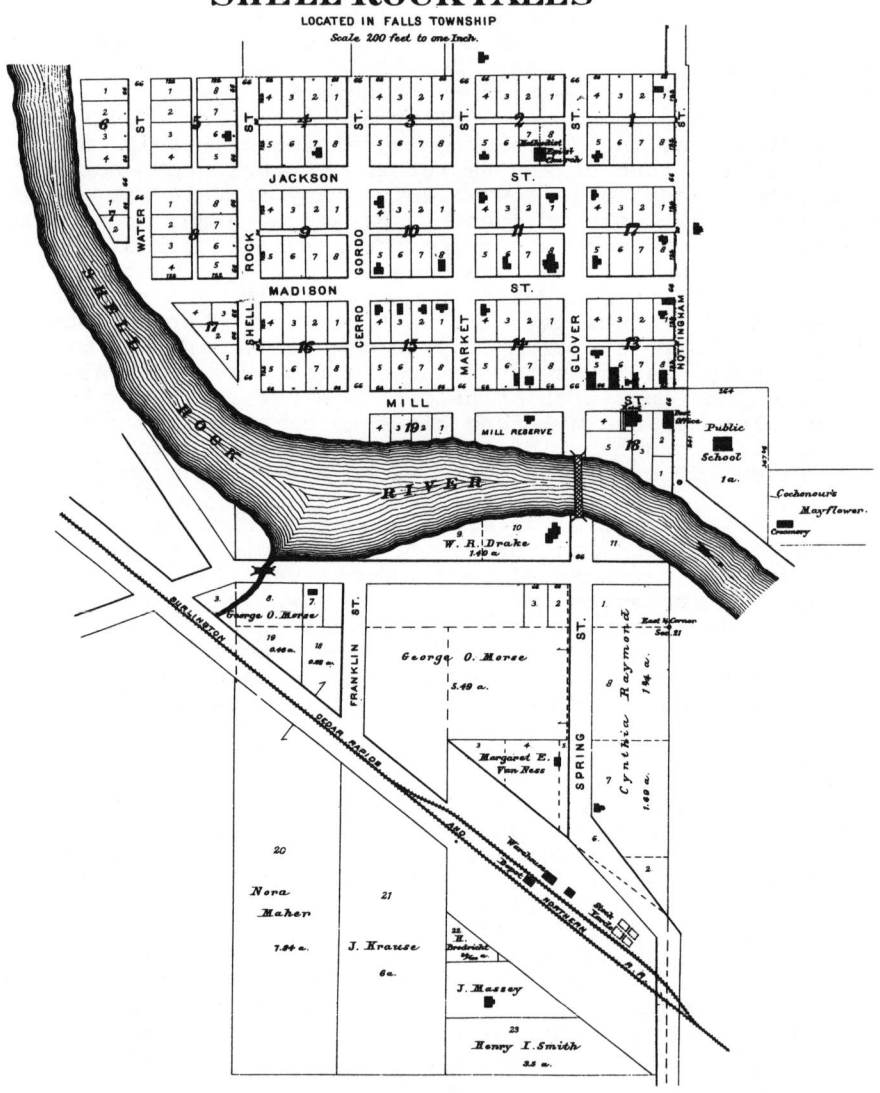

MAP III
(Source: Rock Falls Historical Book, 1977)

miles by 24 miles, and it contained 16 square Townships, six miles by six miles. In 1856, the County was indeed a part of the far western frontier, with but three settlement clusters -- Shell Rock Falls, Masonic Grove, and Clear Lake all in the County's northeast corner. The nearest United States Post Office was in Cedar Falls, Black Hawk County, 71 miles down-river from Shell Rock Falls. Nonetheless, as mail was eagerly sought by the frontier settlers, a few unofficial carriers quickly came into service. Soon, however, the federal government employed regular carriers on fixed routes. Charley Johnson was the first of these in the whole County, carrying letters, packages, and sometimes passengers when weather permitted a team and buggy. Most often, he travelled the route to Osage in Mitchell County and Nora Springs in Floyd County by horseback, and in the dead of winter Charley, wearing snowshoes, brought the mail through by foot.

In an 1860 issue of the Clear Lake *Independent*, Charley advertised that he was running a mail and express route between Clear Lake and Cedar Falls (presumably with a stop in Rock Falls) and that he would be at Clear Lake every Friday morning. Charley, a native of Sweden, had no known relatives in America. It is said that he was shy, unsocial, industrious, economical, and with a "ruling passion" for acquiring land. He eventually married one Adaline, and they went to live in Charley's log house in the woods along the Shell Rock River above the town. Charley was quoted as saying that someday he and Adaline would be able to ride all the way to Mason City on their own land. Sad to relate, a bad cold that turned into pneumonia took Charley away in 1869 at age 51, before he could get all of that land. Adaline and their three sons seem to have vanished, as no word of them remains.

Water power to turn the wheels of the Wiltfong grist mill, producing corn meal and flour, fixed the town's central location. Just downstream of the place where a small creek flows into the river on its south bank (see Map III) there was a natural waterfall extending north and south across the Shell Rock, Wiltfong's waterfall, so to speak. The fall of water over this rock ledge was only about three feet, but the river continued downstream in a modest riffle or cascade to just about opposite the end of Market Street. This provided a total descent of the river of perhaps ten or twelve feet over this short distance of some 1,000 feet -- from above the falls to flatwater at Market Street. It is not known precisely where the original mill was situated, nor the dam to raise still higher and divert the water, but a later and larger mill would soon be build, receiving water from a new dam. The new dam was built at the natural falls to add 18 feet more of "head," then to divert a part of the river's flow into a long, narrow flume or "race" on the north bank. This flume sloped very gradually, sufficient only to move the water by gravity, to the mill where flume water would be some 20 feet over river level at the mill site. Here, water flowing from the flume would come against the paddle wheels of the grist mill to turn those grinding stones that made the farmers' grains into flour and meal. This simple operation was the original <u>raison d'etre</u> for the community of Rock Falls.

Hundreds, perhaps thousands, of such grist mills all over the midwest served a vital need before the days of steam and electric power. In the same year when Elijah was constructing his first mill dam and mill on the Shell Rock, Elisha Randall was erecting a dam and mill on Lime Creek, eight miles across the prairie to the southwest. A new town had been platted nearby in 1853 called Masonic Grove after the pioneers of the Masonic Order who first settled there. It would become Mason City, Cerro Gordo County Seat, and a prairie metropolis that rapidly outgrew its neighbors. There was another mill built the same year at Nora Springs, seven miles below Rock Falls, and soon thereafter two mills near Plymouth, three miles upriver, still another at Osage, 15 miles away on the Cedar River, and two on the Winnebago, at Fertile and Portland.

Datus E. Coon, owner and publisher of the <u>Cerro Gordo Press</u> in the thriving community of Mason City, sent his editor on a visit to Shell Rock Falls in 1859. The following was soon printed:

> The Grist Mill at Shell Rock Falls is now doing a fine business and promises to manufacture a good quantity of flour and corn meal during the summer. We called on Mr. Wiltfong, the proprietor, and found him rushing business forward on the big site. On calling at the store of Mr. Eager, we found him also busy. He has a fine, well-assorted stock of goods and is progressing in business finely."

From 1840 to 1880, the development and operation of water-powered grinding mills were vital to the settlement of the agricultural heartland. These were roughly the four decades from earliest settlement until the coming of the railroads. The growing of wheat by the earliest farmers was essential to their lives, and a grinding mill was essential to converting the wheat into flour, so that it could be baked into bread and cakes. Indians managed to grind their meager grain crops by hand over stones, but the white man saw the potential of the energy in falling water. By 1860, 12 grist and flour mills were producing within a 20-mile radius of Rock Falls. A less frequently applied use of water-powered mills was to saw logs, primarily rough cuts for heavy structural framing, supported posts, and planking for buildings and bridges.

For either use there were two basic mill styles. The

more common, but less efficient, was an overshot-undershot wheel. As the water struck the wheels horizontally, much potential energy was wasted by not becoming realized energy. The other mill style was the turbine, in which water from the race entered a penstock and was dropped onto a circle of turbine blades enclosed in a shaft, spinning a turbine wheel by hitting all blades at once and vertically rather than a single paddle, thus enhancing the realized energy of the falling water.

The mill at Rock Grove, now a ghost town, two miles down the Shell Rock from Nora Springs, was a typical low-head flour grinding mill of the 1870s. Farmers hauled in their sacks of wheat by the wagon loads, and the miller could produce some 75 barrels of rough-ground flour a day. Most labor at the mill was provided by the farmers themselves. They also had to give one-eighth of the wheat to the miller as a toll for grinding.

Why is Rock Grove no more? The coming of the railroad through Nora Springs by-passed Rock Grove. This was its death warrant, as was the routing of railroads for most of Iowa's more than 700 flour and grist-mill towns and 300 saw-mill towns. The tiny hamlet of Portland was another victim of progress in railroad transportation. It was too close to Mason City and didn't get a railroad. A like end was suffered by Freeman, Winnebago Heights, Burchinal, Hanford, and Emery, all Cerro Gordo County ghost towns. Another even more far-reaching death warrant for the small towns was the development of great milling centers in the large cities, such as in Minneapolis and St. Louis, where mechanized grinding operations produced higher quality finely-ground baking flours and whiter bread flours in larger volumes. Thereafter, as long as the vagaries of weather allowed the old mills to stand along side the mill streams, they were limited to grinding buckwheat, cornmeal and rough feed for livestock.

The land speculators did their best to attract settlers to Rock Falls and to make a fast buck as well. One Mr. Lamson Corey placed the following advertisement in a January 1858 issue of the <u>Cerro Gordo Press</u>:

> "There is in this village a good state of society, a school house and place of Religious Worship, regularly occupied. Shell Rock River, as its name indicates, passes over a <u>rock bottom</u> and has a water power of sufficient <u>fall and volume</u> to propel four runs of stone. There is now in operation at this point a Store, Saw Mill and Grist Mill doing a good business. Shell Rock Falls is located 170 miles northwest from Dubuque, and is on the stage route passing Dyersville, Strawberry Point. . . . through Shell Rock Falls and on to the State line. Lumber is furnished by the saw mill and an inexhaustible Stone Quarry of the

choicest material is located immediately upon the bank of the river in this beautiful and healthy little village." (underline added, no pun intended)

Another advertisement stated that land was "...extremely cheap, ranging from $1.25 to $10.00 for prairie land" and that the "...country around is extremely beautiful and a prettier location for a town cannot be found anywhere."

Well, as it turned out, the quarry was not inexhaustible, nor even very large, as were the huge clay and limestone deposits that were one day to make Mason City the "Brick and Tile Capital of the World" and location of the largest cement plant in America. Still, Rock Falls grew at a measured pace through the late 1850s. A decent one-room schoolhouse was built on the east edge of town overlooking the river in 1859. The first bridge to span the river was in place in September of that year as well, a fine iron archbridge that cost the County $960. A congregational Church organization was launched by the Reverend Thomas Tenney in 1856, and plans were made to buy land and build a church, plans that soon had to be put on hold by the outbreak of the Civil War in 1861.

Rock Falls (let's now call it by its later name), was only indirectly affected by the tragic four-year conflict. From a purely economic viewpoint, the war was a favorable event for the Iowa farmers. They were far removed from the battlefields, but demand for and prices of their grain and meat rose greatly. Coupled with unusually favorable weather conditions for crop production and the rapid introduction of substantially improved farm machinery, primarily the all-important sod-buster plow, the prairie farmers of Falls Township enjoyed abundant crop yields, ready markets and high prices. They could pay for their $1.25 and $10.00 per acre investments in land, a team of good work horses, and some machines in a season or two, with money left over to build decent housing for the family and barns for the livestock. Labor became very scarce as the war dragged on, and with a scarcity of lumber and nails, a farm construction boom had to await the post-war years.

On a personal basis, the war was far less favorable, as Falls Township sent its share of soldiers into battle. When President Lincoln issued his first call for troops in 1861, Iowa's Governor Samuel Kirkwood asked Iowans to contribute one regiment. Ten times as many as were needed to fill out a single regiment offered themselves for enlistment. Still, in 1864, when President Lincoln issued a nationwide (northern, that is) call to another 300,000 men the Cerro Gordo County Board of Supervisors, whose job it was to see that the County's quotas of soldiers were filled (and their dependents cared for during the war) became concerned. The Board ordered that a bounty of $500 be paid to any volunteer in order to fill the quotas. Sitting on the Board from Falls Township were the well-known citizens of Rock Falls: C. W. Tenney, David Butts, George Morse, Richard Morris, and Thomas Perrett.

Cities, towns, and hamlets throughout the midwest and far beyond experienced this national tragedy. By February of 1861, seven "lower" southern States had seceded from the Union, soon followed by Virginia, North Carolina, Tennessee, and Arkansas. Three "border" States in the heartland -- Kentucky, Missouri, and Kansas -- harbored strong but divided loyalties, and they stayed in the Union. Kentucky declared for neutrality in May, but when Confederate troops occupied Columbus, the State stayed with the Union. A sharp contest in Missouri between disunionists and nationalists was resolved when a State convention in July deposed a pro-southern Governor and declared for the Union. In kansas, the earlier free-state choice held for the Union, despite bitter opposition. During the war, officers and men in the Union service numbered 2,675,000, about equally divided between the 13 heartland States and eastern States.

By war's end, Iowa had furnished 48 regiments of infantry, nine of cavalry, and four artillery batteries -- 80,000 men, all of them volunteers. The 32d Regiment received many Cerro Gordo County volunteers, with many familier Rock Falls names. Let it be recorded for posterity that the following answered the very first call:

    David H. Butts H. I. Smith (Captain)
    George O. Brown Marqus Brown
    Joseph Morris   Edwin Morris
    Cyrus Morris   Ira Williams
    H. A. Gregory   Peter Smith (Lieutenant)
    Charles Senior   Hiram A. Wiltfong
    Uriah A. Wilson David A. Butts

Later, Horace and Sally Gregory furnished more than their share -- six sons called the "fighting Gregorys," and all served with distinction and apparently without casualties. Lieutenant Smith was killed in Mississippi. Hiram A Wiltfong and David A. Butts were killed in Tennessee.

Another young midwesterner to serve with distinction in the Civil War was George Magee. He came from Canada to settle on a Minnesota farm in 1858. He enlisted in Company G, the First Minnesota Regiment, and served for three years, fighting in the battles of Bull Run, Ball's Bluff, West Point, Fair Oaks, Peach Orchard, Salvage Station, White Oak Swamp, Mavern Hill, Vienna, Antietam, Charlestown, Fredricksburg, Gettysburg, Bristow Station, and Mine Run. Some service! Wounded at Gettsburg from a musket ball, he carried it with him to his death at the age of 83 on his farm back in Minnesota. He had a son, John, who had a daughter, Mary, who married John Dezell. They had a daughter, Jane, who married John Wilkinson, the Yorkshire miller, from which union they raised five children, their youngest being Rufus Verne. He married Edith Krug, and they had three children who grew up in Rock Falls during the Great Depression. Faint footprints through the woods and fields of the prairies!

In the spring of 1865, local disasters resumed with the temporary termination of national disasters. The original Wiltfong saw and grist mill was washed downstream. So vital an industrial centerpiece for the town had to be replaced. Alfonzo Brown, who had bought the mill the year before, was quick to rebuild it, but in 1866 the mill dam and iron bridge were swept away in the spring flood. In 1868, George Heaton bought the mill's water rights and set about building a more substantial structure than its predecessors in the river valley. Known to townspeople as "The Stone Mill," distinguished as it was from the typical wooden structures, it was "one of the finest mills in the whole country." Standing four stories high and 40 feet by 60 feet in length and width, it was made of solid limerock quarried right from the site, the high ledge of limestone overlooking the river on the corner of Glover and Mill Streets.

Operations began with two runs of grinding stone in the mill, getting water from the upstream mill dam through the race or flume. This facility consisted of a two-inch planking, seven feet in diameter and tubular in shape, 30 rods long. Three more runs of stone or "burrs" were added in June of 1873. Adjoining the mill was a coopers shop in which flour barrels were made. Aiming for a 50,000-bushel production run that year, the mill's operator offered 77 cents a bushel for wheat, and the mill wheels ground night and day. As this was a handsome price for the times, one suspects fierce competition from grist mills in neighboring towns -- Mason City, Nora Springs, or Plymouth -- for the wheat crop of Falls Township farmers. With hardly more than 50 farms in the Township, an average thousand-bushel crop would provide a fine return of some $770 for a year's labor on the soil. Lots of money for those days!

During and after the Civil War, two related national movements or policies were of considerably greater impact upon Rock Falls (not to mention the entire midwest) than the Civil War had been. These were the accelerated disposition of the public land and the railroad-building era. In a race to secure the American Empire from its potential enemies, much land that had been bought from France at low fire-sale prices, taken from the Indians, or handed over by treaty, all to become the U.S. public domain, had soon been given away by grants of various kinds in a deliberate effort to foster settlement and expansion of the country. Such were most grants to builders of canals and turnpike roads, to improve harbors, to drain swamps, and for military installations. This is not to say that private greed had not played a dominant role in formulating public policy. Much land had been sold, but revenue to the national treasury proved to be insignificant, and the slow parcel-by-parcel selling of it seemed to be impeding dispositions at a pace desired by builders of the American Empire.

While the public land laws passed in 1820 lowered the purchase price and the minimum size of purchase, they did require a survey and a public auction sale before titles could legally be secured. But surveying proceeded slowly, and the tidal wave of settlers often carried many beyond lands surveyed and open for sale. These came to be called "squatters." It is quite probable that such a condition developed in Falls Township, although the records are unclear. When tracts of land so occupied were later offered for sale at public auction, the squatters who had improved their lands were forced to bid a higher price to secure title against other bidders because of the very improvements that they themselves had made. This led to demands by the squatters for "preemption rights" and passage of a national Preemption Act in 1830.

This Act provided that squatters who had improved the land and built a dwelling upon an acreage should have the right to buy it at the minimum price of $1.25 per acre before it was offered at public auction. The effect was to stimulate the scattering over and squatting upon the best tracts of unopened public domain. This merely accelerated the waves of immigration to the rich midwestern farmlands. The Graduation Act of 1854 further cheapened the costs of settling and reduced the risk as well, providing that land remaining unsold ten years after it had been opened for sale was to be gradually reduced in the minimum price to a mere twelve and one-half cents per acre. Thus, odd lots of less desirable lands, some timbered but easy to clear and farm, could be had for a virtual song, further inducing the rapidity of settlement.

As if these were not sufficient inducement, the western block of politicians, rapacious speculators, and private land "lords" succeeded in providing the ultimate magnet -- gifts of land. The demand for free land grants had been voiced among the working-class groups of the East for many years, but it was not until the agrarian reformer Mr. George Evans and the promoter Mr. Horace Greeley (go-west-young-man Greeley) had joined forces that legislation was introduced and gained national attention. The Homestead Act of 1862 came after the Republican Party had adopted a free land issue as one of its 1860 election planks. Under the law, citizens or intended citizens could, for a nominal fee, obtain title to a tract of 160 acres after residing upon it and improving it for five years. A further clause designed to protect the settler who for unforeseen reason was unable to meet the five-year residency requirement permitted a preemption right to obtain title after only six months on the land by payment of a $1.25 per acre public auction price. This clause was like a green light to speculators with no interests in developing the land to acquire it and profit from a quick resale. We do not know if our law-abiding ancestors in Falls Township were among these reprehensible opportunists, but we suspect they were not. They wanted to till the soil and establish homes.

It has been written that the Homestead Act, coupled with favorable conditions offered for the railroad builders, settled the West with the "rapidity of a prairie fire." Before 1850, railroad construction had been confined to regions east of the Appalachian Mountains. The interior was barely penetrated by railroads in the following year, first by the Atlantic & Western from Savannah and Charleston to Chattanooga, then by the New York & Erie to Lake Erie. From the outset, it was a story of big city commercial rivalry -- between Boston, New York, Philadelphia, Pittsburg, Savannah, Chicago, St. Louis, and others, to capture the two-way traffic in goods and commodities. These were surplus midwestern commodities (surplus because of rapid technological advances in crop production) that needed to be shipped east, and the surplus eastern manufactured goods (surplus due to technological advances in factory production) that needed to be shipped west. Cities paid the railroad companies handsomely to influence routing plans, donated land for rights-of-way, gifts of money, favorable tax treatment, and public bond issues to finance the trackage for the companies at low interest rates.

Quite apart from these inducements, consider the competition among newly-appointed U. S. Senators and Representatives in 16 or more midwestern States, each of whom was anxious to build a solid voter base with his constituency back home to assure his reelections year after year. Developed into a fine art in later years, "pork-barreling" and "log-rolling" became an integral (and scandalous) part of American governance. Senator X would say to Senator Y "You vote for a railroad land grant through my State and I'll vote for a military base in your State." Add rivers and harbors improvements, waterways, and dams and irrigation projects, and the powerfully entrenched bureaucracies of the Army Corps of Engineers and Bureau of Reclamation are understandable. Also understandable is the massive overbuilding of the American railroad systems in the 1800s and early 1900s.

The railroad building fever spread rapidly, becoming both a national and a local issue. At the urging of many western States, the U. S. Congress had begun in the early 1850s to make grants of the public domain to most States. These States in turn made grants to the privately-owned railroad companies. It became one of the most fabulous of all-time giveaways of public resources -- some 200,000,000 acres of free land, primarily to the great east-west continental lines. The Northern Pacific, building from Chicago to Seattle, was given 42,000,000 acres, probably the largest private recipient of government largesse in the history of any nation.

The original scheme, similar to earlier land grants of 4,500,000 acres to the canal builders, was to give a strip of land 100 feet wide for the railroad right-of-way itself and in addition alternate land sections (each one square mile) in two more strips, one on each side of the roadway. As six miles was a common width for these side strips in the grants at the time, the railroads received six square miles, three on each side -- a total of 3,840 acres for every mile of track laid, and often it was rich and valuable land! Later, to hasten the giveaway and get the country settled or populated (and the very rich even richer), the strips were widened to 15 and 20 miles. To this day the assets of many railroads remain swollen with farm and ranch land, mineral land, timberland, and choice urban real estate, such as much of downtown Los Angeles.

At the local level, Counties, Townships, and Towns also competed actively with gifts of land, loans, and even grants of money to persuade railroad companies to build through their jurisdictions. The railroad companies came to dictate a Town's location in the first instance or its very survival, if it had had the misfortune of having itself platted before the railroads came through the region. An Iowa historian asserts that the railroad lines dictated Iowa's future, first by the routings, and then by preferential freight rate practices, at times involving bribes and kickbacks. In response to what was going on among the States to the east, the Iowa Constitution was amended in 1857 to limit assistance that any community or an organization might furnish to the railroads as they pressed westward across Iowa.

As soon as the Civil War ended, railroad's extensions into Iowa and beyond accelerated. The Northwestern reached across the State to Council Bluffs in 1867. The Chicago, Burlington & Quincy spanned the State in 1870, and the Illinois Central crossed to Sioux City in that same year. Four east-west trunk lines, 3,000 miles of trackage, all within five years. Imagine the feverish building activity, laying all of those rails, with thousands of railway bridges, road crossings, underpasses, sidings, depots.

It remained to complete the network system with many more miles of north-south trunklines, junctions, and feeder lines. Before it was over, the residents of Iowa noted with pride that not a town in the State was more than 12 miles from a railroad. In Rock Falls, excitement grew as the Burlington, Cedar Rapids & Northern penetrated north and west as far as Rockford, 20 miles downstream along the Shell Rock River. The concern was that the routing would veer west to Mason City, which already had the Northwestern and Rock Island lines, leaving Rock Falls to wither and die. But Falls Township called an election in August of 1871 to raise a five percent property tax to subsidize (i.e., persuade) the railroad company to build into Rock Falls and on to Plymouth, three miles upstream, where it could connect with another line there. No land grants had been made to this line. The measure passed, the rails and the siding were laid along the south edge of town (see Map III) in 1872, a fine depot was built by 1876, and there was much rejoicing in Rock Falls.

Until this greatest event in the town's history, not much had happened since the boys came home from the war. Farmers continued to arrive and work the land, marked by increasing numbers of Germans, Austrians, and Bohemians in contrast to earlier English, Irish, and Scots. The railroad era had brought thousands of Irish to the State, first as construction crews, then as locomotive engineers, firemen, brakemen, station agents, and maintenance crews, and Rock Falls became a home to many Irish families. The railroad companies continued for decades as major employers because, in haste to beat competing companies into new territory, trackage was literally thrown into place, the measure of accomplishment in each day having nothing to do with quality. It was the miles of rail laid per day that counted. This meant poor alignments, poorly leveled track, poor banking and cutting and filling, poor drainage, unstable roadbeds, weak bridges. Such conditions meant slow trains, frequent derailments, flooding, and washouts, and the great technological improvements to locomotives outpaced those to trackage, necessitating more and faster upgrading of the rails, ties, and roadbeds. No sooner was a line completed than a major rebuilding effort was needed, as James J. Hill, the master builder of the Great Northern empire, was quick to realize. All of this meant more construction and repair jobs, more homes and businesses, and more trade for Rock Falls. The future of the town seemed secure, or so they thought.

John Bliem and his family emigrated from Westenburg, Germany, back in 1864. After working for a brief period in New York City, Mr. Bliem and his family came out to Iowa. They moved into a small house on Mill Street (Lot 6, Block 13) in March of 1866, and there he resumed his old-world skill and trade of making and selling boots and shoes. He and his sons became valuable additions to the growing town for many years to come. In the same month, a Cemetery Association was formed to buy burial grounds. In 1867, construction of the beautiful stone church high up on the far north edge of town was begun, a new iron bridge was built across the Shell Rock, Henry Stowe bought the blacksmith shop, and George Heaton's new Stone Mill was doing a land-office business, as they used to say. Construction of the fine new church building was completed in 1869, and Reverend J. D. Mason arrived to become the first minister, a Congregationalist. While surrounding farmland was rapidly being taken up by homesteaders, the town's permanent population was little more than at its founding 15 years ago -- about 50 or 60 people.

Beginning in the 1870s the railroad and the new flour mill made a great difference in the fortunes of the town. Construction workers required board and room, so new housing was constructed, and Reverend Mason began operating his place as a boarding house (Block 18, Lot 3). As recorded by the Rock Falls Historical Book Committee, "In January 1872, the iron horse steamed through town providing many conveniences not previously available." These were very probably a daily mail service, a bulk carrier to bring products in from faraway places and take commodities out to faraway places, and daily passenger service. After all of those cart-and-oxen years, what a thrill and a comfort it must have been to be able to ride the trains for hundreds of miles in a day's time. It was at this time that Shell Rock Falls had to change its name to Rock Falls by orders from the Burlington, Cedar Rapids & Minneapolis railroad to avoid confusion in its time-tables due to the nearby town of Shellrock.

Back in 1858, Datus E. Coon had forded the Shell Rock River at Rock Falls on his way from Osage to Mason City. He was bringing a printing press and related materials by three wagons pulled by two yokes of oxen. Soon, he would start the County's first newspaper, the Cerro Gordo Press. The press was "an under toggle, 'Foster,' hand lever, back breaker, and is thought to have been the first printing press to cross the Mississippi River into Iowa," wrote the Rock Falls Historical Committee. Now, 13 years later, in November of 1871, and as Editor of the City Express of Mason City, Mr. Coon revisited the little village, and his full account of the visit tells it all (or nearly all):

> "We passed a few hours pleasantly and profitably at Shellrock Falls a short time since, and as it was our first visit to that charming sister town within two years, we were greatly surprised at the changes and improvements that have taken place and are now going on there.

> "We went 'all rail' to Plymouth, at which place we halted but a few moments, as our business was at the Falls, and time was pressing. Respectfully declining a kind offer from friend C. W. Tenney, to furnish us a wiry colt to make the short distance over fine roads, we started out on foot, a western Weston in imagination, and had accomplished the three and 1/2 mile feat before we hardly knew

it, so intent were we on the beauties of the
scenery -- rich farming lands of the valley, and
picturesque bluffs, which at points bound the
pretty stream on our left.

"Not withstanding the fact that over 6,000 bushels
of wheat were shipped from this valley during the
month of October, we noticed much grain yet in
stack, on the well-kept farms along the road.

"Arrived at the Falls, and crossing the river on a
fine wagon bridge, we made direct for the residence of our good friend Brother Mason, where we
were scarcely allowed to brush the dust of travel
from our clothes, till welcomed to the dining room,
for which our walk had given us a fine appetite;
and we believe we did ample justice to the fresh
fish just caught by the Elder himself, from the
clear waters of the Shellrock. Elder Mason's
folks are, as they ever were, the hospitable friends
of all, and Mrs. Mason well sustains the position
of hostess, to which she finds herself nearly every
day exalted by their own hospitality and the absence
of any regular hotel or any other so comfortable
stopping place.

"After dinner we started out to take a look at the
town, Mr. Mason kindly volunteering to introduce us.
We first visited the fine new flouring mill of Geo.
Heaton, which, now nearly completed, stands as a
monument of that gentleman's wide-awake energy, the
finest mill building in the whole country. It is a
beautiful dark limestone, 38 x 62', and 3 stories
above the basement -- designed for four run of burrs.
We were shown all through it, from the dark basement, where the workmen were quarrying into the solid
masonry of nature to make room for the water power,
to the 3rd story, where Mr. Heaton is already storing grain. Mr. Heaton informed us that he expected
to get in two run of stone this winter. His enterprise in the short time he has been here, aside
from speaking for itself on every hand, is highly
spoken of by the entire community so fortunate in
securing his permanent location among them.

"Emerging from the mill, we were hailed by a well-
known voice, and went across the street to find
Geo. Sumner and Will Harding, of this place, engaged in fitting up the cellar of a commodious room
to be occupied by Mr. H. D. Cadwell with a stock
of general groceries. Mason City has since opened
out a fine stock at that point, and is doing a
flourishing business.

"From here we took a general tramp, accompanied by

the Elder. Met Mr. Beyer, a well-to-do farmer
of the valley, who gave us his name for the
paper, when we journeyed on to the residence of
Mr. James McLeod, who gave us a friendly welcome,
a few moment's chat, and his name for the Express.
Next called on Mr. Reuben Kinney, whom we found at
work storing vegetables in his garden, shook his
hand for $2 worth of Express, and then conducted
by the Elder to see his pride of the town, "the
little church around the corner." Nestled con-
fidingly in the timber on the north side of town
is as pretty a stone church, 35 x 55, as the
country can boast of. It was erected by the Con-
gregational denomination, liberally aided by the
good people of that town, and was dedicated to
divine worship, some 3 years ago. During the past
season the Ladies Church Aid Society have completed
the furnishing of the house in truly fine style,
carpeted aisles, and pulpit -- sofas and chairs,
rich chandeliers, and everything complete to lend
an air of neatness, not to say elegance, to the
interior of the fine edifice. A large bible, the
gift of Mrs. Merrill of Milwaukee, graces the pulpit. As we notice the glow of honest pride on the
Elder's face while he showed us his sanctuary, and
talked of the liberality of the people in endow-
ing it, we felt sure this little 'temple in the
grove' was well attended each Sabbath.

"On the hill in the east part of town, we noticed a
fine two-story stone schoolhouse, in which a first
class school is taught the year around. It will
thus be seen that educational interests are not
lost sight of.

"From here we next visited the house of Mr. T. W.
Lane, to whom we were introduced. Mr. Lane was
busily engaged in putting in a new pump on his premises but not too busy to chat awhile, and give us
his name for the paper. Mr. Lane has a fine location, good house & territory enough to not be
crowded when the railroad and other enterprises
have made of Shellrock Falls a city.

"The busy ring of an anvil directed our steps to the
shop of Mr. H. W. Stowe, a young man whose untiring
industry and application to business has made him a
good run of custom, and many warm friends in the
town, and entire valley. And this is the only blacksmith and ironing shop in the place, Mr. Stowe is
crowded with work, and we were informed he could
crowd through as much of it, in good shape, as any
man on the Shellrock. He said he had $2 for the
Express, and time on Sunday to read it, and we in-
audibly murmured "Bully for you," as we put his

name down for a year.

"At the store of L. S. Eager, pioneer merchant of the town, we were next made welcome, and stopped a moment in converse with the proprietor and Mr. S. H. Sheldon, his gentlemanly clerk. Mr. Eager has kept store at his old stand on the corner, a number of years, and is a citizen well-known throughout the county -- his store having accommodated a large scope of country up and down the river. His stock is now full and being enlarged, with dry goods, groceries and general merchandise. Our call here was necessarily brief, as it was getting near train time at Plymouth, and we tho't of the walk thither, so taking the name of Mr. E and Mrs. S. for the paper, we prepared to start back on the "home run," when Brother Mason informed us that he was intending to take us back to Plymouth, but as he was busy himself, he could send his horse & buggy to take us up to the train. As we had depended so much on the Elder's courtesy during the brief stay, we made purely a business visit, we felt some delicacy in accepting this last proffered kindness; but he would hear no refusal, and hurried away to give directions for hitching up the pony, returning with a subscription from Mr. Reuben Barret, a carpenter at the mill. Many warm thanks for your kindness, Elder.

"It was with a feeling of regret at the shortness of our stay, that at 3 p.m. we took seat in the carriage, and were hurried away from this pleasant little town. We had been there but a few hours -- moments, it seemed -- and had made many valuable acquaintances, and 'got a subscription' out of every man we met.

"On the west side of the river, the B.C.R.& M.R.R. is graded, and probably by this time receiving the ties; the depot grounds, if the town succeeds in securing a depot this season, will be just west of the bridge. On this side of the river the scene is changed greatly since our last visit before. The heavy timber felled & cleared out for the march of improvement in grade, cut and "embankment" which is lined with the shanties of the laborers.

"Verily, Shellrock Falls of today bears little resemblance to the point at which, just 13 years ago, we crossed the river, with the first printing press ever brought into Cerro Gordo County, and pushing west, proudly felt that we

> 'Crossed the prairies as of old
> Our fathers crossed the sea,
> To make the west, as they the east
> The homestead of the free.' "

Clearly Mr. Datus E. Coon was not one to be caught at a loss for words! And he had a sharp eye for subscribers, as well as a need for copy.

Meanwhile, the Town of Rock Falls was coming alive. In 1873 George O. Morse, one of the original land tycoons, having bought Elijah Wiltfong's claims and other lands in Sections 20 and 21 (see Map III), joined with H. D. Cadwell in a grocery and drygoods business. Mr. Cadwell was also the Postmaster. Henry Stowe, the blacksmith, put up a warehouse and became a grain buyer, calling himself the Stowe & Co. E. W. Ford built a hotel on Block 14, and Lot 7, running a hack service to the depot to accomodate the guests. He built a livery stable behind the new hotel. A woolen mill was organized by Mr. Dean and others as a company called the Rock Falls Manufacturing Co. with $100,000 capital, $25.00 per share. The stock was immediately subscribed by 20 gentlemen taking 200 shares each. Named to the Board of Directors were Thomas Perrett, Joseph Perrett Simon Calvert, J. B. Kelly, George S. Heaton, George Morse and John Wilkinson.

The Town was not without its problems. As reported by a correspondent who contributed copy from time to time to the City Express, signing his news dispatches "Quill," the following chronicles the drama of the saloons, legitimate ventures at the time before the Town incorporated.

> "Messrs. Welcome & Gill have taken the contract
> for excavating Mr. J. B. Kelly's cellar, for a
> large store, corner of Main & Mill streets.
> Hauling dirt to end of new bridge." (Nov 3, 1873)

> "Mr. B. W. Harr purchased business lot fronting
> Main of Kelly & has commenced building 18 x 26,
> 2 stories -- rumor says for a billiard hall &
> saloon." (Nov 18, 1873)

> "New building of a small pattern has been put up
> just east of the Exchange Hotel, said to be for
> a saloon. We were in hopes we could remain
> free from such a curse." (Nov 26, 1873)

> "Our citizens were quite surprised this morning
> when they beheld the building, to be used for
> a saloon, lying in Mr. Kelly's cellar, sills
> upward. From the commencing of said building --
> created some indignation among citizens. We are
> not in favor of mob violence, & parties who did
> it, no doubt, were little too fast, as there was

nothing in the building to justify them destroying it. We claim to be a strictly temperance community, & would hope that parties will take warning from this, & in future not impose upon our citizens by putting a low-lived doggery upon our streets. Quill."
(Dec 3, 1873)

"Col. Scrihner, who is partial to a morning dram, came down as usual Saturday morn, & looking over door of saloon, staring him in face -- words 'Baptist Church.' His astonishment knew no bounds. Turned on heel & not seen entering old place since." (Dec 9, 1873)

"Assault & battery Saturday evening. Saloon object of assault. Windows broken & door broken in. No arrests." (Dec 16, 1873)

"The effects of two saloons in town are daily seen on the streets." (Jan 13, 1874)

"Billiard table arrived for new saloon." (Jan 27, 1874)

"One of our saloons has come to grief & the other probably will follow, two of our prominent citizens having sufficient evidence against them for selling liquor to minors & habitual drunkards, caused a notice to be served, that unless they were immediately closed they would be prosecuted. One of them quietly took the hint & took his departure for Osage. We hope that saloons have had their day in Rock Falls." (June 16, 1874)

The forces of temperance prevailed. Ah yes, the good old days! The town would remain dry for years, although not forever.

On the fourth of July, 1874, the first celebration of many to come was held with an all-day program of speeches, musicals, reading of the Declaration of Independence, parades picnic dinners, games, boat races, and a dance. Early in the year, with the Kelly building completed, but, with no saloon, three or four merchants sold groceries out of it from time to time. Then Dr. J. B. Conley came to town, rented the building for an office and drug store and added a soda fountain -- something the townspeople did not vandalize. Cadwell built a new two-story grocery business on Block 18, Lot 1, that year, and the Reverend Mason's wife opened a millinery shop in the front room of their house-hotel. Preachers pay was not good, so Reverend Mason had rented another building and opened a furniture and hardware business, but he soon sold that to Cadwell. In the fall, Henry Stowe, the blacksmith, couldn't pay his mortgage so he sold his shop. The new mill company put up a warehouse, elevators, and cooper shop as the flour milling business prospered.

For several years thereafter, a bewildering change of renting, owning, operating, and closing grocery, drygoods, hardware, furniture, millinery, and variety stores continued as enterprising men came to town, stayed, or moved on. The rise and decline of so many hotel ventures suggests that there were wide swings in employment during and following completion of the railroad through town. They suggest also the very transient nature of small-town activities in this still relatively new period of settlement of the prairies.

In June 1875, a terrible rainstorm took out the mill race and the iron bridge, and another bad storm a few days later nearly took out the mill itself. Still, the town put on another celebration of the Fourth of July that year but with some difficulty, as lumber for all the booths and seating were hard to ferry across the river. Meanwhile, the versatile Mr. Silas S. Lewis, an early editor of the Mason City Times, joined his friend Dr. Conley as a druggist, and when the doctor sold out and moved away, Silas moved his stock of drugs to L. S. Eager's grocery and drygoods store. On December 15, Silas married Elizabeth Dezell, one of 14 children of John and Mary (Magee) Dezell and younger half-sister of Jane Dezell. At the wedding at Edgewood Farm, north of town, twenty guests came to the little log house for the occasion. The ever-active Reverend Mason moved to Forest City to preach, selling his hotel-house to Silas Perry, who enlarged it considerably and sold it to H. W. Morse. H. W. called it "The Morse," but lacking capital, or perhaps an adequate cash flow, he sold it to George O. Morse, the land tycoon, who rented it to "Judge" Ingersoll. Ingersoll already owned and operated the "South Side Hotel," which was also his home just south of the river.

A few words about Silas Shelton Lewis are in order. Known to many as "S. S.," he typified the life and times of the settlement era and the good old days. This distant cousin of the Wilkinsons by marriage was a Welshman. His great-great-grandfather, Thomas Lewis, migrated from Wales to Philadelphia, then to North Carolina, in 1750. Abraham, son of Thomas, soldiered in the Revolutionary War. He moved on to Kentucky, probably taking the Comberland Gap route over the Appalachian Mountains, in 1794. There he bought a large acreage of land and became acquainted with Daniel Boone. Isaac, son of Abraham, a frontiersman distinguished for bravery in the Indian wars, moved with his family to Indiana in 1809. He was appointed a lieutenancy in the territorial militia during the Blackhawk War. Then Isaac moved to Illinois in 1817. William, son of Isaac, married Ester White, said to be "connected by blood" to the Todd family, of whom Mary Todd, Abraham Lincoln's wife was the most prominent. William and Ester were parents of Silas Shelton Lewis, born in Darlington, Wisconsin in 1850. Shortly after the Civil War, the family moved to a farm in Mitchell County, Iowa.

Silas entered the Seminary at Osage and there made friends with A. T. Conley. Both thought they would become doctors, but Silas soon decided against that, becoming a pharmacist and settling in Rock Falls. Conley became a doctor, and settled in Cannon Falls, Minnesota. Early in 1880, the Cannon Falls Beacon, a weekly newspaper, came up for sale. When Silas heard this from his friend Conley, he sold his Rock Falls drug store, bought the paper, and moved with his beautiful wife Elizabeth (Dezell) to Cannon Falls. Thus began a distinguished journalistic career for S S., as editor and publisher of the Beacon for 50 years. They raised six children, a daughter becoming a Dalton, another a Doebler, another a Roseing. More of S. S. later.

In January, 1876, Town of Rock Falls inhabitants numbered 258 people and 65 dogs, by official count, a fivefold increase (in people, that is) in just six years. It was a good year for construction and business activities. A great boost came when the mill dam at the falls upstream was raised to 21 feet, creating a much larger mill pond. This not only provided a more certain flow to the enlarged mill but started a new winter business, the cutting and selling of blocks of ice for refrigeration. The rail siding to the grist mill now became especially useful, as ice could be harvested and towed by the teams of horses to the railcars and shipped to markets. Sheds had to be built to store ice for later shipment, and another spur of the rail siding was added to the mill siding so that blocks of ice could be put onto slides and loaded to cars. During 1880, Todd, the subsequent mill owner who had bought out Heaton in 1876, contracted an astonishing 1,000 railcars of ice and employed 100 men and 40 horses. The good old days had gotten better and better for the little village.

Rock Falls really took off in the late 1870s. Wages were at $1.75 to $2.00 a day for laborers, and farm prices were rising -- 90 cents-a-bushel wheat, 20 cents-a-bushel oats, 30 cents-a-bushel corn, 18 cents-a-pound butter, 10 cents-a-dozen eggs, and 20 cents-a-pound lard. A number of new businesses were launched by the end of the decade: a new lumber company with a livestock buying business and stockyards, built along the rail siding, a marble-cutting service for making gravestones, another new drugstore and soda fountain, a meat market, a jewelry and watch shop, another millinery shop, a brickyard and kiln atop a small clay deposit. The first "burn" yielded 60,000 bricks, but it was the last as well. The clay deposit played out.

Robert Todd was a "go-getter," as they say. After he acquired the Stone Mill, he made several improvements and additions. The original burrs were replaced to provide ten double sets and a single set of rollers. Roller processed flour was considered the finest produced, and the Todd mill was the first and largest complete roller mill in the whole State of Iowa (yes sir!), with a daily production capacity of 250 barrels of flour. In 1877, Todd also built a 30 by 60 foot, two-story frame addition to the Stone Mill and installed equipment enough to fill an additional three railroad cars of flour a day. There was good reason for the town to celebrate the Fourth of July in that year, this time with a ringing of bells, shooting of cannon, a five-piece Pickford String Band, the gifted Rock Falls Choir, a baseball game, races, and the parade. The event was attended by an estimated 1,200 people. How good they were, the good old days! But could they last?

CHAPTER III

THE NOT-SO-GOOD OLD DAYS

J. B. Lippincott & Co, publishers, came out with a fascinating book of 2,478 pages in 1880, 25 years after the founding of Rock Falls. Befitting a large book, it carried a very large title, as follows:

LIPPINCOTT'S GAZETTEER OF THE WORLD

A Complete
PRONOUNCING GAZAETEER
or
Geographical Dictionary
of the
<u>WORLD</u>
Containing Notices
OF OVER ONE HUNDRED AND TWENTY FIVE THOUSAND PLACES
WITH
Recent and Authentic Information Respecting the Countries
Islands, Rivers, Mountains, Cities, Towns, Etc,
in Every Portion of the Globe

NEW EDITION
Thoroughly Revised, Re-written, and Greatly Enlarged
BY A NUMBER OF ABLE COLLABORATORS

In this fact-packed book, a paragraph on Mason City, described all of its railroads plus "2 banks, 5 churches, a school-building which cost $30,000, 2 flouring-mills, and a pottery. Two weekly newspapers. . . .Pop.1703" And for

Nora Springs, it described the railroad, a bank, a newspaper office, four churches, a high school, two grist mills, and an iron foundry, with "Pop.742" For Rock Falls, the following in full:

> "ROCK FALLS, a post-village in Falls Township, Cerro Gordo Co, Iowa, on Shell Rock River, and on the Burlington, Cedar Rapids & Northern Railroad, 24 miles W.N.W. of Charles City, and 9 miles N.E. of Mason City. It has a church, a newspaper office, and 1 or 2 mills. Pop.350"

Lippincott's "Pop.350" may have been an exaggeration. The 1880 census put it at 230, a slight but disappointing decline from the 258 residents of 1876. Clearly, it had already lost ground to Mason City.

Generally, Iowa had prospered greatly in the 30 years following statehood. All of its agricultural acreages had come "under the plow" or were grazed by cattle, hogs, and sheep. Beneath its rich soil, deep veins of coal, clay, lime, gypsum, sand, and gravel were being mined. Large cities were forming -- Des Moines, Davenport, Dubuque, Sioux City, Cedar Rapids -- as the grain processing, meat packing, and minerals industries flourished. Railway mileage neared its peak of 9,000 miles statewide, connecting with growing highway networks and barge traffic on the big rivers. Population surged to 192,214 in 1850, to 1,194,020 in 1870, and to 1,624,615 in 1880. Even the essentially rural Cerro Gordo County had a population density averaging well over 60 per square mile. Falls Township farmers and townspeople numbered at least a thousand by 1880. The Township's 36 sections offered 144 family-size farms of 160 acres. These were being snapped up in a hurry. No question about it, the liberalized public land law had accomplished its purpose. Iowa was settled. Lippincott's "Bible for the traveling salesman" must have sold well.

From the beginning, education had been a primary interest of Iowa settlers. This interest was attributed in part to the many arrivals from New England, bringing with them their strong Yankee traditions of culture, religion, and self-government. Also, the ranks of the large migration from old England, Scotland, and the northern European States of Germany, deprived of educational opportunities, brought with them the hunger for learning as much as for freedom. The results were quite amazing. They extended beyond the countless one-room schoolhouses built for their first eight years (grades) of study. They extended beyond the many small seminaries, equivalent of four more years of study pending the statewide support of an educational "system." A further level of learning opportunity emerged quickly in the form of colleges.

Even before statehood in 1846, Iowa Territory could

boast of a few colleges. In 1839, Loras College, and in 1843, Clarke College, both of them affiliates of the Roman Catholic Church and both in Dubuque, were founded. Iowa Wesleyan College at Mount Pleasant was founded in 1844, followed soon by Iowa College at Davenport in 1846. In 1847, the State University of Iowa at Iowa City was established by act of the First General Assembly. During the next decade, seven more college level institutions came into being: Coe College at Cedar Rapids (Reformed Church of America, 1851), University of Dubuque (Presbyterian, 1852), Central College at Pella (Presbyterian, 1853), Cornell College at Mount Vernon (Methodist, 1853), the great Iowa State College of Agricultural and Mechnical Arts, established at Ames by State law in 1858, Upper Iowa University (formerly a college) at Fayette (1857), Grinnell College at Grinnell, formerly Davenport College since 1846 but moved in 1859.

Small colleges with a religious affiliation continued to be founded in the 1860s and 1870s: Luther College at Decorah (Lutheran, 1861), Wartburg College at Waverly, (Lutheran, 1865), William Penn college, at Oskaloosa (The Friends, 1873), Parsons College, Fairfield (Presbyterian, 1875), and Drake University in Des Moines (Disciples of Christ, 1881). With such emphasis on high learning and with the obviously widespread support rooted in religious institutions, it is hard to believe a summary comment appearing in the report of the Public Lands Commission, published near the close of the century:

> "Of all the motley crowd that helped themselves
> to public land during the boom of the eighties
> not one in three had the slightest intention of
> remaining upon it; not one in five remained more
> than long enough to prove up and sell out, or
> 'mortgage out'; and not one in ten has left a
> permanent mark upon the landscape..."

Such a generalization could not have applied to countless thousands of the heartland farm-town communities where the evidence is clear that most who came, came to stay. As for Falls Township, Iowa Map II, circa 1895, shows names that would have appeared on the township map 25 years earlier and 25 years or much more later.

Despite a drop in the population of Rock Falls to 175 in 1885, new businesses continued to open and others to expand. A town election was held in 1882 and voters passed a measure to incorporate the town, with Todd, the miller, as first Mayor. At the lumber, livestock, and grain company near the depot, T. W. Lane added machinery to his inventory for sale. John Bliem opened a fine new Boot and Shoe Store next to his home on Mill Street. A fine new creamery was opened in town in May, 1882, but in September Mr. Carney and Mr. Hay, the proprietors, closed it up and skipped town, owing a lot of money to farmers. It was reopened by Orcutt and Brown in October, closed for the winter, and reopened in April. By May they were churning 500 pounds of cream a day, shipping butter all the way to New York. For some reason, perhaps high rail freight rates, it couldn't make it, soon closed for good, and sold everything in 1890. After the good times, the town was now in a struggle to stay alive.

So, there you are, the town after a quarter of a century. The seventies had brought their share of social and economic ups and downs to Rock Falls, and these continued into the eighties. The church was used by four denominations (not at the same time, mind you), but the Methodists were the most active, despite a succession of ministers, each of whose stay in town was brief. The pay apparently didn't improve, as Reverend Dego had a jewelry and watch shop in one corner of Mr. Hillyer's store for a time.

In 1878, Miss Minnie Hamlin opened a millinery shop, this one in the front room over Cadwell's Store, and Cyrus Blair opened yet another drug store, this one in part of Cadwell's store as well. There seemed to have been a lot of turnover in businesses, and each was short-lived. There were three barbers in town in the seventies at different times and several meat markets, including Bosley & Ford, Simon Calvert, Hall & Treadwell, L. D. Kidder, Mr. J. C. McLead, Mr. Keith, Mr. Bosie, W. Burlingham, Mr. Bice, Mr. Kitchum, and C. W. Young. Rock Falls residents must have been hard to please about butchering! For a time the Tiffany & Wright Store, a branch of its Mason City store, occupied the Eager Store, with A. B. Huntley as manager.

Mr. Cadwell was the correspondent for the Mason City newspaper for some time, and he also briefly published a Rock Falls newspaper, called the <u>Union</u>. Later he ran another called the <u>Rock Falls Star</u>. Levi Helm operated a general merchandise store and was also a dealer in grain and coal. He also published a newspaper, <u>The Rock Falls Courier</u>, at least one copy of which, undated, has been saved for posterity. Its four full pages consist largely of thinly disguised advertisements for Chamberlain's Proprietary Medicines written as news stories with such intriguing headlines as "Chamberlain's Colic, Cholera, and Diarrhoea Remedy," "Worth More Than its Weight in Gold for the chronic diarrhoea," "A Valuable Discovery" which was Chamberlain's cough remedy for croup, "A Severe Cold cured in Two Days Time," "Chronic Diarrhoea," "A Very Bad Lung Trouble," "Sore Nipples Cured," (!), "A Cure for Piles," and a dozen more "How-to's" and many testimonials for the Chamberlain cures for dysentery, blood flux (whatever that was!), scald head, eye and skin itch, chest pains, and the rheumatism. Not-so-good times, all right!

The women of the Ladies Aid Society, those very dear,

sweet, quiet, tireless, unsung pioneer heroines, met frequently and prepared church suppers once a month, for ten cents a plate to help pay the ministers' salaries. For a short while, one of the many ministers to serve the town was a Mrs. Hawkins, but she too left for greener pastures. The church acquired a new organ in 1877, paid for by the ladies of the church. They also conducted Thursday Night Prayer Meetings which, it was recorded, "were usually well attended." Singing schools were held for adults, an archery club, a literary society, and Good Templars Lodge were formed, the latter holding frequent lectures and educational meetings on the subject of temperance.

Contagious diseases were an ever-present menace, with tuberculosis, pneumonia, scarlet fever, diptheria, small pox, and whooping cough being the worst. Many large farm families lost two or more children in epidemics. The town had a hard time keeping a doctor in residence. Dr. J. B. Conley departed, to be followed in turn but at long intervals between, by Dr. Allen who stayed five months, by Dr. Murphy, who stayed less than a year, by a Dr. Wright (who was also a preacher) who stayed nine months, and by no one else for many years thereafter. In 1880 Dr. Pool, a Mason City dentist, made monthly visits to the village to repair teeth. Tramps were a continuing problem in those days as well. Arriving by railcars or wagons, they would beg and move on. Crop diseases hit the wheat farmers hard, causing many to shift out of this basic grain crop to raising livestock. The not-so-good old days were ever-present.

More bad luck in 1884. One night the old Stone Mill, the economic mainstay of the town, was destroyed by fire. Todd saved little of his possessions in the blaze. Most papers, records, sacks, and some flour were saved but his 2,000 bushels of wheat, 100 barrels of flour, much other feed, and all of the machines were destroyed. Only the stone walls remained and a basement full of rubble. Todd rebuilt the mill somewhat, but it was far from the output of the original Stone Mill. He sold out to H. I. Smith, leaving town to manage his other mills in Manly, Iowa, and Albert Lea, Minnesota.

In that same year, the always enterprising John Bliem began operating a rural delivery wagon "exchange service" that would endure for over 50 years and become very profitable. He would head out nearly every morning for the country byways with his horse-drawn wagon loaded with his stock of groceries and drygoods. He would trade his goods for the farmers' eggs and butter, which he would then sell in Mason City, assuring a nice profit on both sides of his trade, one from the farmer and one from the city retailer.

The worst luck to hit the community occurred on the morning of April 11, 1888. In the spring of every year, with temperatures rising, the prairie snow cover and the thick ice covering on the frozen river would begin to melt rapidly, swelling the flow, then breaking up the ice cover on many miles of the river, causing huge ice jams and bank overflows. It was an annual event. This time there were heavy warm rains overnight, adding immense flows and pressure on the frozen river. Suddenly, all hell broke loose. The 21-foot-high mill dam collapsed, and within minutes the entire south side of the town was under water and huge chunks of ice. Houses were crushed, the 155-foot-span iron bridge was washed down stream several hundred yards, and the mill was badly damaged. It was a devastating blow to the local economy, coming so soon after the mill fire. The town would be the rest of its life trying to recover.

But the town kept trying, despite the odds it faced. In 1891, Mr. Smith formed the Standard Oatmeal Company and fixed up his damaged mill to operate it as a small oatmeal mill. He built a large warehouse and cooper shop, installed mill machinery and erected storage elevators, helped financially by leading citizens in town - George O. Morse, Richard Moore, Joseph Perrett, and B. A. Brown. The mill did well for a year or two, but in 1893 it was sold at a loss of every penny that local investors had put into it. That was also the year that the new schoolhouse was struck by lightning and burned to the ground. Whatever next!

In 1894, Mr. Cochonour of Nora Springs built a brand new creamery with an ice house out back, and it prospered from the start. Delos and Sloane Stickney opened a variety store featuring jewelry, watches, clocks, repairs, sewing materials, and candy on Madison Street (Block 17, Lot 6), not a particularly good retail location. The cobbler and harness shop was closed down and was moved to Tennessee. A handsome new grain elevator and large corn crib were constructed at the rail siding, down by the lumber and grain business and stockyards. The farmer could now market his oats, wheat, and corn for shipment to Minneapolis, Kansas City, or St. Louis for milling. And Mr. T. M. (Tom) Perett became the area's leading livestock commission man, buying live cattle from farmers for shipment to the big packinghouses in Chicago and Kansas City. In December, walls of the old Stone Mill (now the oatmeal mill) were blasted out for safety reasons. That ended the local milling business for good. Only the stone foundations and bits of the wall remained as reminders of the good old days.

The May 1895 census revealed the town having only 145 residents, a very discouraging drop from the 350 reported in Lippincott's publication. The hand-writing was on the wall, as they say, because Mason City, just eight miles across the prairie had grown to 5,700, almost all of it in the 30 years since the Civil War. However, John Bliem was continuing to prosper in the grocery and drygoods business and in 1896 he added a large storage house for goods and ice behind the store and changed the name to Bliem Brothers General Store. This was because his sons Ferdinand, Valentine, and Leonard, now grown, wanted to buy him out.

Another son, John Junior, joined in the partnership for a time, but he moved to Plymouth to operate his own store. Leonard was the youngest of eleven Bliem children, four of them dying in infancy, three of diptheria and scarlet fever in one year. At the new store, Ferdinand handled the traveling egg wagon route, Valentine handled the in-store post office as the new postmaster, and he also helped his brother Leonard to "wait on trade," as the expression was. Leonard, one of the all-time nicest of men, would one day marry Mabel, second daughter of John and Jane Wilkinson.

Back in the autumn of 1871, the year before the iron horse arrived in town, a young woman of 31 years with a five-year-old daughter and a nine-month-old son arrived in Rock Falls. She had come from Wisconsin (presumably by stage coach) to have a look at a 72-acre piece of farmland in Section 16 north of town that she heard was for sale. English friends who had been on the same boat to America with her husband had settled in Falls Township. They had sent back an account of "...wonderful chances to get land cheap and rich quick," causing her and her husband to be restless and dissatisfied with things in Wisconsin.

The husband had arrived in America on May 22, 1856, from his birthplace in Shepley, Yorkshire, England, and had found work first as a laborer in Chicago, then in two or three woolen mills in nearby Wisconsin. He had worked in the Shepley woolen mills as a young man. Now having to hold down a good job as boss miller in Waukesha, he had to stay behind with the older son, aged seven, when his wife set off for Rock Falls, knowing that she would be welcomed at the homes of their English friends, the Seniors, Roebucks, and Holdens near Rock Falls. They were all Yorkshire people from near Shepley.

The young woman's family had migrated to Wisconsin in 1845 from her birthplace in Prescott, Canada, near the St. Lawrence, to which her father (a Dezell) and her mother (a Magee) had emigrated from Counties Armaugh and Tyrone, Ireland, in about 1839. In March of 1863, she had married the Yorkshire-cum-Wisconsin miller, John Wilkinson, third of eight children of the Jeremiah and Hannah (Batty) Wilkinsons of Huddersfield, near the Yorkshire moors.

The young woman liked what she saw in Iowa. It was indeed a beautiful farm setting, good land bordered by the woodlands at the western edge. They would one day call it Edgewood Farm (see Map II, Section 16). It was only two miles from the center of Rock Falls. She soon returned to Waukesha, and in the spring of 1872 the papers were signed by John Wilkinson and Jane Dezell Wilkinson. The farm was bought for $1,000, with $500 down and the balance at five percent interest. With son Wendell Waldo, daughter Jessie Ellen, and son Theodore Dezell, Jane and John Wilkinson moved to Falls Township that spring. They stayed with the George Roebucks east of town (Section 22) for a spell until the old log cabin on their own farm could be repaired and made fit for the family. They bought a team of horses, two cows, and some pigs and chickens, and started farming. They would soon have two more children to raise as well, Mabel Alice and Rufus Verne.

Another young woman born in 1830 in Hessen-Darmstadt, Germany, and married there at age 25, came to America with her husband in 1856. Conrad Krug and Anna settled somewhere in Canada and farmed the land. In 1865, with the Civil War at an end, they pushed on into Iowa and in 1866 settled onto Section 36 in Falls Township, probably among the earliest of the homesteaders. They built a house and stable in that first year and bought a pair of horses and some farming equipment and tools, but in the fall of that year, all was destroyed by a fire. They moved to Portland Township, rented for two years, bought 40 acres, sold it in three years, and bought 180 acres in Sections 14 and 15 of Falls Township, about a mile southeast of town. They farmed there for 33 years and they raised eight children. Three died in infancy, Mary married a preacher, and Anna Katherine married a Rockford farmer. Peter farmed in Plymouth, and William and Henry farmed near Rock Falls. Henry married Anna Keidle, whose parents also came from Germany, and the Henry Krugs raised two daughters, Edith Amelia and Myrtle May.

Clearly, the Wilkinsons and the Krugs and millions of European families like them in the mid-19th century must have shared a dream of some land to call their own and a "new start" in the new world. Getting it and keeping it would prove to be a struggle against great odds, as an account of the times written by Jane Wilkinson suggests:

> "My experience in starting life had nothing very romantic in it. John Wilkinson and I were married forty years ago in Atica, Green County, Wisconsin. Like most young married people of them days we didn't have much to start life with but willing hands and a strong faith in the future.
>
> "It was in the midst of the Civil War and there was plenty of work to do but money was scarce. So we had to consider what would be best to do to get a start toward getting a home of our own. John had been working for farmers for two or three years after he came from England and had saved up two or three hundred dollars. But we did not think that would be enough to start housekeeping and buy a team and start farming on shares.
>
> "But just then an old couple that John had been working for the year before wanted him back and also wanted a hired girl. So here was an opportunity to have what we had and earn some more.

John hired for $12 a month and I had a dollar a week. We stayed eight months, and after that we went to Monroe and bought us a nice little cottage for three hundred dollars. John had plenty of work by the day for a $1.00 and $1.25. We lived very economical and saving -- but still it did not seem possible to save anything, for everything was to buy and everything was very dear. When we had lived there about a year and a half, he was offered a place in a woolen factory in Illinois at a dollar and seventy-five cents a day and house rent. So we sold our house and lot for four hundred dollars and move out.

"But that was not satisfactory for he had to be idle all winter. We stayed one year and then moved to another place for a year and from there we moved to Waukesha to work in a factory. The work was steady the year around and the pay good so we stayed there nearly four years. But we were both tired of the factory and we both thought we could do better if we were out west on a farm. I used to think I was living a very useless life. If I were on a farm how many things I could do to make my own spending money. I thought how nice it would be to make butter and sell it and raise lots of chickens and what lots of money there was in eggs, everything looked flattering. I fairly envied the farmers wife.

"We had friends out here in Iowa who were urging us to come. It was such a beautiful farming country. So....we came to Iowa and bought the little farm where we are still living....But I cannot take up your time now to tell you of our success and failures and homesickness and disappointments. We had our share for a few years."

In 1891 John Wilkinson and his wife Jane of Edgewood Farm, north of town, added 160 acres to their holdings -- a quarter section of the prairie cropland in Section 11, Falls Township (see Map II). It was just next to a quarter section that their English friends, the George Roebuck family, owned. The Wilkinsons had built a comfortable, new home to replace the log cabin at Edgewood in 1878. As rapidly improving farm machinery and farming practice had developed, they needed more land than 72 acres at Edgewood in order to farm more efficiently. What they came to call the "Prairie Farm" was a valuable addition, although it meant more than twice the farm work.

To say that John and Jane had worked hard and saved while raising their five children would be to understate the facts. When not in his fields, during the planting and harvesting seasons, John worked in a woolen mill in

Mitchell, 18 miles to the east, walking the whole distance on Monday mornings and back home on Saturday nights! On the Prairie Farm, they broke up the soil a bit more each year, raising several crops of flax, an excellent cash crop at the time. In 1895, wanting some pastureland, they added to their 72-acre Edgewood Farm the eight-acre plot of wooded land at the southwest corner, paying George Roebuck $50.00 an acre for it. In 1896, Isaac Lewis, brother of Silas, sold the Wilkinsons his 80 acres bordering the south line of Edgewood Farm. This made John and Jane the proud owners of the full quarter section close by on the north side of Rock Falls, plus the quarter section Prairie Farm. The 320 acres kept them harder at work than ever.

The township map referred to herein shows owner names in about 1895. These names recall the many families who settled here to form the farm-town community. They raised large numbers of children, nearly all of whom went through the Rock Falls school. The English contingent included the Senior, Holden, Roebuck, Perrett, Wilson, Kendrew, Edgar, Woodall, Boothroyd, Calvert, Ingersoll, Pryor, Duff, Lewis, Morse, White, Smith, Dunton, Raymond, Stickney, Brown, and Wilkinson families. These were about equally matched in numbers by large and prominent German families: Gildner, Gashel, Helm, Schnartz, Jensen, Bahnsen, Hansen, Christiansen, Siewertsen, Isaacson, Hinrichsen, Bliem, Wetter, Brodrecht, Bistline, Schlobolm, Bernhardt, Bohn, Wegener, Lair, Fox, Krug, Minott, Stebens, Struchen, Weitze, and Steil. The Bohemian and Czech families were outnumbered: Wyborney, Eygabroad, Jost, Michalek, Wasechek, Navoritil, Yezek, and Dedina. So too were the Irish: Craw, Coonrod, Davison, O'Donnell. The Petersens represented Sweden, the Gorkowskis represented Poland, and the Italian representative was the very fine Tony Napoletano family.

The definitive compilation for Iowa's European-born residents for the first century of the State's history is by Professor Leland Gage, University of Northern Iowa. His listing shows a remarkable diversity of 24 nationalities. Reproduced on the following page are countries of origin and numbers of foreign-born as of the first <u>Census</u> after statehood, 1850, through the peak <u>Census</u> year, <u>1890</u>. By 1900, all major country totals had begun to decline as the State's population growth came increasingly from generations of the native-born.

Clearly, the principalities that ultimately comprised Germany supplied Iowa with the greatest number of immigrants in the nineteenth century, nearly one-half of those from all major European nations. The Germans, primarily a peasant stock, came intent on farming the rich soil in the state. The Irish built the railroads and stayed to maintain them. The Scandinavians were mostly dairymen, while the Brits and Scots a mix of farmers and shopkeepers, except for those who manned the woolen mills.

Country of Birth	1850	1890
All Countries	20,969	324,069
Germany	7,101	127,246
Ireland	4,885	37,353
Sweden	231	30,276
Norway	361	27,078
England	3,785	26,228
Canada	1,756	17,465
Denmark	19	15,519
Austria	13	12,643
Netherlands	1,108	7,941
Scotland	712	7,701
Switzerland	175	4,310
Wales	352	3,601
France	381	2,327
Russia	41	782
Italy	1	399
Belgium	4	384
Poland	0	383
All others	19	476

And in the hamlet by the Shell Rock River, south of where John and Jane Wilkinson farmed and raised their five children, the last decade of the century came to a finish quietly. In 1891, a harness and shoe shop took its place near the oatmeal mill and meat market near the river. And Miss Lizzie Perrett caught a 31-pound, 33-inch-long eel in the river, had it stuffed, and sent to the museum in Ames. In 1892, the January temperature plunged to 32 degrees below zero, causing the loss of many stored vegetables. In March, John Bliem moved into his fine new drygoods store on Mill Street. In 1893, John Schnartz and Jack Edgar quarried stone by the river bank south of town, Mr. Cochonour built an ice house next to his creamery, George Gehring bought the old Morse Hotel and reopened it for business, and the new schoolhouse was struck by lightning and burned to the ground. In 1894, several retail shops were bought and sold, a 1,000-bushel corn crib was built near the depot elevators, and the Edgar Opera House became a popular dance place. In 1895, not much worth mentioning happened.

In 1896, Ed Payne and John DeNewt opened a harness shop. Perrett and Cochonour launched a poultry business, shipping chickens, ducks, and turkeys to many parts of the country. In 1897, the Mayflower Creamery was sold to William Keidle, George O. Morse, Conrad Krug, and William Meire, local farmers. Their creamery butter, again shipped to New York City, commanded top prices. A railroad ticket from Nora Springs to California was said to cost $25.50 and Ed Payne, the harness maker, opened a barber shop.... really!

In 1899, final year of this great century of discovery and settlement of America's heartland, we record Levi Helm doing well in merchandise retailing (including cures for all known maladies), the Bliem Brothers General Store continuing to prosper, Mr. Daly operating his lumber yard, Delos Stickney and his wife Sloane operating their jewelry, watch, sewing materials, candy, and assorted variety items business, the blacksmith shop and the creamery doing well, the name "Morse Hotel" now the "Rock Valley House," Tom Perrett buying hogs and cattle in large numbers for shipment to Chicago, Rock Falls community housewives being harassed by book agents, pack peddlers, and tramps, the barber shop being taken over by Mr. John Brodrecht from Ed Payne, and Mr. Brodrecht becoming Mayor of Rock Falls.

What was happening was that the farming population of Falls Township was increasing, evident from Map II, but that of the town was decreasing. The reason? Well, the coming of the railroad was not the blessing everybody expected. It rendered obsolete the town's centerpiece, the flour mill, and with it the cooper's shop. Without a mill, no need for a mill dam; without a dam, no mill pond ice to cut and ship out. No jobs, and people had to move on.

It must have been worrisome for the leading citizens in town and particularly its merchants to watch their town languish as the prosperity of the surrounding community's farms surged ahead. And what a contrast between the thousands of agricultural hamlets and villages whose high hopes for growth turned to disappointment, while such explosive growth of heartland cities continued. Chicago, hardly a good sized town in 1855, rose to a great railroad and industrial center of two million people by 1900. The great river cities of St. Paul and St. Louis, unrivaled in location on the inland waterways network, needed only the rail links to make them metropolises by 1900. And even smaller prairie cities, hardly more than hamlets in 1850, enjoyed phenomenal growth. Interestingly, the largest of Iowa's cities by 1900 were on the rivers: Burlington (23,201), Clinton (22,111), Davenport (35,254), Dubuque (36,297), Sioux City (33,111), Council Bluffs (25,802). How important were the great rivers! Little rivers like the Shell Rock promised only an obsolete mill dam site, as the railroads shipped the farmers' grains to big city flour mills. And most worrisome of all for Rock Falls was Mason City, also founded in 1855, but a tiny hamlet now grown to 6,746 residents in 1900.

All in all, it had been an eventful, even turbulent, half-century for the nation and the heartland, indeed for the village of Rock Falls. And there were plenty who were happy to see it closing on a note of prosperity fueled by ever-increasing technical innovations in agriculture. Few in number were those concerned for survival of the smaller farm-towns amid such prosperity. To be sure, the tragedy of the Civil War, then the brief Panics of 1857, 1873, 1884, and 1893 triggered by an unstable currency and by an unregulated banking system had contributed to hardships in the midwest. But despite temporary setbacks, an agricultural revolution in the midwest to rival the earlier industrial revolution in England in terms of strides in productivity served to lessen the hardship and brought security to the farmers...if not to the farm-towns.

This period of 50 years began primitively on the farm but then came developments in machinery and methods that would amaze and bewilder the immigrant settlers of Falls Township. Dramatic improvements came in rapid succession. Among the first was John Deere's vastly improved plow. In the 1830s, this Illinois blacksmith made a single-piece, all steel plow share and a moldboard plow to replace the old iron and wooden share. This was said to have cut by one-third the animal power required to break and turn the sod and soil. In 1868, the sulky or riding plow replaced the ones that farmers had to walk behind and laboriously guide through the furrows. Then, the magnificent threshing machine to separate the seed heads or grains in plants from the stalks, straws, and seed pods replaced the centuries old flailing of sheaths of grain and handrolling of seed heads on threshing floors. This enabled millers like Robert Todd to aim for his 50,000-bushel flour milling run supplied by a few neighboring farmers. Crude threshing machines were available to the local farmers by 1850, from earlier inventions in Scotland, but by 1900 these machines had been greatly improved and continued in use through the mid-1930s.

Other labor-saving machines quickly followed: seed drills, corn planters, row cultivators, sod harrows, discs and drags, binders, hay mowers, hay rakers, hay forks (to hoist hay into barn lofts above the livestock stanchions), corn huskers (one of the all-time great labor-saving devices but the spoiler of one of the prairie communities' all-time great social events -- the husking bee), windmills for livestock watering in pastures, manure spreaders and dozens more. Improved seeds, cultivating practices, harvesting techniques, and management helped to swell the on-farm surplus production and give the midwest names like corn belt, wheat belt, and the nation's breadbasket.

A generous federal government had given 36 million acres of public domain to a State called Iowa. This acreage included an astonishing 14.4 million acres already earmarked by federal authorities as "military bounties," lavish rewards to favored soldiers for services in major wars and minor skirmishes against Indians. Most of this, unwanted by soldiers except for its cash value, was soon sold to land speculators. Cash sales by State Land Offices to settlers disposed of an additional 12.2 million acres, some for as little as 12½ cents per acre. Grants to railroad companies were an added 4.2-million-acre giveaway.

The educational land grants for school and college grounds added 1,860,000 acres to Iowa's favors to its inhabitants. Surprisingly, only 900,000 acres -- a mere 2.5 percent of the total -- were earned by homesteaders, living on and working the prairie soils.

And the railroads came -- 200,000 miles of them coast to coast by 1900, bringing millions of jobs to shape the roadbeds, lay the rails, and build the depots, bridges, and tunnels. The magnificent big-city railway terminal stations of the midwest, in St. Louis, St. Paul, Kansas City, and the three stations in Chicago, were elegantly and massively designed, built to last a thousand years. Importantly, the railroad lines linked the farm to distant markets, inducing growth of cities as milling and meatpacking centers, using larger and more mechanizations coupled with large pools of cheap immigrant labor and large pools of capital.

State and County roads were laid out along the surveyed section lines, and while still just plain dirt, and gravel surfaced, they too gave jobs to the builders of the roadbeds, bridges, culverts, rail crossings, and fences. The nation's natural resources were located, dug up, cut down, and processed: Minnesota's Mesabi Range iron ore, cooked and shaped into millions of miles of rail and great girders to support the skyscrapers; Illinois' immense coal fields to heat the homes and fuel the factories; gold and silver to fuel the financial houses; copper and lead and zinc deposits for industrial fabrication; endless expanses of forests, cut and shaped for a thousand uses, and clay to dig up and shape into drain tiles for farmers' fields.

Yes, all in all, it was a dizzying, enchanting, amazing age of unparalleled development. It did indeed seem to be the good old days for nearly half a century in the prairie cities and most rural towns, especially where the <u>community of spirit</u> of town <u>and</u> farm flourished during the <u>changing times.</u> But they were nontheless years that began to sow the seeds of decline and decay for small-town America, and the process was irreversible. At the turn of the century, the first faint clouds were gathering on the distant prairie horizon.

CHAPTER IV

THE GATHERING STORM

In the midwest, perhaps everywhere, a disturbing calm settles across the land, quietly softening the atmosphere, before a threatening storm. The signs are always the same. A faint, slightly oppressive weight seems to press against the temples and eyeballs -- barometric presure, they say. You look at the trees, and hardly a leaf is stirring. You watch the horses, their heads held higher than usual, as they whinny softly, their feet stomping nervously. Cattle huddle together, wild-eyed. Your dog maintains steady eye contact with you as though seeking some kind of assurance. Only the placid pig gives no hint of impending turbulence. Dogs and cats, possibly cows and horses too, can sense a storm long before a person hears the distant thunder. In humans, the sign is an uneasiness, impossible to explain.

There were no clear indications of serious trouble in America's rural heartland at the turn of the century. A series of financial squalls -- "panics," they were called, were experienced in the 19th century. There were seven of them during the century, the last and longest from 1893 to 1897. Each had arrived without much warning, had broken sharply, and had passed along, leaving only minor damage. They were short-lived corrections of maladjustments in a basically unstable financial system, rather than weakness in the economic system, so it was believed. They were but temporary interruptions in an ever-rising tide of prosperity. In 1900, the rapidly rising farm commodity and real estate prices and renewed national prosperity were proof that the nation was again on course. More good times.

Was there any faint evidence of another storm gathering, however distant? If you had put that question to a strapping young German farmer in Falls Township who had a name like Martin Hinrichsen, or to his strong and robust young neighbor, Chris Bendicksen, each would have thrown back his head, roared with laughter, jarred your teeth by a friendly whack on the back, and said, "Vot you talkin' 'bout, fellow?" The joy and freedom that they were experiencing, tilling the fertile, black soil on their own Iowa farmland, was not to be spoiled by any concerns about another mild panic some time down the road.

In little more than 100 years, America had come from colonial status to a world power. It had started the century an agrarian society. It ended the century a predominantly industrialized society. It had been a nation of farmers...subsistence farmers, mostly. It became a nation of commercial farmers. Heartland America had achieved industrial might and agricultural supremacy around a circle of great cities -- St. Louis, Chicago, Minneapolis, St. Paul, Omaha, and Kansas City, all of them linked together and to the rest of the world by the greatest rail and waterborne transportation network on earth.

The subsistence farmer had lived off the land, selling locally only a modest share of his crop that might be surplus to his own needs, exchanging it for basic supplies such as salt, sugar, soap, and cloth. The commercial farmer produced much, much more and sold it all in a distant market, exchanging it for factory products and a higher standard of living. Early settlers and homesteaders had been independent, virtually self-sufficient. More recent commercial farmers were dependent on uncontrollable, global supply-demand forces, fluctuating currencies or prices, and credit to finance ever more expensive and technically efficient farm machines. The earlier farmers had been unorganized and saw no need to be otherwise. The 20th century farmers tried to band together for better rail rates, credit terms, and crop prices, but with no more success than industrial workers had in seeking better wages and working conditions.

By 1890, the value of American manufactured products exceeded the value of American agricultural products for the first time since the nation's founding, and soon the number of factory workers would exceed those of farmers. In 1902, the ranks of employed were 30,400,000, but only 500,000, or 1.6 percent, were unemployed. The agrarian-mercantile democracy was slipping away. The captains of industry and finance (some called them the robber barons) held sway -- Astor, Vanderbilt, Drew, Cooke, Gould, Carnegie, Morgan, Rockefeller, and many more -- in a golden age of more production, consolidation, speculation, and manipulation. Mark Twain aptly named it The Gilded Age.

From 1850 to 1900, the nation's population had tripled, from 25 million to 75 million. In little more than 50 years, Iowa had gone from territorial status to an agricultural giant and an emerging industrial State of some 2,232,000 inhabitants. In the same 50 years since Elijah Wiltfong had driven his team of oxen from the Mississippi upstream by the Cedar and Shell Rock to found Rock Falls, that little town had prospered. In a flurry of activity, it had peaked at 350 residents in the 1880s before declining to 140 residents in 1900. Was this a hint of the beginning of the calm before the prairie storm?

It was a disappointment for the growth-oriented merchants and other townspeople that Rock Falls had settled back into relative economic stagnation. They had hoped for an expanding population in the Township to bring not just new wealth and financial security but better school buildings and teachers, a stronger church, a newspaper, a bank, a small industry or two, better streets and roads, perhaps even a movie house and cafe, and at least a doctor, dentist, lawyer, and a barber or two. Surrounded by such incredible progress throughout Iowa, why had Rock Falls begun to falter and decline?

There were many reasons that made the decline inexorable. It was not so much the rotten luck with the unmanageable Shell Rock River, as temporarily destructive as it could be, and despite its scenic attractions. It was not the quality of the farmland or the farmers, although Cerro Gordo County soils were less than Iowa's best. It was not the fault of the railroad entirely, for its arrival in the town was timely and its services adequate. Rather, Rock Falls was disadvantaged, as were thousands of other small communities, by a combination of three basic shortcomings. First, it was not favored with any natural resources that would stimulate and sustain community growth. Second, its location was too close to a community that was so favored, thus it could not become a "market town," in the English sense, serving a large surrounding area as distinct from a village or hamlet. Third, it was not geographically centered in the County, such that it might be chosen as a seat of County government or a location for County facilities.

Virtually all of midwest America's major cities are river-port cities or lake-port cities: "astride the crossroads and gateways of commerce," as a famous early Supreme Court decision described Chicago. The great midwestern cities are on the Mississippi, Ohio, and Missouri rivers or the shores of the Great Lakes. Water is their abundant natural resource. Lesser cities, not blessed with a navigable waterway, are State capitols -- Des Moines, Springfield, Lincoln, Pierre, Madison, Lansing, Independence, Columbus, and Indianapolis. Less favored, smaller cities are often the seats of County government. While not cathedrals and abbeys in the European sense, the County courthouses of the heartland, many of them architectural gems in themselves, were the 19th century American equivalents.

Mason City, Iowa, was uniquely favored. It had no navigable waterway to stimulate growth, as did the great metropolises of Davenport, Burlington, Cedar Rapids, Council Bluffs, Sioux City. Mason City was an early rival of Rock Falls, a mere nine road-miles northeast, and a dozen other Cerro Gordo County farm-town communities. All were founded and settled in about the same year and, for most outward appearances, with identical conditions and circumstances. What favored Mason City? It was what was just beneath its fertile prairie loams and not elsewhere that made the crucial difference. It was the 30-foot deep and extensive deposits of limestone, clay, sand, and gravel. What a difference a few miles make...and a few feet! The young John Wilkinson of Shepley, West Yorkshire, might have become rich beyond the dreams of avarice, while the rich Hanford McNider remained an unknown farmer.

In particularly mixed proportions, these limestones, clays, and sands would launch and sustain for four decades what became the largest single cement plant in the world. This plant and a second nearby developed a 12,000-barrel per day production capacity. Similar mixtures would launch and sustain what became the largest brick and drain-tile factory in the world. The hut-shaped kilns dotting the landscape developed a combined annual capacity of 200,000 tons of manufactured clay products in Mason City.

Cement is a chemical binder vital to the construction industry. When cement is combined with water and sand, it makes mortar. Mortar is the stuff that binds clay bricks and concrete blocks together. When cement is combined with the water, sands, and gravel, it makes concrete. Mortar and concrete are components of a great variety of man-made structures. In 1824, Joseph Aspdin patented "portland" cement, a unique mixture which he said resembled the limestone quarried in Portland, England. The principal ingredients of portland cement are limestone, clay, and a little gypsum. A combination of the right qualities of these ingredients makes a finely ground powder with a large content of anhydrous calcium silicates. This reacts chemically with water to produce a strong, hard coherent mass. In the building boom of the 19th century Charley McNider's Northwestern States Portland Cement Company on the north side of Mason City was a big winner from the start, and it was a springboard to national prominence for Charley's son Hanford, but that's another story.

Clays are hydrous aluminum silicates, and their properties, hence their uses, vary widely in nature. The clay deposits under the south side of Mason City, between 7th and 19th streets (practically down town), were uniquely suited for building materials, bricks, roofing and flooring tiles, and most importantly drain tiles. Clay was in great and immediate demand, in the cities and on the farms alike, and more than for building materials. Midwestern soils do not drain well naturally. With excessive surface and sub-surface moisture due to snowmelt and heavy spring rains, rolling prairie soils are slow to drain into water courses. This can delay the planting of crops or prevent plantings entirely on otherwise good croplands. The clay beneath Mason City was brought out, baked, and shaped into millions of clay tiles, rounded into hollow tubes about 18 inches long and eight inches in diameter, then put back in the ground on thousands of Iowa's farms. When laid end to end beneath the surface of the ground perhaps two or three feet deep, drain tiles served a vital purpose on most midwestern farms as underground passages to speed the flow of excessive water from the soil. Mason City's Brick & Tile Company was also a big winner from the very start.

The first brickyard was launched in the city in 1871. It was operated by N. M. Nelson and Henry Brickson and was located about a mile south of the city's central business district. Bricks were molded from the thick clay mined from the immediate area. They were then dried in the sun. Later, modern bricks and tiles were dried in gas-fired kilns at temperatures exceeding 1,800 degrees. The Mason City Brick & Tile Company was organized in 1884. At its peak of production in the early 1900s, there were as many as nine plants producing bricks and hollow tile products simultaneously. These plants and the cement factories attracted great numbers of immigrant laborers. A section of the city came to be known as the infamous "Powder Street" neighborhood, where the brick and tile company provided worker housing of the typically cheapest kind for the poor labor force. It was said to be a section of town to avoid because of its fights, prostitution, and such attractions.

The city's limestone and clay attracted not one but five railroad lines, making the city a major rail center virtually overnight, as growth induced more growth. Other industries were inevitably attracted, providing thousands of jobs. Among them was the American Beet Sugar Refining Company. Using lime in its processes, it handled 100,000 tons of beets a year, all grown under contract between the sugar refinery and a hundred or more surrounding farmers.

Another big new industry was the Jacob E. Decker Meat Packing Company. Here was a German-born immigrant who knew how to make sausage. He developed a large slaughter house and processor of beef and pork, which employed 1,200 workers at its peak. Still another striking boost to the Mason City economy came with the surge in demand for lime as a vital alkalinity additive to midwestern croplands to offset and balance against the soil's naturally excessive acidity. What a fortuitous gift of nature in time and in place for the young midwestern city in the heart of the agricultural midwest! And what a bad break for Rock Falls just nine miles away and with superior water-power, but with hardly enough limerock to build and Old Stone Mill.

The city was almost embarrassed with its riches and the number of its railroads. Before the railroad building binge had ended (and it was a binge, resulting in outragious over-building of needless trackage, as lines competed ferociously for dominance over trade territory) Mason City had acquired four depots. The one on 2nd Street NW served both the Chicago Great Western and the Chicago Rock Island & Pacific Railroads. The one on South Pennsylvania Avenue served the Chicago Milwaukee St. Louis & Pacific. The one on 1st Street SW served the Chicago & North Western. The one on 3rd Street NE served the Minneapolis & St. Louis.

Of course, all of this railroad activity meant a lot more construction, operations, and maintenance jobs. With all of these advantages, and having the additional honor of being chosen as the County Seat (over some competition from Clear Lake), Mason City was poised for growth from its modest total of 1,703 residents in 1880. By 1900, it had quadrupled to 6,746 and would triple from that number to over 20,000 in 1920. The little hamlets surrounding it didn't have a chance.

If the 1800s could be called America's Railroad Age, the early 1900s could be called the Automobile Age. Not that some kind of power-driven, rather than horse-drawn, vehicle was especially new to the world. A steam-powered tri-cycle built by Cugnot of France in 1769 is recognized as the first "automobile," and for a century it was the accepted way throughout Europe and America to be mobile on three (and later four) wheels.

Two Germans, Carl Benz and Gottlieb Daimler, launched the first gasoline-powered autos in 1885 and 1886. They later merged to form Daimler-Benz, one of the great names in automobile history. In the United States, Ransom E. Olds and James Ward Packard, also familiar names for later models, were active in automobile research, and by 1898 more than fifty automobile companies existed. In 1901, the three horsepower Oldsmobile was the first commercially successful car; there were 425 of them sold in that year, and 5,000 of them were sold in 1904.

It was Henry Ford who turned the car from a luxury or a sportsman's plaything into a necessity. He had borrowed ideas from the others to achieve mass production of inexpensive cars. Mass production *per se* was an old idea in Ford's time. In 1776, a certain Jeremiah Wilkinson of England had invented the fixture or jig, a means of making parts in series, which is the root principal of mass production. (Not to be confused with the clothier, Jeremiah Wilkinson, seventh son of cloth-weaver James Wilkinson and father of woolen miller John Wilkinson, all of Shepley,

West Yorkshire, England.) Henry Ford's Ford Motor Company, organized in 1903, applied this principal to automobile production, but more important was his genius and concept of the automobile as a necessity. Within two decades, the country was on wheels, as was said, and Ford's Model T car of 1908, durable, simple, and inexpensive, would be reproduced 15,000,000 times!

And what had this to do with Rock Falls? Quite simply, first the railroad, and then the automobile, placed Mason City and Nora Springs and Manly and Osage a good bit closer to Rock Falls than when there was not any traveling option to the horse and buggy or wagon. Put another way, the automobile saved the farmers and townspeople around the village of Rock Falls about five hours of preparation and travel time for a round trip shopping visit to Mason City. The team of horses was a lot more useful in the hay fields than on the roads to town, and so were the farmers.

What's more, it soon became a settled fact that the farmer would go to the city to see a doctor, dentist, and barber, and to the movies, now that he could zip down the country roads at 25 to 30 miles per hour. A hundred and one farm and home necessities could be purchased at a good choice of stores in the city. A carpenter, plumber, veterinarian, minister, or medicine man could cover two, even three or more near by towns as his "territory", and make it back to his own home town by nightfall. The automobile would profoundly and permanently alter the economic and social structure of America, and most of all the small-town trading centers of rural America.

But all of this was not to happen over night. Meanwhile, events in Rock Falls continued to occur at a measured pace, and as with most revolutionary changes in the making, rare was the individual who foresaw their coming soon enough to do much about them.

Still, while the town was certainly not growing, it was nonetheless a veritable beehive of activity. The game of musical chairs continued over retail store space, with various establishments moving into and out of homes, up and down streets, changing hands and adding new goods for sale. The more or less permanent barber offered services over the blacksmith shop. The elevator and lumber businesses continued to prosper. A small office building was added at the lumber yard, down by the tracks, not large enough to rent out office space to others, mind you, but a good place for the lumber yard operator to "wait on trade" and keep the books and haggle with customers about prices. Up town, Delos Stickney, believing in the future, took down his ageing shop and built a new and larger one on the jewelry store site. The Bliem brothers added Doran (apparently gas) lamps to their drygoods and grocery store. In June of 1901, "the town's first automobile whizzed by through the settlement," to quote from the Rock Falls Historical Book.

In 1902, C. L. (Charley) Calvert bought out the lumber business. Two years later he bought the grain elevator near by. He kept both for a short while but then sold out to a Minneapolis outfit. It installed a manager from out of town, something that didn't set so well among the local folks. Why not a local man to be the manager? In 1902, also, consideration was first given by local businessmen to the organization of a new banking institution. Those named in support of the venture were the Bliem brothers, Tom Perrett, the livestock commission man who was averaging about $80,000 per year in purchases and shipping 80 carloads of cattle to Chicago, William Brodrecht, the farm implement dealer, Charley Calvert of the lumber yard, Levi Helm, the general merchandiser, H. P. Gildner, also a livestock dealer shipping about 25 carloads of cattle each year, and Delos Stickney. Together, they about constituted the town's census of businesses in 1902. Strangely, nothing more was decided about a bank for another twelve years, difficult to understand, as the community certainly could have used a bank. It would have helped local trade as well by keeping the folks in the home town rather than trading in communities that had a bank. Yes sir.

In early 1903, the first telephone company was organized to connect many farm homes and the towns of Plymouth, Rock Falls, and Portland. Bliem Brothers General Store was given custody of the first local switchboard to be installed. It and others like it throughout the heartland, came to be called "central," and Leonard Bliem operated the central facility for a time. It was a delicate position to be in, as the central operator, once having connected the caller to the callee, so to speak, could then listen in on the conversation. You wanted someone of the highest integrity as central, and Leonard Bliem was certainly that. It was not a job for a gossip. No sir.

In that same year, Bert Olden opened a blacksmithing shop and became a mainstay of the community for more than 35 years. Levi Helm's store burned to the ground. Brodrecht added windmills, organs, and "other implements" to his goods for sale. The Rock Island Railroad discontinued telegraph service at the depot only to restore it the following year. The Modern Woodmen of America, a social, insurance, and benevolent fraternity, issued a charter to Falls Camp in 1904, listing 18 charter members. The Order built a lodge hall in 1905 on Lot 1, Block 15, on Market Street, and it became a useful meeting hall for the town for the next 50 years.

The next four years were painfully slow ones for the town. While farmers prospered with good prices for those times (72 cents a bushel for wheat, 38 cents a bushel for corn, 37 cents for barley, 33 cents for oats), the town stood still. The only recorded activity in 1906 was sale of the Mill Reserve property along the river by the County Board of Supervisors for $50 for back taxes. Sad to say, the only remaining evidence of the old flour mill was the stone foundation walls. The end of another era. In 1907, Charley Calvert was delivering dressed poultry to eastern markets, small pox closed the schools for three weeks in May, the railroad put in a sidewalk from the depot to the town center, and Rock Falls was connected to Mason City by a telephone line. That, at least, was progress!

In 1908, the inveterate Mr. Stickney built a new combination store-house, adding more merchandise to be sold. His wife Sloane, who had taken on the switchboard job in her home and operated as "central," had her wages reduced from $60 to $45 per month, not for a lack of adequate or proper performance, but because of the meager early returns from phone calls and rates and the generally depressed local economy. In 1909, the Ladies Aid Society held an Ice Cream and Apron Social, bringing them $30, which helped to pay the pastor's salary of $200 a year from the Rock Falls church. Plymouth Church, with which his services were shared, paid him $600 annually. Together, it wasn't much of a salary, but it was augmented with quite a bit of payment in kind, such as in eggs, chickens, pork, vegetables, fruits, chopped wood, and that sort of thing.

A close look at the township map (page 24) reveals eight school districts, numbered 2 through 9, and the locations of each district schoolhouse. A ninth, which was District No. 1, not numbered on the map, surrounded the Town of Plymouth, in the northwestern corner of the township. It was the first to be established, on August 11, 1856. District No. 2, surrounding Rock Falls, was established a month later, on September 10. Education in the township was restricted to eight years of attendance at these one-room prairie monuments scattered over the landscape. Amazingly, they remained in service through the late 1930s, for more than 80 years. Meager financial support came from County property tax monies and intermittent levies by the township on the same properties. Needless to say, the educational opportunities offered for little blighters improved rather dramatically with the demise of the country schoolhouse and consolidation of all schools in the town.

The State of Iowa as a whole was tardy in developing a public educational system. It wasn't until 1909 that a State Board of Education was established and until 1911 that State laws provided "free high school education extending to all qualified pupils." This encouraged, but did not mandate, four more years of attendance, not especially attractive to parents in many farm families. They needed the child labor on the land. Similarly, a lengthy duration of attendance every year was never popular, and for the same reason. The need for helping hands was often crucial during the planting and harvesting seasons. Thus, the school year developed into one of nine months only, with the three summer months excluded, and it remains so today. Of course, it is safe to say that all blighters heartily endorsed that development and custom.

The small but handsome schoolhouse built on the east edge of Rock Falls in 1893 for District No. 2 had survived storm, flood, and fire longer than its predecessors. However, it would be at least two decades before more than eight years of schooling would be available for the town. In 1912, the community received a big boost when the Township Board of Education recommended and the populace voted 175 to 32 to establish their own free high school. With this approval, the Board voted to build an addition, eight feet by ten feet by twelve feet, to the present structure for the High School of Falls Township. How about that?

The President of the Board at the time was W. B. Calvert (Charley's uncle), the Secretary Elizabeth Perrett, and Directors included Henry Krug, Charley Calvert, S. H. Wetter, Geo. Christiansen, E. E. Hersey, and Frank Wherry. Henry Krug's daughter Myrtle was the first primary teacher and her sister Edith was a teacher in District No. 7, then called the Ernie Stebens school after the farmer owning a quarter section on which the schoolhouse was built. However, Edith's marriage to Rufus V. Wilkinson was to take place on May the 8th of that year, so she would soon leave the teacher rolls of the township. Both Edith and Myrtle had earned teaching certificates after completing studies at the Roosevelt Institute in Mason City, an excellent private alternative to free State-supported high schools.

The John Wilkinson family, as well as the Henry Krug family, went in for school teaching. Wendell Waldo, the oldest son of John and Jane, taught briefly in Falls Township, before moving to Lime Creek Township and the Mason City area, where he farmed and followed the carpenter's trade for many decades. Jessie, an older daughter, taught school for several years, first in the Rock Falls primary grades in 1891 and 1892, then in Plymouth primary grades for 15 years, and then in District No. 8, near her father John Wilkinson's Prairie Farm, across the road from George Senior's place. Mabel, the other daughter, taught in No 8 in 1898, after attending the Nora Springs Seminary. She then taught in the school in Rock Falls and No. 5 district until her marriage to the town's enterprising merchant, Leonard Bliem.

The Seminary in Nora Springs, basically a teachers' preparatory school (not quite a college, more than a high school) filled a distinct need of the times, namely as an institution of higher learning for young people in rural communities. Like many other small institutions of similar purpose in Iowa, it was privately-owned and operated, as the arrival of a State-wide publicly subsidized system was awaited. The little promotional booklet dated 1900 which

Edith Krug had acquired set forth the courses of study offered. They were the rough equivalent of a higher school and early college education, at the time not widely available. The courses were as follows:

> "THE NORMAL COURSE prepares fully for county and state certificates, and fits for success in the school room.
>
> "THE SCIENTIFIC AND CLASSICAL COURSES prepare for college in the shortest time and most thorough manner. These also prepare the theological, medical, dental, law, pharmacy and engineering courses.
>
> "THE COMMERCIAL AND SHORTHAND COURSES in the Business College prepare to fill successfully positions in the business world."

This delightful booklet also listed "Ten Points in our favor" as being Convenience of Access, Location, A Christian School, Students, Teachers, Personal Oversight, Expenses, Courses, Equipment, and True Manhood. Three of these are noteworthy for their forthright clarity:

> "A CHRISTIAN SCHOOL. A christian but non-sectarian school is a better place in which to be educated than in one of any other kind.
>
> "STUDENTS. Students from the country and smaller towns have stronger bodies, clearer brains, better habits and a more wholesome influence than those from the cities.
>
> "TRUE MANHOOD. We believe in symmetrical education. We wish that our students may develop the best type of manhood and womanhood."

The cost for a three-term year was modest. For a ten weeks term, and there were three terms -- fall, winter and spring, the total cost was $29.75, which covered furnished room ("bring sheets, towels and pillow cases only") board, tuition, and book rent. For those who could not attend during the entire term (the farm boys), there were special inclusive rates of $1.30 a week. For those wishing to take advantage of the offer, a certification of character from the home County's Superintendent was required. It is uncertain and nowhere recorded why Edith and Myrtle Krug chose the Roosevelt Institute in Mason City over so fine an institution as the Nora Springs Seminary. Perhaps the Krugs felt more than did the Wilkinsons that the reward of higher education at a city institution would prove greater than from those catering to "country and smaller towns."

John and Jane Wilkinson's two younger sons, Theodore

and Rufus, were not attracted to the teaching profession as a career. Rather, after eight years of schooling and a lot of hard farm labor, they were interested in leaving the farm to become merchants. They seemed to be on the right track. Theodore was 39, and Rufus was 29, and both were unmarried when, in 1910, they launched the Wilkinson Brothers lumber and implement business by buying what remained of the less than successful ventures by the many previous owners of these businesses in the town. Rufus, expressing a life-long fondness for fancy letterhead stationery paper, was quick to have printed on a fine grade of paper an Indian chief's full-feathered head as his colorful logo and the words "Wilkinson Bros THE CHIEF DEALERS, in Lumber, Coal, Mill Feed, Implements and Harness" and in four different type faces.

The business was widely known as simply "The Lumber Yard," but there was a lot more to it than shingles and boards. There were milled doors and windows and moldingboard, hardware tools and paints and nails and bolts, rope and binder twine, barbed and woven wire fencing and fence posts, everything that a team of horses could ever want or need, from feed bags to hang under their noses to collars and halters and saddles, and much, much more. Newly-constructed sheds made up the yard complex, including a ten-bin coal shed along the rail siding, such that different grades of coal, from the very soft Iowa coals to the best of the Illinois hard coals, could be unloaded into chutes from the rail cars. There was a feed storage house, similarly located close by the siding, in which sacks of various cattle, hog, dog, sheep, horse, and chicken feeds and sacks of cement were stacked. There was a large extension to the machinery show room attached to the office and harness shop, and it contained spring-toothed harrows, manure spreaders, side-delivery rakes, grain wagons, hay mowers, hay forks, hay racks, discs, and drags.

There was a drive-on scales out front onto which the teams of horses and (later) the trucks could ascend to be weighed with loads of grain hauled to the elevator and for Theodore and Rufus to weigh the many loads of coal that they had sold. There was the old elevator with its chain-driven lift to raise the grain into rail cars for shipment to the great milling centers of Minneapolis, St. Louis, and St. Paul. The dimension lumber -- everything from the 1 x 4s through 1 x 12s, 2 x 4s through 2 x 12s, 4 x 4s, and 4 x 6s, and in lengths from 6 to 18 feet -- was stacked in a two-story shed with one side open for easy loading and replacing of stock, and a wide eave or protective overhang to keep rain and snow off the lumber.

And last but not least, there was the office, with a pot-bellied stove, red-hot in winter for the loafing clientele, a nice old roll-top desk of solid oak in which to keep the sales slips and other records, the demonstration model of the fascinating new De Laval Cream Separator, and assorted literature from the companies that made machinery and produced feeds and seeds. What a place! And it was all within a hundred yards of the Rock Island Depot, past which the great iron horses, belching steam and smoke, pulled their hundreds of railroad cars throughout the day. It was the most exciting place in town.

Meanwhile, John Wilkinson's family shared abundantly in the golden age of agriculture by working both the home farm, Edgewood, and the Prairie Farm, about a mile northeast of Edgewood. Farming had always been hard work in the days before tractors replaced the teams of horses, and before other mechanizations. It became particularly arduous work for John Wilkinson in his eighties as manager of the planting, cultivating, harvesting, and marketing activity on two 160-acre farms after his sons, Theodore and Rufus, moved to town and started the lumber yard business in year 1910. The two farms were kept in operation by the father and sons with hired help, but a lifetime of hard work for the father, starting as a West Yorkshire woolen mill worker 65 years earlier, finally exacted its toll.

On March 16, 1911, John Wilkinson died. He had taken sick, wrote his daughter Mabel, while in Manly to attend the funeral of William Holden, his old friend and companion on the voyage from Liverpool to New York in 1856. Back in Edgewood, John died a few days later, age 85 and a few months. Reprinted here is a copy of an original printing that appeared in the Cannon Falls Beacon and in the Mason City Globe Gazette over the signature of Jonn's uncle, Mr. Silas Shelton Lewis.

LINES
On the death of John Wilkinson
March 16, 1911

We know he has gone to return to us never,
   But the love he bore for us went not to the tomb,
And all that he was has not vanished forever
   And left us alone, overshadowed in gloom.
He lives tho the chain that long bound us is broken,
   And his chair by the ingle is vacant, alone,
Yes, still is he here in the word kindly spoken
   And deeds of devotion for years we have known.

As the wildwood conceals in its shade the lone flower,
   Faraway from its kindred that blooms in the vale,
How little it dreams in its deep covered bower
   That its fragrance is wafted o'er meadow and dale.
So is it with him, who is silently sleeping
   In the grave where we left him with sorrow and tears,
Fond memory holds him fore'er in keeping
   And his lifework like incense our solitude cheers.

> He trusted in God and his faith was well founded, —
> > He believed God is Love, 't was the thought of his soul,
> And that Love universal, for all it abounded,
> > To last while the ages eternally roll.
> And the love in his heart had the Father in Heaven
> > Bestowed for a blessing to all of his kind,
> And to family, friend, it was lavishly given
> > By a conscience enlightened, a purified mind.
>
> Let the love of the Father now lighten our sorrow,
> > And words of our Savior now scatter the gloom,
> Though we parted today he will on the morrow
> > Meet us in realms far away from the tomb;
> Meet us where farewells are never more spoken,
> > In a haven of rest that he hoped for while here,
> Where the chain that unites us can never be broken
> And our joys never marred by a sigh or tear.

G.S. Lewis

The prairie Farm had for some unexplained reason been deeded by John and Jane Wilkinson to Theodore and Rufus at the time when they launched the partnership in the lumber yard business in 1910. After their father's death, the two sons rented out the Prairie Farm on a crop-sharing basis. However, Jane Wilkinson continued to operate Edgewood with help from her sons when they were not at their lumber yard and with some hired hands.

On May 8, 1912, after a long courtship, Rufus married Edith Krug, the beautiful daughter of Henry and Anna Krug. Rufus was 31 years old, Edith 26 years old. She resigned her teaching position in a one-room Township schoolhouse and they moved into Rock Falls, buying a small home in the woods just across the Rock Island tracks from the railroad depot and very convenient to the lumber yard. Theodore, still single, continued living at Edgewood while working at the lumber yard. In 1919, Jane, Theodore, and daughter Jessie rented the home place and moved into a handsome new home that Jane had had built on the northeast edge of Rock Falls. With Mabel married to Leonard Bliem and living now just next door, and with the oldest son, Wendell, having moved to a farm near Mason City, the Wilkinsons had left the scenic farmland that they had worked for 47 years. It could not have been easy for Jane to leave it, but she had the memories.

The timing of the business venture by brothers Theodore and Rufus was excellent. In spite of worsening times for small towns due to the coming of the automobile, which shortened travel time to the cities, the period from 1900 through the first World War was a "golden age" for farming in that it was a time during which prices were high and rising, while productivity soared and costs of farming were low and falling. Two decades later, when the federal government devised programs to rescue the American farmers with subsidized crop prices, the benchmark years for farming that federal New Deal policy-makers chose in efforts to achieve a "parity" in prices and costs for the farmers and urban workers during better times in the past was the period from 1910 to 1914. In other words, cost-price parity in that period was indexed to 100; if the cost-price relationship dropped to, say, 80 in 1933, the feds would support the commodity prices to make up the difference.

In this golden age for agriculture, the Wilkinson's lumber yard did well. It was a time following the passing of the frontier, when cheap midwestern land only stayed cheap so long as cheaper land could be had near the frontier to the west. But with settlement of the western High Plains and intermountain valleys, land values in the midwest began to rise. It was a time also when explosive industrialization and population growth created unprecedented demands for farm produce, with consequent upward pressure on commodity prices. At the same time, however, farm production costs were still declining, as more and more could be produced with better techniques and less labor. It was just too good to last.

While it did last, it was a decade when the farmers of Falls Township paid off debts taken on to get started in the late 1800s, and when they could place some profits into improving the homestead. First, and typically, these improvements were for new barns, livestock sheds, silos, machine sheds, and fences. Some better housing for the wife and kids came next. The farm animals were no longer raised just for meat for the farmers' tables. Livestock was fed out with processed grain supplements milled in the big cities, and herds of cattle and hogs were then sent to packing houses. That is how Tom Perrett, local raconteur and livestock commission man, made his very comfortable living. Theodore and Rufus made out all right too.

Large dairy herds produced thousands of ten-gallon cans full of milk every year in Falls Township. The cans of whole milk would be set out along the roadsides each morning for early pick-up by the local milk-run trucks and delivered to creameries. With all of this new commercial farming, Theodore and Rufus brought a steadily increasing stream of building supplies, livestock feeds, seeds, coal, and machinery from the railcar siding, through the lumber yard complex, and out to the farms, always at a nice (but of course reasonable) markup in price.

Some prosperous dairy farmers even invested in those clever new De Laval Separators, after looking at the demos and reading the literature on it in the Wilkinson Brothers lumber yard office. This ingenious machine could separate cream from milk right out there on the farm, enabling the farmer to sell his cream at a high price and use the skim milk to swill or slop the hogs. Depending on the relative prices of hogs on the hoof and skimmed milk at the creamery, the farmer would either slop the hogs or put out the whole milk for the milk-run. Farmers caught on fast; and they were becoming good businessmen.

There was no question about the improved prospects in farming in the early years of the 20th century, what with expanding markets, higher demand, better machinery, better farm management, better crop strains, and greater variety of crops. Much of this was due to research at the States' "aggies." These were agricultural colleges, one in each of most States, founded in the late 1800s under the provision of the Morrill Act of the U. S. Congress to promote better farming practices. One result of the better practices was that farm land prices were escalating. The $2-per-acre homesteader prices were long gone. The $12.50 per-acre paid by John Wilkinson in 1891 for the Prairie Farm and the Edgewood Farm were long gone. By 1910, good land was going for $60 an acre and more in Falls Township. By 1920, the average of all land, good and poor, in the midwest would sell for $75 per acre and higher. In the same year, the value of farm machinery had climbed to an estimated $1,500 per midwest farm. Prices received for farm commodities were better than ever. From 1900 to 1914 wheat rose from 55 cents a bushel to 93 cents, corn from 32 cents a bushel to 69 cents, oats from 23 cents a bushel to 42 cents. These nearly two-fold increases for the three big grain crops were matched by higher prices gained for cattle, hogs, and sheep on the hoof. Clearly, these were pretty heady times down on the farm...and in the lumber yard as well.

While all of this made some difference in Rock Falls, the biggest change that predomonated over the fortunes of the little community was the automobile. No longer was Rock Falls and its surrounding farmers a self-contained economic unit more or less isolated from the rest of the world. In earlier times, farm produce had been grown for consumption on the farm -- subsistence farming, as it was called -- or at least sold locally. Grain was brought to the miller, then taken back to the farm as baking flour or horse and cattle feed.

With automobiles and trucks, locally available goods no longer restricted the farmers' choices. Neither the farm nor the town was any longer self-contained and self-sufficient. They were commercial units integrally linked to the rest of the world. Warner Gildner could get into his Model T, have his hired man crank it up out there in front of the engine (at risk of breaking his arm when the motor started and the clutch engaged), and drive off to Mason City or Osage, bigger towns with bigger stores. Some would say it wasn't very loyal to Rock Falls to do that, but it was done. The local farm-town did remain loyal to the local lumber yard and related businesses, year after year, maybe because Theodore and Rufus had been local farm and town boys themselves.

Nevertheless, the rising tide of agricultural activities in Falls Township carried with it good increases for the amount of money and the velocity of its circulation. This spurred the good merchants and the civic spirits of Rock Falls to resurrect an old idea. They banded together to revive the earlier consideration that had been tabled, that Rock Falls really should have its own bank. It was a little like the notion so well expressed years later by Mason City's very own Meredith Wilson. In his famous muscal <u>The Music Man</u>, he wrote that "...every town has got to have <u>a boys' band</u>, yes sir, with trombones, tubas," etc. Similarly, it was a matter of pride for a town to have its own bank, and the sooner the better. Well, this was fine, if the need existed, and if the size of the bank was carefully considered under existing and prospective business circumstances.

Basically, banks have performed two vital functions in more or less the same ways since those money-changers held forth in the temples of biblical days. First, they provide a safe place in which those with money temporarily surplus to their needs can deposit it. Those who deposit earn interest. Second, the banks provide a place at which those with temporary shortages of money can hire the use of those deposits. Those who hire money pay interest. As Calvin Coolidge said, without sympathy, of countries that couldn't pay their World War I debts, "They hired the money, didn't they?"

Many additional services were quickly to develop for these quasi-public institutions called banks. For example savings deposit accounts earned interest, but did not have check-writing privileges, checking accounts did not earn interest, and other early arrangements. For a time during the 18th century, banks could even print and circulate their own money in the form of paper currency, but that privilege came in for so much abuse, confusion, inflation, and panic that the federal government had to take over the function of currency issue exclusively.

Also, borrowing could be short-term or long-term and in small amounts for, say, a new manure spreader, or in very large amounts for, say, a whole farm. These simple functions have throughout the ages enormously increased the efficiency with which money or capital is used. Imagine how inefficiently capital would be distributed for use in an economy if each holder of surplus cash had to find and deal with each person short of cash. As a result, a bewildering array of additional services, all variations on the theme of saving and lending, were devised and offered by banks, not all of them serving a public interest so much as the banking interests. That explains why banks have had to be regulated by governments -- more or less -- from the earliest days.

The self-contained Rock Falls community of the late 1800s needed a full-service local bank with adequate lending power to meet the needs of the farmers for short-term production credit and long-term real estate mortgages. However, for the essentially open, commercial, community economy of 1917, such a need was somewhat questionable. There were full-service banks in Plymouth, Manly, Nora Springs, Mitchell, and Mason City, all within short travel time by automobile. Any one of them could have established a small branch in Rock Falls, perhaps open for three days a week, to receive surplus money for deposit, make small loans on approval of the home office, and provide savings, check-writing, and other services as well.

So, what was done under the circumstances? Needed or not, on April 19, 1917, a newly-organized Farmers Savings Bank of Rock Falls, Iowa, secured a charter from the State of Iowa banking regulatory authorities and was opened for business. However, and for unknown reasons, it was capitalized at only $10,000, among the smallest in the State. This effectively prohibited the fledgling bank from making long-term farm real estate loans, backed up by the land as collateral. A single mortgage loan on a small (say 120-acre) farm or any larger farm at current land prices of the time would have exceeded the bank's capital, not a safe position for any bank to be in. Therefore, the Farmers Savings Bank was limited to dealing in small production-type loans to farmers for feed, seed, fertilizer, harness, machinery, and building materials, and perhaps for a short-term loan now and then to a local resident for home furnishings or to a merchant for purchase of his stock in trade. In short, undercapitalized as the bank certainly was, it was restricted from the outset to being sort of half a bank. That was too bad, in a sense, but in the mid-1930s, perhaps it was a blessing for the community and for those who had a stake in the bank.

Among the Board of Directors was W. G. C. Bagley, (we called him Alphabet Bagley), who was also to be named its first president. He was a very large wheel in the very large First National Bank of Mason City. The vice-president was Valentine Bliem of Bliem Brothers General Store and an excellent choice for the position. He was also a director, as was J. B. Graham, the cashier, Pete Jensen, a prominent farmer in the community, and C. H. (Charley) McNider, one of the richest men in all of Iowa. A leading Mason City entreprenuer, chief executive officer of the Northwestern States Portland Cement Company (world's largest, don't forget), Charley was the father of Mr. Hanford McNider, who would one day become prominent in State and and national affairs of the Republican Party.

To many Rock Falls folks, Charley McNider was just another "one of the outsiders," as were Bagley and Graham. With all of those heavyweights, however, the Rock Falls Historical Book Committee quotes: "A fine brick building was erected on the corner of Mill and Glover streets, and a very fine vault is a feature of the bank." In the <u>Mason City Globe Gazette</u> of August 22, 1917, the following:

> "Rock Falls is proud as a peacock these days over its new bank. The institution is called the Farmers' Savings Bank and it certainly is a credit, not only to Rock Falls, but to the entire State. The building has been constructed in the very latest style. It is furnished inside with quarter-sawed oak and the appointments throughout are strictly up-to-date. There is a fine banking room, a neat private office and a good sized directors room. The vault was made by Victor Safe and Lock Co. and is of the screw door type. The officers of the bank are W. G. C. Bagley, president...," etc, etc, etc.

Well, maybe there was a justifiable need for a few of the region's heavyweights in the banking industry to have things properly launched. Certainly, there wasn't a lot of banking expertise available locally. Still, it didn't seem right to a lot of the farmers and townspeople that Val Bliem was the only local man chosen as a Director.

There was abundant evidence in 1917 that the town and township were no longer a self-contained economy. On the 6th of April, 1917, two weeks before the Farmers Savings Bank was chartered, the United States entered the murderous fray in continental Europe that had been under way for nearly three years, and the local community would soon be involved. The United States entry at long last made it a <u>world</u> war, the war to end all wars. This meant registering of potential soldiers under the Selective Service Act of Congress, a necessity for building an army on the pitifully small peace-time regular forces of only 200,000 men. Ultimately, the universal draft recruited 4,800,000 Americans of the 24,000,000 registered between the ages 18 and 45 years. Of those called up, about one-half would get to France, and two-fifths or 800,000 of those who did would go into battle in the front line trenches.

Even before the United States entered the conflict, American industry became involved. As early as August of 1914, France asked J. P. Morgan Company, the distinguished banking colossus, for a $100 million loan. Secretary of State William Jennings Bryan disapproved on grounds that it would violate President Wilson's neutrality policy. Jack Morgan, J. P.'s son, determined to help the Allies anyway, became in 1915 a purchasing agent for Great Britain and France. He immediately by-passed Bryan, got Wilson's tacit approval, and loaned France $30 million. He then syndicated a $500 million bond issue involving 1,570 U. S. banks to finance munitions purchases. By the time the U. S. was in the war, Morgan had lined up $1.5 billion in credits for the Allies, engineered a switch in industrial production to munitions, and transferred $3.5 billion worth of armaments to our European Allies.

It was a short but vicious slaughter for "our boys," a mere 19 months in the fight, compared with the four-year devastation for England, France, Germany, and Belgium. American lives lost number a very low 122,500 of the total for all countries of 7,450,000. The State of Iowa contributed 113,000 men to the Army, Navy and Marines, including the famous 42nd or Rainbow Division, and many of them were trained at Fort Des Moines or at the huge cantonment at Camp Dodge. Iowa was fortunate in sustaining only 2,000 casualties in the war, and as many of these were from diseases as from battles. Only six World War I veterans are at rest in the Rock Falls Cemetery -- John Dedina, J. W. (Fanny) Duff, George Hansen, William Maher, Lee White, and Frank Gildner, and none of these was a war casualty.

Far greater impacts of war on the farm-town community than that on personal life came in the form of sharp rises in prices of farm lands and farm products. On top of the run-ups in grain prices earlier in the golden age of agriculture, wheat advanced between 1914 and 1917 from just 93 cents to $2.20 a bushel (the legal limit under price control law), corn went from 69 cents to $1.49 a bushel, and oats from 42 cents to 79 cents a bushel. Land prices skyrocketed with the wartime food demand and the government's urgings to increase production to feed Europe as well as America. Herbert Hoover, a name to become familiar on the political stage, was one major mover in expanding on-farm production and industrial food processing. He was head of the National Food Administration which undertook a campaign to conserve food in the home. Called "Hooverizing," it promoted the idea that to make do with less food was a patriotic duty.

As from the beginning of time, a major cause of wartime inflation was politicians. Always mindful of winning the next election, they decided, after protracted debate in the Congress, to raise the $18 billion needed for fiscal year 1917 by raising taxes by only $3.5 billion and borrowing the rest by sale of war bonds. For fiscal year 1918, they voted to finance outlays of $19 billion by tax increases of $2.5 billion and borrowing the rest. How better to inflate still more an already inflated economy?

To make matters worse, the government, through that mysterious new institution called the Federal Reserve System (mysterious to all but the bankers), had greatly expanded the nation's money and credit to provide for widespread purchase of liberty bonds by individuals, thus further financing the war with credit rather than by taxes. Banks were even encouraged by the government to lend money at low interest rates to investors in higher interest rate liberty bonds, accepting the bonds as collateral for the loans! (That's a bit like perpetual motion.) So, too much money chasing too few goods fired more and more inflation. The index of wholesale prices soared from a 98 in December 1914 to a 272 in May 1920.

Escalating commodity prices fueled the fires of inflation in land prices even more. Seeing the government's liking for mortgaging the public's future, the farmer was hardly able to resist mortgaging his own. His talk with the banker would be somewhat as follows: "I've got this quarter section with the buildings on it about half paid for. The quarter next to it, I can buy for about $200 an acre, which comes to $32,000, if you give me a mortgage on it for $24,000. That's only three-fourths of its value at today's prices and it's sure to go up."

To this line of reasoning, his very friendly banker could hardly resist replying somewhat as follows: "Well, now, are you sure that $24,000 is enough for you. It's prime crop land and you need lots of new machinery to work it best. Why not write up a 20-year mortgage for you for $30,000 at nine percent?" The result of this kind of deal was that the bank pocketed the difference between the nine percent that the farmer pays in interest and what the bank pays its many small depositors on their savings accounts, about four percent at the time, and the bank's officer receives a fat raise and buys a membership in the golf club.

Then came the armistice -- November 11, 1918 -- and great rejoicing throughout the uncivilized world. When the news reached Rock Falls, the townspeople started to celebrate. Everett and Merle White (Ed's son and daughter) climbed into the old stone church's steeple and rang the bell for hours. Someone rang the school's bell for hours. Whistles from as far away as Mason City could be heard, presumably fire trucks and locomotive whistles. A large bonfire was lit on the corner of Glover and Mill Streets in front of the new bank building. There was rejoicing on the farms and in the homes to know that "our boys" were to be home soon.

With the return of peace, plenty, and overproduction of farm commodities, prices collapsed. By 1921, wheat had plummeted from $2.20 to $1.03 a bushel, corn from $1.49 to 47 cents a bushel, oats from 79 cents to 32 cents a bushel. Live cattle and hog prices plunged to pre-war levels. Land prices fell below amounts of the mortgages written by those generous bankers. The only thing that didn't come down was the interest rate paid on the cussed mortgage loans. In short, the result was the beginning of disaster for the farmers. The agricultural depression of the twenties was under way. The Great Depression of the thirties would not be far behind. For urban America, it would be a 10-year Depression following the Roaring Twenties. For rural America, it would be a 20-year Depression <u>including</u> the Roaring Twenties.

Iowa's historian Leland Sage believed that the period from 1897 to 1920, known as the Golden Age of Agriculture, might well have ended in 1913, had not the onset of World War I in Europe solved the American farm problem of mounting crop surpluses. Europe's wartime imports of American grains and meats, then America's increased demands to support the war in 1917, revived the agricultural sector, indeed the whole American economy, from a noticeable downturn in 1914. However, it was but a temporary solution, preventing an attack on the problem of crop surpluses, and postponing the day of reckoning.

CHAPTER V

ROCK FALLS IN THE TWENTIES...
WHAT IT WAS

Picture in your minds a stranger -- maybe in a pinch-back suit, wearing a flat-topped, flat-rimmed straw hat, wide suspenders, and high-buckled shoes -- coming to Rock Falls to have a look around in the summer of 1920, possibly with a view to launching a small business or professional practice. Chances are he would arrive at the Rock Island Depot on "63" northbound at about 1:30 in the afternoon. Unlike the big smoke-belching steam-driven monsters roaring through with 50 freight cars and a caboose in tow, "63" would arrive quietly, a small locomotive pulling a coal car, a baggage car, and a passenger car.

The stranger would need to hesitate while the little train's conductor went ahead down the steps of the passenger car and to place a small metal stool on the station's platform. The stool was to bring his detraining passenger safely down the last high step to the platform. The conductor would be wearing a well-worn dark blue work jacket, shiny at the elbows and with bright brass buttons, matched dark blue trousers, thick-soled black shoes, and a round dark blue flat-topped and flat-billed cap, a bit like the French army officers' cap, with the word conductor on it.

Looking around, the stranger would see another uniformed employee of the Chicago, Rock Island, St. Paul, and Pacific Railroad, widely known simply as the Rock Island, tossing some pieces of luggage and maybe some packages of freight onto a four-wheeled, high-bottomed cart, just the height of the train's baggage car floor. Thus the station agent could position this sturdy cart just against the car door for convenience while unloading and loading cargo.

Ahead, in the locomotive's cab, the train's engineer could be seen leaning out of the cab's open side window. He would be dressed in his blue striped denim overalls and shirt, a bit like a convict's uniform, a blue scarf around his neck, a billed blue denim cap on his head, and gauntlet shaped blue denim gloves shielding both his hands and wrists. Very probably, he would not have removed his big goggles, as "63" made a very short stop. It would take no more than five minutes for the baggage man to toss a mail bag or two and some pracels from his car onto the cart and pause to chat a moment with the station agent. Behind the engineer in the cab, leaning on a long-handled shovel, the soot-blackened face and white eyeballs of the fireman were to be seen in the background.

No idle chit-chat now. The "Rock Island" took pride in running on time. Quickly, the conductor would wave his hand to the engineer, whose head by then would be twisted backward as he watched impatiently for the signal. The engine would immediately stop wheezing and begin to make strange rythmic, chugging noises, the baggage car's door would be slammed shut, and the conductor would pick up his little stool and hop aboard the now slightly forward moving passenger train.

If the day was one when children had gathered to see the train passing through, as they often did, the stranger might see the conductor walk forward for a word with the engineer just before giving his signal to move out. Then, as the train moved past him, the conductor would pretend to miss his grasp for the hand rail by the front-end door of the passenger car. Then, while the train was gathering speed, he would grab the back-end platform hand rail just in time and gracefully swing up the steps at the very rear of the car, giving the awe-struck children a big wave and smile. What an act! Within a minute at most the stranger would be all alone, in complete silence near the baggage cart on the long, well-surfaced platform, a platform with boarding space enough to accomodate at least a twelve-passenger train. The railroads built things for growth and to last forever.

Standing on the platform, facing across the tracks which the train had just left behind, our stranger would now see wooded areas in which two houses were just visible through the trees. Joe McKee lived in one of them. Joe and his wife had come from Ontario, Canada, farming in Falls Township for 50 years, raising eight children, and at last in much deserved retirement in Rock Falls. Rufus Verne Wilkinson and his wife and two children lived in the other house. In 1920, Rufus and brother Theodore continued to operate the lumber yard complex by the rail siding.

Had our stranger looked down the tracks to the southeast, in the direction from which he had arrived, he would have seen the stockyard with dozens of roofless pens and a loading shoot that extended from the pens to the siding. Closer in along the rail siding toward the depot, was the Wilkinson Brothers coal shed with its 12 large bins (for differing grades of coal) lined in a neat row. Closer in toward the depot was the Wilkinson Brothers grain elevator with its high metal conveyor pipe that could be swung out and over the rail siding. Almost next to the depot was the Wilkinson Brothers feed-seed-and-cement storage shed. Chances are there would be no hack service to transfer the stranger the short distance into the town's center, as the New York House with its livery stable and hack service had gone out of business. But the rail company had put down a fine concrete sidewalk all the way from the depot into the center, making for a nice walk up town for arriving passengers, a distance of no more than half a mile.

Let us assume that the station agent had provided the stranger a copy of the old Shell Rock Falls map, with its street layout (Map III, Chapter II, page 26) to guide him around the town. He would then grab his suitcase from the baggage cart, check it in at the luggage and waiting room, stroll past the Wilkinson Brothers lumber yard office and grain-weighing scales, turn left and head for town. To get his bearings, he would first spot the nice house where John Isaacson and his family resided, just across Spring Street from the Wilkinson Brothers farm machinery sheds on the Van Ness property. As he walked on north toward the old iron bridge crossing the Shell Rock, the Dave Gildner pasture would come into view on the right of Spring Street with a fine stand of oaks to provide summer shade for the cattle herd. Bert Morse, George's oldest son, owned the pasture and the old team of work horses standing asleep in the August sun just on the left of the sidewalk.

Soon the visitor would approach where the road into town from the west along the river dead-ends into Spring Street. He would see on his left nearby the bridge a very fine old structure, the Woodall residence. Mr. Woodall, a traveling salesman at the time, was scarcely seen in Rock Falls. His home was once the Todd House, run by Mr. R. M. Todd, the miller, a rugged Perthshire Scot. The place was later the South Side Hotel, run by "Judge" Ingersoll, but it had gone out of business also. The stranger would be out of luck for a room across the river and into town, as the old Ford Hotel, sometimes called the New York House, was now the "teacherage" and would, with start of another school year, be occupied by school teachers and their families. (The School Board provided this housing, a fringe benefit to augment modest salaries). And the Morse House on Mill Street went out of business as a commercial Hotel long ago, becoming the private dwelling of Oscar Morse, Bert's younger brother.

Walking on up the grading to cross the bridge (graded

up on the south side to make a level bridge span reaching over to the high limestone bluff on the north side), he would cross a graceful old iron bridge with thick planking for its roadway. He would find the bridge a bit rickety and rusty in 1920, but he would linger there nontheless, appreciating the splendid view upstream on the Shell Rock. Just upstream of the bridge, the river flow moves slowly, but further upstream riffles of broken whitewater could be seen and beyond them the three-foot rock falls, the very raison-etre of the town's founding 70 years ago.

The river's banks were heavily wooded on either side with willows and oaks, and they were thick with underbursh and tall weeds in the flat bottomland. Looking downstream to the east, he would be presented with a pretty picture as well -- more riffles for a distance past Dave Gildner's pasture on the right, with steep limestone bluffs on the left. Higher on the hill overlooking the bluffs and river, he would see the ageing wooden schoolhouse, District No. 2 of Falls Township Schools. On the hill even further east and out of town, he could make out the house and barns of the Dave Gildner farmstead, headquarters for his 280-acre cattle and grain spread.

At the north side of the bridge, the stranger would be getting very close to the center of town. Glover Street and Mill Street intersect in an unusually broad expanse of gravelled roadway, somewhat like a town square, except that it wasn't square. On his immediate left, and almost touching the bridge railings, were the remnants of an old stone grist mill that flood and fire must have taken long ago. What remained were limestone rock foundation walls, overgrown with brush and trees, but obviously one of the finest sort of places for a serious all-day game of cowboys, Indians, cops, and robbers.

If our stranger chanced to look just beyond the mill site, and over a row of well-worn hitching rail and posts (the town parking lot of 1920), he would have seen a new house under construction about in the middle of Mill Reserve. It faced Mill Street to the north, with the lot sloping to the river in the back. It was the only structure between the street and river. Once there had been a blacksmith shop and coopers shop along this street, where barrels were made in which premium grade baking flour was shipped. Faint evidence of remains of a blacksmith forge and shop foundations showed in a flower garden near to the handsome new bungalow-style house being built.

On the visitor's right side, just across the bridge, was a donkeys' pasture, which took up all of Lots 4 and 5, Block 18, from the corner of Mill Street toward the bluff above the river, except for what was the Morse House Hotel until it became Oscar Morse's residence. These two fine lots were probably the prime commercial locations in the entire town. To the east, the post office shown on the old map had long since been moved from the corner lot opposite the school grounds into Bliem Brothers General Store (back by the stove), and the land to the river, more prime commercial real estate, had reverted to pasture.

Walking straight into the town center, he would face the modern red brick building on the northeast corner of Mill and Glover Streets. The bank, now three years old in 1920, was the first brick structure in town. In 1919, the brick frontage style was continued in two new additions to the east along Mill Street, cn Lots 5 and 6, Block 13. The one next, and attached to, the bank became a combined pool hall, barber shop, and soda fountain. The next addition attached to these became an automobile service and repair shop. Just to the east beyond the garage was Bliem Brothers General Store -- groceries, drygoods, confections, meats, you-name-it-we've-got-it. The post office back by the stove was not far beyond the shelves of canned goods. Beyond these commercial establishments along Mill Street, there were three old residences, and east of them, across Nottingham Street, was open pastureland.

By taking a moment to poke his head into the Farmers Savings Bank building, the stranger would find it everything that the Globe Gazette had said it was in the newspaper account of its opening -- directors' room, lobby, and two tellers' windows, the president's desk, and vault, all within the space of some 30 by 50 feet, in the center of which was a large coal-burning stove. Had he been curious about the pool hall, a look through that front door would reveal a barber's room and chair occupying about ten square feet of partitioned space in the immediate left of the entrance. The soda fountain with ten pedestal-style stools at the counter and cigar and candy cases were at the right. Straight ahead beyond another partition was an extremely smoke-filled back hall, windowless and dimly lit by some shaded gaslights hung low from the ceiling, one or two green-cushioned pool tables, pool ball racks on walls, and three or four circular card tables covered with green felt cloth. Over the opening in the partition to this dinghy appearing room hung a sign: "adults only."

Proceeding down main street past the grease encrusted auto repair shop for a look through the large display window of Bliem Brothers General Store, the visitor would see a long narrow room, walls lined with shelves to the ceiling on the left containing a great assortment of bolts of cloth and other drygoods (gloves, caps, hats, work shirts, boots, and the like), and walls lined with shelves to the ceiling on the right stacked with canned fruits and vegetables, flour, cereals, and a hundred other packaged food. The rear of the store was cluttered with packing boxes and stack upon stack of crated eggs either waiting to be candled or, having been candled, waiting to be shipped out to

Mason City. For those uninformed, to candle an egg is to view it when it is placed in front of a bright light, thus to reveal whether its insides are good or bad, and perhaps containing a partially developed chick.

To one side of the candling process was the post office. This fascinating little space consisted of a high, wide, wooden frame with some 100 pigeon-hole compartments, "boxes" as they were called, open in the back side so that Valentine Bliem could sort the mail into the proper boxes of each of the town residents, but closed off by glass on the front side to preclude unwarranted pryings into other people's mail, while still permitting one to see if there was mail in his or her box. A one-foot square opening and counter in the framed center enabled Val to hand out mail and through which the townspeople could acquire stamps and postal money orders...or just chat with Val. A small slot beneath this stamp window was where mail could be inserted for sending out. Such was the Rock Falls Post Office.

Next to the post office area was the old massive iron National Cash Register where sales were rung up. It was the check-out counter of the 1920s, probably the most ubiquitous of America's new machine age machines, and source of immense wealth to its inventor. The store owner would press some keys to add the prices of the goods purchased. Then, he would press a final button that would propel the cash drawer rapidly toward the owner's stomach, and at the same time ringing a bell and having the total price of the sale spring up on a card facing the customer. What a fine machine! Opposite this modern-day marvel was a very large coal or wood-burning stove, providing a popular place for loafing when the crops were in and the harvest work done. Curiously, the floor of this long, narrow store swept upward about midway to the back, giving the effect of two levels but with no step, possibly the result of a sinking foundation. Also, viewed from the front the store revealed a distinct list to the east, a condition that seemed to worsen with each passing year.

At this point in his stroll about town, the stranger might well have stopped and asked, "Well, now, is this all there is?" And the answer could have been, "Well, nearly but not quite." He might be encouraged by local residents to continue on up Glover Street to its intersection with Madison Street. Here he could see the Modern Woodman and Royal Neighbor Hall, and what an imposing one-story wooden structure it was, on the southwest corner of the intersection (Block 14, Lot 1). Bert Olden's fine blacksmith shop stood on the southeast corner, facing west (Block 13, Lot 4). The old stone house, oldest structure in town, probably built by T. Lane in 1867, was in clear view, on the northeast corner (Block 12, Lot 5), and just to its east was the Delos Stickney Watch, Clock, Jewelry, Gun Repair, Candy, and Sewing Materials Store (Lot 6). The Henry Krug residence built on the northwest corner (Block 11, Lot 8), was a sturdy and imposing old house perched on the hillside, and with a concrete retaining wall built around the sidewalk on the east and south sides of the lot.

Proceeding north toward the crest of the hill and the intersection of Glover and Jackson Streets, our stranger might well miss seeing an important small structure on his right, just north of the old stone house. This structure housed a four-wheeled and brightly painted red wagon with several buckets hanging from its sides and a long tongue of wood attached to the front. A "tongue" was the common name for this protuberance which served to hitch a team of horses to anything that needed pulling. This particular tongue had several crossbars attached, which were for men to clutch, rather than horses to be hitched to. This was the Rock Falls Volunteer Fire Brigade fire wagon, equipped so that a few men could pick up the tongue at the crossbars and pull the bucket-wagon off to the fire. It was strategically positioned, our visitor may have taken note, within no more than three blocks distance of any house in town. He may have questioned whether men would be available at all times to pull the wagon, but the answer would no doubt have been that there were plenty of strong women accustomed to hard labor and available during working days when men were away at their jobs, so not to worry.

On reaching the top of the hill at Jackson Street, he would see the handsome old stone church, built 53 years earlier, and in fine condition still, standing serenely on the corner of Block 2, and with a grand view of the entire town and flock. To his right and east of the church, facing south on Jackson Street, was the large white framed house of Tom Perrett, cattle buyer and commission man, and beloved raconteur (Block 1, Lot 5). Further east on Lots 7 and 8, near Nottingham Street, stood the beautiful new home of Leonard Bliem, of Bliem Brothers General Store, where he lived with his wife Mabel and their two daughters Mary Jane and Jessie. Our stranger would certainly pronounce it the finest house in town. Mabel's brother Theodore, her sister Jessie, and their mother Jane Wilkinson had moved in from Edgewood Farm the year before, following John Wilkinson's death, to live in the fine new home just to the north, on the way out of town on Nottingham Street (Block 1, Lot 1). All of the land to the east of Nottingham was pastured or cultivated farmlands, except for the District No. 2 school grounds near the river. There were no visible remains of the Cochonour Mayflower Creamery.

Walking on past the church to the west, where Jackson crosses Market Street, the stranger would find himself to be almost out of town. He could look west to Block 4 and see Bert Olden's farm where he lived with his dear, sweet wife Lizzie. North on Market Street was the Ed White home place, (Block 3, Lots 7 and 8), more a farm than a town home. Had it not been for a fairly heavy growth of timber to the west and south, one might have glimpsed the river flowing down and over the falls. North on Market Street, beyond the platted blocks and lots, was a brick gate and wrought iron fence, entrance to the Rock Falls cemetery. This tranquil setting occupied the highest ground in the entire area, affording a magnificent view of the prairie to the east and of the Shell Rock River valley to the west and south. The stranger may have been tempted to walk the quarter of a mile to this cemetery on the newly laid concrete sidewalk, but he probably felt at this point in his tour that he had seen the town, and indeed he had.

It would have been entirely unnecessary, he may have reasoned, for Elijah Wiltfong to have had surveyed and laid out Blocks 3, 4, 5, 6, 7, 8, 9, 16 and 17 in timber lands and along the river, for after some 70 years as an established town, there was not a dwelling to be seen on those blocks. Great expectations of growth had not been realized. Still, growth isn't everything. An observant visitor would surely have noticed several amenities not as available everywhere. For one thing, because of the many vacant lots -- at least 30 of them on the northern side of the river, and much pasturage and open space on the south side within the platted boundaries, some large vegetable gardens and apple orchards were growing in healthy profusion. It seemed that everyone had taken advantage of the fertile soil and abundance of free manure from the cattle and horse populations to enjoy the rewards of gardening.

Quite apart from these outdoor amenities, there was a definite sense of openness, a spaciousness, and a scenic beauty among the town's dwellings. There was an abundance of open park land for children to play upon. The natural setting was unspoiled by those usually intrusive works of man, such as electric light poles and wires, street curbs and drains, sidewalks (except the long one from depot to cemetery), fire hydrants, billboards, and other garish signs, smokestacks, parking lots, stop signs, telephone lines, and four-land highways.

The natural environment of the river valley is in all respects scenic, with the river as the central attraction. Large trees of great variety were everywhere to be seen. Most of the houses were well tended and the lawns and the shrubbery neatly maintained, except perhaps for the utter dilapidation and junkyard scene presented by the Oscar Morse residence (formerly the handsome Morse Hotel) facing onto the very commercial center of town, right across from Bliem Brothers General Store. All in all, it must have impressed our visitor as a genuinely pleasant little village nestling in an attractive river valley of clean water and clear air, a quiet, peaceful place indeed.

This late summer day in August would surely be a warm one but probably one less sultry than are the hot, humid, days of spring and mid-summer in Rock Falls. A steady but gentle westerly wind would follow the stranger, wafting a sharp, pungent smell of pigs and pig-pens across the town from Bert Morse's farmstead, just visible through thick woodlands on the west shore of the Shell Rock River above its falls. It would be a dry and dusty wind. With school out and harvesting in progrsss, the late summer would be a more than usually quiet time in the village, with few people out and about. The blacksmith's hammer might be heard shaping a bit of iron on the anvil for a farmer. A horse or two might be tied to the hitching rails, stomping and twitching the flies away. Even the song birds would stay quiet at this time of day in the dog-days of August.

The village might have struck the stranger as a place in which to marvel at the utter stillness and peacefulness of it all, but was it a place in which to start a business or practice a profession or teach school or raise and educate children? Hardly. He might have lingered a while, pondering the question, but not for long.

There was, however, the problem of his evening meal and a night's lodgings. Therefore, the stranger could be excused for walking quickly back down the slope toward the river on Market Street, past the intersection with Madison Street near which stood the homes of Laura Raymond, Clarence Kendrew, and brothers Ray and Will Edgar, past Will's barns, sheds, chicken coops, rabbit hutches, and cow pasture. He would pass between the teacherage and the fine house under construction on the Mill Reserve, turn right and over the bridge, then south to the depot. He would be about in time to see "64" southbound at 3:30 p.m., standing in the station as if waiting for him and expecting him and letting off a bit of steam as it rested.

With only a moment to spare, he would buy his ticket through a little sliding window between the depot's waiting room and the station agent's office, a tiny, cluttered office where telegraph machines clicked away steadily all day. He would quickly reclaim his suitcase, then hop onto the conductor's stool and up the three steps into the passenger car, there to choose from probably 40 empty seats. If he chose one with a left-side view from the train, he could, after passing the stockyard pens and road crossing at Spring Street, catch a brief glimpse of a rather weed-infested baseball playing field, pock-marked with cattle droppings spread pie-shaped about the infield among piles of horse turds. It was in the Dave Gildner pasture. Was this the only recreational feature offered by the village? He might well have asked. Of course, there was the river to swim and fish in, but not in the low, sluggish, smelly streamflow of August. Then there was the winter's ice to skate on. That was about it.

He might then have leaned back in his seat, to close

his eyes and to reflect upon what he had seen in the small village. He would have to admit that prospects for, let us say, a barber, carpenter, plumber, electrician, doctor, lawyer, dentist, preacher, teacher, or real-estate agent, among others, were limited at best. There were in all a mere 33 human dwelling places, three livestock barns, the livery stable, and 12 assorted shelters for horses, cows, pigs, sheep, chickens, and rabbits. There was a church, a cemetery, a Royal Woodman Hall, five commercial establishments, a bank, a railroad, and a depot. As for public services, there was the four-room schoolhouse with twelve grades, a nearly defunct volunteer fire department, telephone service through a branch of the Plymouth system, the cow-pasture baseball diamond, and the post office in the rear of Bliem's store. Not at all promising. Still, the 1920s in America, and particularly in the rural heartland, were not years for providing the public facilities or social welfare services or even for any expectation of them. There were, however, signs of better days...next year.

Having missed lunch and without a dining car on "64" for so much as a snack, our visitor would no doubt be happy to pull into the thriving industrial city of Waterloo, Iowa, by sundown for a good meal and a night's rest. Two things might have been suggested to the visitor earlier that he missed but might have enjoyed. One was a pause to watch Bert Olden at work in the blacksmith shop shoeing a team of Percherons. The other was an interlude in the back room of the pool hall for either a game of eight-ball at the pool tables or for a few hands of five-card draw at one of the green felt-covered tables.

Now, if the stranger's brief reconnaissance of Rock Falls on that summer day in 1920 had happened to be on the 19th of August, it would have been the day when an event was being experienced at the house in the woods across the tracks from the depot -- the one next to Joe Mckee's. Some time during our visitor's walk through town, there would have been a message brought to Rufus Wilkinson asking him to drop his work at the lumberyard and cross the tracks to his house. His wife Edith's sister Myrtle would have been at the house earlier and perhaps had already made a batch of cookies as she was inclined to do to settle her nerves. Edith's mother, Anna Krug, would have come in from their farm east of town with husband Henry. Carolyn and Jerome, Edith's and Rufus's children, would have been placed out of the way for the day, perhaps up town with their Aunt Mabel Bliem. During that afternoon a second son was born to Edith and Rufus. They named me John, after grandfather Wilkinson, the West Yorkshire miller.

CHAPTER VI

ROCK FALLS IN THE TWENTIES . . .
HOW IT WAS

The village of Rock Falls may not have been appealing or even very interesting as seen through the eyes of some out-of-town stranger. Still, that is only one perspective. How about another -- through the eyes (and ears and nose) of a small local boy? Rock Falls may have seemed a bit uninspiring to the grown-up visitor, but one must remember that his visit, while at the beginning of post-war prosperity in America's cities, was during troublesome times for small-town America. The mature outsider, making comparisons in the context of a larger setting, might judge the pace in Rock Falls from sluggish to downright torpid for his tastes. A less mature, less worldly-wise insider, indeed a very young observer on the scene, might see things in quite a different light.

PEACE, POLITICS, AND PROSPERITY

Consider for a moment the larger situations confronting rural Americans in 1920. The agricultural outlook was uncertain to most, very troublesome and even distressing to many. Farm prices had collapsed, heralding the new post-war decade on a somber note. An agricultural depression would soon settle on farming communities everywhere, long before the Great Depression would engulf the American cities as well. Hard times for the farmers did not begin with a single, resounding event, but rather as a silent, creeping series of incremental changes that lulled rural America with a false sense of security. Then, as the good times after the war began to roll in industrial America, they merely served as further deception for the agricultural "next-year country," where things would surely turn better next year. After all, had not the American farmer survived half a dozen "Panics" and gone on to ever greater prosperity?

If there was an emerging farm problem, few perceived it as such in the glitter and exhilaration of the Roaring Twenties. A climate of optimism sprang from America's new industrial might, borne of wartime expansion. Also, two interesting post-war social issues came to occupy the public's mind. The long, drawn-out temperance crusade against demon rum was finally won in January, 1919, when New Hampshire became the 36th State to ratify the 18th Amendment. Overnight, prohibition made outlaws of distillers, brewers, saloon-keepers, and drinkers of alcoholic beverages. Then, in early 1920, the 19th Amendment was ratified after an equally protracted crusade, giving all women the right to vote. Further, as the decade began, political affairs took front and center stage. International issues in the aftermath of war and a forthcoming national presidential election had captured the nation's attention. The resulting era of peace, politics, and prosperity came to haunt the world far longer than the decade of the Roaring Twenties.

"PEACE SIGNED IN PARIS AND THE TREATY IS NOW IN FORCE; WILSON TO SUMMON FIRST LEAGUE MEETING FOR FRIDAY; LODGE REBUFFS KENDRICK COMPROMISE PROPOSALS." (The New York Times, January 11, 1920)*

The political question that loomed largest was that of a just and lasting settlement of hostilities among the world powers. Woodrow Wilson, U. S. President during the senseless European slaughter and its immediate aftermath, was determined to close out his second term in 1920 exercising world leadership in promoting a new world order for lasting peace. The key institutional vehicle for this was to be a League of Nations. A liberal democrat and intellectual out of Princeton University's faculty, he faced a conservative, meat-and-potatoes, main street U.S. Congress whose representatives and senators in turn faced constituencies back home where demands were insistent for the so-called "return to normalcy." Normalcy to main street and heartland America alike meant a return to the golden days of pre-war isolationism from the damned foreigners, to agricultural prosperity, to empire building by railroads, to cheap labor, to high profits, to gunboat diplomacy, and to unbridled, unregulated, uninhibited pursuit of riches.

Wilson lost. Under his resolute leadership, the Peace Conference among the world's powers, meeting in Paris in 1919, achieved agreement on the "Covenant of the League of

*All newspaper headlines quoted hereinafter are from The New York Times for dates indicated after the quotes.

Nations," adopted unanimously in April 1919. This would create an international, cooperative, consultative body to settle disputes peaceably and stop wars before they started. But it required ratification by each of the signatory powers. The majority of main street U. S. senators could block the two-thirds vote required by the Constitution to ratify such an agreement. They did, in November 1919, and again in March 1920, but by the tactic of forcing such unacceptable U. S. reservations into the treaty in a ratifying resolution that the treaty's purpose would be nullified. This tactic prompted Wilson to urge voting against ratification until post-war sentiment had changed and the Senate's objectionable reservations could be removed. But the hope for United States membership in the League disappeared completely when Wilson's Democratic Party lost the White House and the Congress in November 1920. Wilson's bitter disappointment broke him physically. He was hardly recompensed by being awarded the Nobel Peace Prize in December of that year.

> "HARDING NOMINATED FOR PRESIDENT ON THE TENTH BALLOT AT CHICAGO; COOLIDGE CHOSEN FOR VICE PRESIDENT." (June 13, 1920)

> "DEMOCRATIC TICKET IS COX AND ROOSEVELT; NEW YORKER UNOPPOSED AS RUNNING MATE; BRYAN IS SAD, BUT OTHER LEADERS REJOICE." (July 7, 1920)

Warren G. Harding, a small-town boy from Ohio, sometimes newspaperman, ward politician, "sport," "slob," or "hack," as he was variously characterized, and ultra-conservative, high-tariff, big-business U. S. senator, was the Republican Party's standard-bearer for the 1920 race. There were much abler Republicans in the Party, but Harding was preferred by the convention's brokers as a potentially more pliable puppet than others. Harding selected Calvin Coolidge as his running mate -- the silent Cal from rural Vermont and from "a long line of frugal, modest, and unpretentious New England farmers and store-keepers." They campaigned on a "return of normalcy" slogan and they won big, with 404 electoral votes to 127 for James Cox and his running mate, the young and attractive Franklin D. Roosevelt. Cox and Roosevelt campaigned vigorously on behalf of the U.S. entrance into the League of Nations. But no question about what the voters preferred in that fateful first year of the 1920s.

With the political situation secured by the Republicans for the balance of the decade -- Harding, then Coolidge, then Hoover -- how about the economic outlook? To generalize, for business and industry, things were beginning to look better and better, for agriculture, worse and worse. For businesses, the return to normalcy meant that John D. Rockefeller, J. Pierpont Morgan, Andrew Mellow, Andrew Carnegie, Arthur Vanderbilt, Jay Cooke, James J.

Hill, Jay Gould, and hundreds more from the robber-baron days of the 19th century would be able to continue their pre-war unbridled avarice and unrelenting quest for ever greater accumulations of wealth. Why?

The overriding reason was an executive administration and a U.S. Senate and House of Representatives overwhelmingly sympathetic to the desires of the wealthiest of industrialists and bankers. These captains of industry and finance could secure from President Harding's administration some sizeable income and corporation tax concessions especially in the higher income levels. They could secure continued restraints on the efforts of labor to organize for better wages and working conditions. They could secure ever higher tariffs on the importation of foreigners' goods that were competitive with domestic goods. At the factory level, when post-war prices for industrial goods dropped, these men could quickly control production and restrict output by laying off workers, by reducing pay and working hours, by cancelling orders for supplies, and by shutting down factories until products were again in short supply. They could then raise prices, as they did beginning in 1922. In short, they couldn't lose!

We have noted how agricultural commodity prices fell in 1920, leaving farmers with sharply lower income to meet mortgage debt taken on to buy land at higher pre-war dollars. The farm commodity price decline could not be halted by five million farmers acting individually, as price declines could be halted by two or three industrialists acting in collusion ("secret agreements, secretly arrived at" was the saying at the time). On the contrary, each farmer tried harder in his individual best interest to produce *more*, using more costly labor and production machines and supplies to do so, in order to meet the bankers' more insistent demands for their nine percent mortgage interest. The result was more commodities came to markets, driving prices even lower. From 1920 to 1922, wheat prices fell from $1.76 to 94 cents a bushel, corn from 47 to 33 cents, oats from 79 to 32 cents. Prices of live cattle and hogs followed the trend downward. The indices of farm commodity prices and of livestock prices plunged by more than 40 percent in the two-year period.

The period from 1920 to 1922 was often called a "depression" at that time. As it turned out, this was only true of the agricultural economy. For other sectors, it was a temporary, short-lived post-war "recession," a word not yet coined in the early twenties, as industry quickly retooled and converted from munitions and armaments production to meet the surge in pent-up demand for home appliances, radios, cars, trucks, airplanes, and all of the machine tools and factories needed to produce for the consumers. The good times in fact returned quickly for commerce and industry, as protective tariffs against foreign industrial imports propped up domestic prices while at the same time reducing foreigners' ability to buy needed farm products from America. Industry expanded under this protection, aided as well by many technical innovations, in particular for transportation, communications, electrical power production and transmission, bringing newer demands for labor and machinery, for capital investments in industrial buildings and factory production techniques.

The wartime housing shortages resulted in a post-war boom in construction of new dwellings throughout the nation, together with all of the furnishings to make these dwellings into homes. Road building and improvements on a vast scale were necessary to accomodate Henry Ford's Model Ts and the models of a dozen other automobile makers eager to capture their share of the surging market. And everywhere, so it seemed, the products of mines and mills were needed for the making of more and better goods. But none of this helped the farmers very much. In fact, the great road building activities meant more State and County government costs, which meant more tax levies on farm incomes (for the States) and farm property (for Counties). Farm expenses increased; farm prices declined. Prosperity had returned to the industrial parts of the heartland, all right, but only to help its cities. The Great Depression was underway in small-town America.

R. V. AND FAMILY

Curiously, while economic disparities on the farm and in the cities widened, Wilkinson Brothers lumber yard saw its related farming business in Rock Falls continue in the early twenties to enjoy the level of prosperity that had been maintained before and during the war. Theodore and Rufus were dependent almost entirely upon the farmers for their sales of feed, seed, fertilizers, machinery, lumber, harness, hardware, and coal, although they did sell all of the coal burned in heating the eight country schoolhouses in the township as well. Why had they continued to prosper? There were two major reasons. First, the farmer was still well off in the early twenties, with his rising productivity and wartime gains in crop prices. Understandably, he would tend to feel that the post-war letdown was to be short-lived, that the good times would roll again as in the past and as in industry. Periodic panics had been just that -- short-lived, one or two down years followed by a resumption of even greater demands for farm commodities. In no way foreseeing 20 years of depression ahead, the farmers continued to bet on "next year" and to invest for the future. This meant good business for THE CHIEF DEALERS. Second, the Wilkinson lumber yard marketed absolute necessities of production to farmers, and they were bent on expanding production to offset lower prices.

The brothers had ten successful years in the lumber

yard by 1920, and were still protected from competition by a day's horse-and-buggy ride in all directions. They continued to ship in rail carloads of lumber, feeds, cement, and coal for distribution throughout Falls Township at a good mark-up. R. V., as Rufus came to be known when his business and civic interests widened, had taken his bride all the way to Minneapolis on their honeymoon back in 1912 and there they bought enough useful furniture to more than fill their small home down by the Rock Island Depot. In 1919, he bought the entire Mill Reserve (see Map III) adjacent to the town center and began building an attractive modern home facing Mill Street. He was becoming a leading Rock Falls citizen, active on the Town Council, the School Board, and in the Methodist Church. It helped his career that both sets of parents, the Krugs and Wilkinsons, were well-regarded in the farm-town community as good farmers, public-spirited, good neighbors, solid citizens.

In the spring of 1921, their new home was completed. R. V. sold the house in the woods near the railroad depot to Paul Hansen. It became the home for the next 30 years of Paul, his brother Edwin, and their sisters Anna and Matilda, four of the nine children of Paul and Emma Hansen of Hussen, Germany, who had come to America in late 1878. R. V., Edith, and the three children made the move up town with the help of neighbors and the lumber yard Model T delivery truck. Annt Myrtle, Edith's unmarried sister, was a great help as well. She had become a nursemaid, nanny, maid, housekeeper, and part-time cook for the Wilkinsons, a relationship that would provide a home for her for nearly half a century.

The new two-level bungalow was built on land sloping southward to the river. The lower floor, cellar, or basement was at ground level facing the back yard and river, carved into the slope from back to front. The main floor was at ground level facing onto Mill Street. It was a splendid little house, very modern in design with features quite new for the area and times. For one thing, it had an indoor bathroom and toilet, only the second of such built-in conveniences in the town. The first was in Leonard and Mabel Bliem's new home on Jackson Street, completed a few months earlier. R. V.'s house had a very nice main bathroom on the street level, while a second toilet only, and without accompanying bath facilities, was in the laundry room in the basement.

Another new feature was the built-in garage. It was also on the basement level, which proved to be a serious design mistake. The lot was large, the equal of nearly three town lots, extending from Will Edgar's cow pasture, on the west to the corner of Glover Street. Advanced as was the garage design, it was a hell of a place in and out of which to get an automobile. It required driving down a slope and into the garage from the west side, and then backing the car out, then driving it around the south side of the house and way up the slope to the east side! Since R. V. never got around to surfacing such a tilted driveway, the car would become hopelessly mired in spring mud or deep snowbanks over the rutted slopes of an otherwise attractive lawn. A great idea but ridiculous without some black-topping, the garage was soon abandonned as such and used as storage space, and the car was parked on the road.

A third feature rare in the town was a wood burning fireplace, for which I developed a great attachment. Not an elaborate fireplace -- no Italian marble, it was simply functional and warming on a winter's day. Leonard Bliem's much fancier one graced his new home. For central heating R. V. had another innovation, a coal-fired furnace placed in the cellar near the coal room, with large round heating ducts, clearly visible in the cellar, leading to registers (why that name?) at floor level upstairs in the bedrooms, bathroom, kitchen, and living room. A pleasure on a cold winter morning was to stand over a floor register and feel the blast of hot air from the furnace. In such weather, R. V., bless his heart, would rise earlier than usual and build the furnace fire. He would also cook a large batch of oatmeal for the family. Then he would shave his whiskers. The sound of him stropping his long straight edged razor against the leather strop served as a wake-up call. He was an early riser (like Thomas Jefferson, quoted as saying "Sunrise never caught me in bed."). After potatoes, eggs, bacon, oatmeal, toast, and coffee, he would be away at almost a trot to his work at the bank or on a farm.

The cellar of the new house was a joy to behold. It included the unused garage, an utterly filthy, windowless coal room, a large storage room lined with built-in cabinets where outmoded possessions accumulated, a laundry room with floor drain, faucets, work bench, and toilet, one not for some reason partitioned off for privacy from the rest of the room. There was also a fruit and vegetable cellar, for countless jars of apple, cucumber, beet, and red pepper pickles, relishes, preserves, jams, and jellies. This room also housed a cistern, an artifical reservoir storing rainwater drained by pipes from the roof. And there was a pump room in which well-water -- pure, plentiful -- was raised for household needs. The old Maytag with its hand-cranked ringer and scrub boards was the centerpiece of the laundry room.

Last but not least was the Delco light plant. This was a marvelous device for its time, providing an electric power supply system for the entire house. The plant constituted a very large storage battery, acting on the same principle as an automobile battery, but it was stationery and larger. To thank for this device was one Charles Kettering, the great inventive genius in automobile developments. It was he who invented the self-starter, an electrical ignition system that replaced the dangerous, kicking hand cranked method to get a car's motor running. The key was the storage battery which provided the electrical energy for both the starter and lights, head, tail, dashboard, and cigarette lighter. The name Delco was for the Dayton Engineering Laboratories Company (in Ohio) which produced the first batteries, both motive and stationery. It was the latest thing at the time.

How this clever plant got recharged was perplexing, but it worked....most of the time. When it didn't, there was the old kerosene lamp to fall back on. At that time, there were few electrically driven appliances, but R. V. soon had a little radio, product of an outfit called Radio Corporation of America (RCA). RCA had been created by another outfit called General Electric Company back in 1919. GE had virtually stolen the technique of radio transmission from an Italian, Guglielmo Marconi, the "father of wireless telegraphy" virtually forceing him to sell American Marconi Company for only $2,200,000. These were the origins of one of the great producers of wealth in history.

A marvel of the age, radio brought the outside world to Rock Falls. The broadcasting of entertainment and information spread like a bonfire. The first broadcasting station, KDKA, from the Westinghouse Electric and Manufacturing Company, in Pittsburg, went over the air in the evening of November 2, 1920, with the voter returns from the Harding-Cox presidential election. This occasion had marked the beginning of radio broadcasting in its modern forms. R. V. missed these returns because he did not yet have a radio, but he didn't miss any later returns, as we shall relate. Radio would soon also be bringing crop and livestock production and price reports into the Wilkinson home, not to mention Big Band sounds of Duke Ellington's Count Basie's, Paul Whitman's, Clyde McCoy's, and several other's bands, the crooning of Rudy Vallee, and much, much more from way out there in New York City!

Whether R. V. had designed this house or had purchased the plans from an architect-builder was never discussed in the family. Possibly he purchased a set of plans, then proceeded to make changes to his liking, as he was an innovative person, full of ideas, and he liked his own way of doing things. At about this time in 1920, as more and more automobiles became affordable in the small-town communities (Ford dropped the price of his mass-produced Model T to only $360 in 1917), R. V. conceived the idea of a snowplow to clear the highways and byways of the midwest. In the autumn of that year, Aunt Myrtle packed R. V. with a lunch box full of sandwiches, hard-boiled eggs, and cup cakes, and his daughter Carolyn walked with him across the tracks from the "old" house to the depot where he boarded "64" southbound. He was off to Washington, D. C. to have his snowplow idea patented at the U.S. Patent Offices. He returned a few days later bitterly disappointed that there were already patents pending on ideas like his. However, the disappointment probably lasted about a day or so.

With his interest in home building, among at least a dozen other things, R. V. later designed and had patented a solid concrete "house-to-earth shelter" to be constructed as an integral part of new homes or additions to existing homes as protection against tornado damage, so severe, frequent, and pervasive in the midwest. He didn't seem to recognize that a large structure as he suggested would be prohibitively expensive to build. He never sold a single copy of his patent.

One reason to suggest that he may indeed have been his own architect for his house was the lack of a dining room, separate from the kitchen, something that a professional would not have overlooked in a floor plan of that vintage. Whether intentional or an oversight, the lack of a dining room meant that the family of five had all meals over a long, oversized breakfast table accessible only by sliding along oak benches on either side of a long table. There were no chairs, just hard, unpadded oak benches. So elegant dining was not a part of the family's routine. The house was otherwise well designed with large closets and many built-in cupboards and cabinets and drawers, and all interior wood trim was clear gumwood. In all respects, it was a first class place. It was probable that, in R. V.'s position as a lumber dealer, he was able to buy all of the building materials at wholesale prices.

"PRESIDENT HARDING DIES SUDDENLY; STROKE OF APOPLEXY AT 7:30 P.M.: CALVIN COOLIDGE IS PRESIDENT." (August 3, 1923)

Harding served two years and five months uneventfully as the nation was more interested in Jack Dempsey's prizefighting prowess than in national or international events. About the most exciting events were: creation of an Irish Free State, a four-power France-Britain-Japan-U.S. treaty settling obscure disputes over Pacific islands, the death of Pope Beneduct XV, an arrest of a supposed trouble-maker in India called Gandhi, the discovery of Tutankhamen's tomb in Egypt. None of these played well in the midwest. The great World War was a tough act to follow. The Republican Party's "return to normalcy" policy was apparently succeeding.

Those early twenties were carefree days for the Wilkinson children. Despite the many indoor comforts, a large lawn, garden, and large untended areas of the Mill Reserve were even more exciting and entertaining in all seasons. The winters were sometimes dangerously cold but there were warm spells with abundant snow. There were long, happy hours of sledding with the neighbor kids, Roland, Russell, and David Edgar, Billy Dedina, and the two Bliem daughters Mary Jane and Jessie. The sled run started with a slight shove on Mill Street, then a fast and perilous route all the way down a steep slope, across the old mill flume, to the river bottom land, coming to a stop across the frozen river on its south bank.

As very young boys, the world of my brother Jerome and me was the house, the garden, and the river. The main attraction was the animal farm. Rufus and Edith must have believed that a good way to start kids off in life was to get them involved with wildlife and domesticated animals. A few chickens -- laying hens actually, with the peculiar names, like Rhode Island Reds, White Wyandottes, and Buff Orfingtons -- were acquired, then came pigeons, probably supplied by Will Edgar's flock, caged close by on Market Street. He raised several varieties. He also raised rabbits, dozens of rabbits -- gray ones, black ones, white ones, brown ones. He was the reason for the Wilkinsons getting into rabbits. Then there were dogs, dogs, dogs, and always they were big, long-haired collies. They were registered purebreds, to be bred for puppies to sell. But purebreds or mutts, it was enough to drive my mother out of her mind having all of those dogs and pups under foot, outside, in the cellar, in the back porch, in the kitchen, everywhere, always.

All of this led to establishment of the ECHO VALE FUR AND FEATHER FARM. My brother was President, I was vice-president, and my sister Carolyn was Secretary and Treasurer. R. V. was great on giving names to farms, cattle, horses, dogs, rabbits, and business enterprises. Also, he fancied printed letterheads and envelopes, at the slightest excuse, including the ECHO VALE FUR AND FEATHER FARM. It must have been intended as a start on business management education, and it certainly kept the young officers of the company out of some, but not all, mischief. There was work and responsibility to all of this: feeding, watering, cleaning, bedding, confining, marketing, and always with the hope and never the realization of profit.

The family was so proud of its lawn and garden. The spring time was a real delight, when the lilac, peonie and spirea, and apple and plum trees blossomed and the dozens of flowers bloomed. The whole family spent many evenings together, keeping the grass mowed and flowers, shrubs, and orchard trees tended. To house the dogs, R. V. had a proper detached doghouse built, about 15 x 20 feet, made of concrete blocks on a concrete foundation and floor. Mr. Millard Gage of Plymouth was the carpenter, a meticulous professional artisan whose work was widely known and respected. He built a doghouse to outlast the family house. The only problem was that the doghouse was unheated, much too cold in winter for dogs, in spite of thick straw bedding that was provided. Surprisingly, R. V. disagreed, feeling that if horses, cattle, hogs, and sheep could survive the Iowa winter without artificial heat, so too could dogs. However, during bitter cold nights, the dogs were somehow smuggled into the warm cellar.

Millard Gage was a mildly gruff man of few words. He would arrive on the job promptly at 8:00 a.m. in his Model T truck. Without a moments delay, he had his tools in his hands, ready to start the unfinished task of the previous day. He was a short, chubby-faced man with a well-rounded belly. Always wearing a hat, clean work shirt, and denim overalls with shoulder straps and countless pockets and places to hang tools, he peered out from behind small metal-rimmed spectacles. He grew a carefully trimmed moustache. Mr. Gage was neat, clean-shaven, precise in speech and movement, meticulous in every respect. There was just the right time and just the right place for everything.

Promptly at noon, he would carefully place aside his tools and go directly to his truck. It consisted of a box-like, two-seated, enclosed cab behind which, resting upon the chassis, was a Gage-built walk-in, box-shaped compartment, his tool house and work room. It contained a small work bench, a vise, and a portable saw. On the walls hung every clamp, drill, augur, brace, bit, chisel, saw, plane, hammer, and other carpenter's tool known to man, and in a long cabinet were dozens of drawers of nails and screws of every size for every occasion.

During lunch, Mr. Gage would sit in the right side of his elegant cab-office-lunch-counter. It contained built-in drawers, nooks, crannies, shelves, racks, and pullouts for all needs. Here, he would devour a full-course dinner from his lunch pail, topped off with steaming hot coffee. He dined in silence, clearly not wishing to be disturbed. At 1:00 p.m., he was out of the cab as quickly and back at work. At 5:00 p.m., just as quickly, all tools were put in their proper places, the workshop on wheels was bolted shut, and Mr. Gage would climb into his cab and chug down the road back to Plymouth. In a day's time he might spend ten minutes joking gruffly with the children who had come to watch him work. He gave a day's work for a day's pay. He built the best damned doghouse that money could buy.

There was one thing about this pleasant home that was unsatisfactory but about which not much could be done. It was the manner of disposing of trash and garbage. In that day and age, small towns had no public disposal places or landfill, no communitywide pickup and disposal service, no built-in kitchen disposal appliance, no townwide sewer system. Each household required its own dump on its own lot and usually not far from the house. The Wilkinson's dump was out back, on the slope toward the river, in a trench-like depression paralleling the river. In fact, this very trench marked the ancient route of the water flume or race from the upstream mill dam to Todd's flour mill, the remains of which were visible on the downstream corner of R. V.'s property line.

The disposal procedure was that everything not combustible went from the kitchen into the "slop pail" placed on the enclosed back porch. The refuse included primarily table wastes, peelings, meat trimmings, and the like. The slop pail was emptied into the dump periodically where the refuse provided scraps of nourishment for rats, woodchucks, skunks, squirrels, raccoons, groundhogs, and other nocturnal creatures. What they didn't fancy would bio-degrade, decay, and smell. All combustibles were burned on top of the dump. It would be 40 years before such shocking procedures horrified the environmentalists and before archeologists would be equally horrified to learn that the historic mill dam's flume channel had been filled to overflowing with refuse along a considerable length of its way to the Old Stone Mill.

The joys of growing up are increased by the grandparents, perhaps more so in a small village than elsewhere, where grandparents are the dearer for a shortage of other attractions. It was my misfortune hardly to have known my paternal and maternal grandparents. As grandfather John, the Yorkshire miller, died in 1911, I only knew him from family photographs. In them, he always seemed positioned front and center, surrounded by his wife and five children seated ramrod straight, and displaying a foot-long flowing white beard, giving the distinct impression of being the quintessential autocrat. He must have led a happy and active life, particularly in America, where he raised five such fine children and was such a successful landowner and respected member of the community. Strangely, I recall hardly a single instance when either he or his wife Jane were mentioned in our family home. Nonetheless, he must have been first rate, if the "Lines" penned in his memory by Silas Lewis for the <u>Cannon Falls Beacon</u> and <u>Mason City Globe Gazette</u> were accurate. It is still hard to comprehend his walking the 16 miles across the prairie on Monday mornings from his Rock Falls farm, to work in the Mitchell woolen mill all week long, then walking back to the farm on Saturdays, all to supplement his farm income.

It was my misfortune as well not to have known an illustrious Silas Shelton Lewis, who authored that rhythmic cadence of praise for my grandfather. We did meet once or twice in the twenties. Vaguely etched in my memories are family motor trips in the summertime to Cannon Falls, Minnesota, a journey of some 100 miles, for a visit with the Lewises and their inlaws, the Daltons, Doeblers, and Roseings. Family photo albums contain some imposing shots of S. S. Lewis, the well-known editor and publisher.

Grandmother Jane Wilkinson would have known me during four years before her death at 84 on April 11, 1924. She must have been a remarkable woman, perhaps the stabilizing influence in the family, as it has been said that her husband was more interested in arguing politics than in farming. The snapshots of Jane suggest a woman of very lively personality, calm demeanor, and grim determination. Her own account of the early years with John and the children support such an appraisal. At any rate, the English-Irish mix seemed to have served the five children well. Jane's life must have been years of very hard labor as a pioneer housewife, child-bearer, and helping farm land. Still, without the distractions of radio, television, telephones, VCRs, "sound systems," and automobiles, it couldn't have been all bad. But without indoor plumbing, electricity, medicines, and doctors, it couldn't have been all good.

A beautifully written obituary eulogizing Jane Wilkinson appeared in the Manly, Iowa, <u>Signal</u>, a weekly newspaper. The unknown author mentions having known Jane for 58 years, first during her early married years with John in Wisconsin, then during the hard years at Edgewood Farm. She was charter member of the Farmers Wives and Daughters Club, oldest rural club functioning for community betterment in the State. She must have been intelligent, warm, gentle, fun-loving, firm, and tough, but there is no mention of religion or an involvement in church activities or organizations in her obituary, a bit of a surprise.

On the Krug side, solidly Teutonic, I have faint recollections of both grandfather Henry and grandmother Anna Katherine (Keidle) Krug. Henry died on April 19, 1930, following surgery for gallstones, and Anna died suddenly on June 17, 1932, probably of a heart attachk, as typical of rural German stock, she had become terribly overweight in her advancing years. My recollections are solely of my grandmother Krug's large kitchen/dining/family room, all in one, a block north of Mill Street, where I would often go with Aunt Myrtle for sauerkraut, hot potato salad, with liverwurst, sausages, cakes, cookies, and other very rich, delicious, and fattening German dishes.

That room in the Krug house to which they had retired from the decades of farming was the only place in a rather large house in which there was ever any activity. It was dominated by a huge black iron stove, fueled by wood and always in use. There were four round iron grills on the surface above the fire box, warming ovens on either side and above the grills, and a compartment for heating water. A mammoth round, wooden table and several chairs occupied the rest of the room, entry to which was through the side porch on Glover Street. The main entrance, front porch, and parlor overlooking Madison Street were rarely in use. From the central family room, doors led to a pantry, woodshed, and spiral staircase leading to upstairs bedrooms. Out of doors, they maintained a huge vegetable garden with a place where I could dig horse radish roots.

Two printed "Appreciations," probably for newspapers to publish, eulogized Henry and Anna at their passing. It is without question, they were rock solid in the community of Falls Township, lifelong church workers, first for the German Methodist Church in Nora Springs, and then for the Methodist Church in Rock Falls, and in the latter, Henry served in a number of official capacities, while Anna was a Sunday school teacher and baked for the Ladies Aid Society suppers for over 40 years. Henry was a member of the local Modern Woodmen Lodge, while Anna was a local social member of the lodge of Royal Neighbors. To the end, they spoke to each other and with farm friends near Rock Falls in their native German tongue. Of the limited possessions passed down from the Krugs, those now in my possession are four beautifully printed and bound Holy Bibles, two psalm books, and one hymnal, all of them in the German language. So much for the grandparents, four lives deeply rooted in the rolling prairie soils of Iowa.

R. V. was something else. I came to know him well in the twenties and thirties. I probably would have known him better had he not been so busy in the lumber yard, and in other businesses and farming enterprises, in organizations and public offices, and importantly in the new and demanding position that he was shortly to assume in the town, of which more in a moment. Despite his many and varied activities, he was an exemplary husband and father, helping his wife around the house diligently, while being careful to divide his time at home among his three children. This didn't allow much time for each, but he was nonetheless a good and generous provider.

R. V. was also one of the last of the big-time spenders. This is strange, because he came from sternly frugal parents in a community and society ingrained with frugality. With successful years as a lumber merchant, the time arrived in 1921 when R. V. must have asked himself why he should not own a seven passenger studebaker touring car with all the trimmings. And his answer being "no reason at all," he did it, he bought one. What a car! It had a long hood covering an engine with eight cylinders, a removable canvas top and side curtains, two fold-out seats in the rear section, a trunk on the back, and a spare wheel back of the trunk. What a beauty!

R. V. would put on cap and goggles and drive his family all the way to the Waterloo, Iowa, Cattle Congress in each year, to Spring Park in Osage, to Pilot Knob State Park near Forest City, to the Little Brown Church in the Vale in Nashua. There were always shorter excursions to Mason City for summer band concerts in East Park each Wednesday and Sunday evening, to annual Music Festivals and to the North Iowa Fair in Mason City each summer. It was even pleasant just to drive around the farmland and up and down the Shell Rock, along the river roads to Plymouth and Nora Springs, and to take the family on picnics and visits to cousins. Yes, the times for R. V. were still very good indeed, and he knew how to enjoy them.

How can I characterize my young father fairly and accurately? He was quiet, taciturn, a man of few words, unlike his father, so we have heard, and not especially articulate. He was by nature sober, even stern, yet good-natured, kindly, outgoing, and with a good, if usually a bit delayed, sense of humor. He didn't joke much, rather was inclined to serious talk. He was a no-nonsense person, in word and deed. He was alert, inquisitive, energetic, restless, tireless, keenly interested in things and events -- excepting art, music, and literature, in which he had no interest. Like all of us, he had some strange mannerisms and ways of expressing himself, and his grammar was appalling, understandable in view of eight grades of schooling perhaps. He walked fast and with shoulders well back, head held high, straight as a rod, and he insisted that his children do the same. He would frequently adjust his step with a little hop and skip to remain in step with others walking at his side. He wasn't good at sports, in spite of his husky and lean five-feet-ten-inch height.

When I knew him, R. V. didn't have time for such idle pursuits as sports and wasn't interested in recreation or vacations. Earlier, according to fading snapshots, the 20-year-old Rufus had travelled all the way to New York to have a look at Niagara Falls in 1901. Snapshots dated in 1904 show him on a western tour, viewing Old Faithful, the geyser in Yellowstone National Park, and irrigation projects near Spokane, and lumber mills and factories in Tacoma, Washington. He was making up for lack of classroom schooling. He was eager to seize opportunities for advancement and improvement in a land of opportunities, and he simply couldn't be bothered with or distracted by anything even slightly frivolous.

At the same time, R. V. certainly wanted me to be a big league, lefthanded baseball pitcher in the style of Lefty Grove, so we often played catch on summer evenings. For winter games, his passion was chess, and he taught me this great game by age five or six. I was beating him by age ten, which I regretted, but I couldn't bring myself to toss a game, and he didn't mind in the least losing to me. We would play chess for hours, year around, without a word passing between us, except for a momentary chuckle after a checkmate. Whatever the hour, he was the one to suggest just one more game.

I am certain that R. V. never smoked a cigarette, a cigar, or a pipe, never chewed tobacco, and never drank an alcoholic beverage, never said a profane word or played a game of cards for money. What's more, he didn't have much time for anybody wo did any of the above. There was in fact an arrogant, aloof, intolerant, even haughty streak in my father, which perhaps stood him well in the new position soon to be his. He was not a religious man either, as he admitted to me late in life, yet he took the family to church and Sunday School nearly every week. During the sermons, he preferred napping to listening. If R. V. worshipped anything, it was all living things in the immense outdoors: dogs, cats, horses, cattle, hogs, sheep, rabbits foxes, chickens, birds, and trees. Fond of Indian lore, he would take me walking in newly plowed fields after a rain, seeking arrowheads and other artifacts turned up and washed into view. And we found a few over the years.

In the home R. V. was not inclined to fix anthing or do odd jobs. If he couldn't hire it done, it didn't get done. He usually hired John Dedina, my friend Bill's dad, to change the storm windows and screens in spring and autumn, this providing some work for his friend, who was limited to life as an odd-jobs man. R. V. could not sing or play a note, but he whistled a lot, and he insisted that his three children take piano lessons (hopeless in my case as pianos were made for righthanders). He also insisted that we each learn to play a musical instrument. He had stocked the house with a dozen or more publications -- the Mason City Globe Gazette, Des Moines Register and Tribune, Nora Springs Advertiser, Manly Signal, Chicago Daily Drovers Journal, Wallaces Farmer, Aberdeen Angus Association Journal, Country Gentleman, American Banker, Saturday Evening Post, Readers Digest, Ladies Home Journal, the Better Homes and Gardens, and Good Housekeeping, and yet he was a slow reader, moving his lips visibly with each word.

Basically, my father was a farmer turned businessman who had an abiding faith in the future growth of this little village on the Shell Rock River. That explains his acceptance of an offer in 1923 to become Cashier and part owner of the Farmers Savings Bank, but continuing as CHIEF DEALER in the lumber yard. At about this time, he split with brother Theodore and dissolved their business partnership (for reasons unknown to the family). Later, he built the first and only gas station in town, and then, as if that wasn't enough, he bought a farm and personally managed it, so that he could raise a herd of purebred Aberdeen Angus cattle. Clearly, managing all of this on his own as the rural depression deepened left R. V. even less time for the family. But he thrived on it all, and he was a very happy man.

> "COOLIDGE WINS, 357 TO DAVIS'S 136; LA FOLLETTE CARRIES WISCONSIN; SMITH BEATS ROOSEVELT BY 140,000." (November 5, 1924)

The burden of child-raising was left in large part to Edith, with many assists from Aunt Myrtle. Judging from photographs of Edith Krug as a student, as a young school teacher, and as Mrs. R. V. Wilkinson, my dear mother was a smashing beauty. She was more than beautiful; she had an aristocratic air and presence, she was handsome, she was attractive. And she seemed to have been more than up to the tasks of raising children in an age of limited domestic services and conveniences. Born to a German farming couple and raised in the relative isolation of the farming and small-town America, Edith had grace, charm, style, and class. I often wondered how or where she acquired it, but she certainly had it.

My mother was outwardly calm, but it was apparent to me that she was an obsessive worrier. Her greatest worries, things she could hardly abide, were summertime thunder storms, lightning, wind, hail and tornados, wintertime blizzards, family illnesses, without help from doctors or medicines, community epidemics, kicking horses, snakes, firecrackers, guns, swimming holes, and river ice-skating. Her concerns were well founded, as there were experiences in this little community to warn that any of these dangers could mean injuries, lifelong cripplings, and death. Despite her fears, my mother was a constant companion for us. She played games with us, read to us, taught us pre-school reading and writing, took us on picnics by the river, made clothes for us, and above all listened to us.

Edith did not have the strong religious faith of her German parents. If she worshipped anything, it was her magnificent flower gardens, in which she spent countless happy hours, and her husband. A rich variety of flowers, flowering shrubs and hedges, fruit trees, and ornamental trees surrounded our house. My mother especially liked iris, and was proud of her 65 varieties. Many were those winter evenings by the fireplace when we would go through the seed catalogs, plan the garden, and fill out the order forms to send off. When my father bought the farm on the south side of town (promptly naming it "Active Acres") my mother planted a large vegetable garden, liberally enriched from the cattle barns close by. She could pickle, can and preserve almost any garden produce, so the summer months were busy ones, and the vegetable cellar was fully stocked for the coming winter. I often felt that gardening was her "safety valve" in the troubled 1930s. She was surely in need of one at times.

How young Edith Wilkinson found the time for it all, I don't know, but in addition to being an avid gardener, and naturally the President of the Garden Club for years, she was President of the Ladies Aid Society, she taught a Sunday School class, she managed the Falls Township Annual Christmas Seal campaign, for two decades, she was a great reader who made the most of the Mason City Public Library, she was an active correspondent with friends and relatives far and wide (displaying an elegant penmanship), and she sewed, knitted, and quilted with great skill.

Like Rufus, she couldn't play or sing a note, but she was intelligent, educated, well-read, and amazingly perceptive, considering the environment in which she had been raised. She had sensed long before my father had that Rock Falls would never make it to metropolitan status. Therefore, she started to expose her children very early to the world beyond, to broaden their vistas, to encourage them to read great books, to instill ambitions in them, and to promote in them some curiosity about careers other than in farming, small-town banking and lumber yard merchandising. She was full of quotable quotes, the most often repeated being, "Not failure but low aim is crime."

To sum it up, I would characterize Rufus and Edith as "prairie aristocrats," in the best sense of the word aristocrat. Unusual to find in decidedly unaristocratic surroundings, it was reflected in their life styles, their public-service orientation, their personal traits and habits, and their friendly aloofness in the community. It shows in the countless family photographs. Their own and the childrens' and grandparents' posed portrait pictures were taken frequently. The family must have been the best customers of Mason City's Kirk, Wright, and Russell Studios. There were many sessions in these studios, one or more of us sitting for a picture, watching some funny man make funny faces to make us smile, then darting quickly under a black cloth over his elaborate equipment on a tripod to snap something that made a flash. Obviously, but with strange results, my parents "ways" came from the inherited traits and environments of their own parents, the English woolen-mill laborer, the Irish farm lass, and the German peasant couple not long removed from serfdom.

THE SEASONS

"BYRD FLIES TO NORTH POLE AND BACK; ROUND TRIP FROM KINGS BAY IN 15 HRS, 51 MI.; CIRCLES TOP OF THE WORLD SEVERAL TIMES" (May 10, 1926)

The seasons in Rock Falls constantly influenced life. We lived close to the weather at all times. The weather was then and remains today of central importance to rural Americans. It was the main topic of conversation whenever two or more people gathered together. In the 1920s, winters were particularly dangerous, primarily because of the primitive roads. A blizzard, never easily forecast, could plug every road in the county within minutes. Iowa always has been subjected to the worst blizzards on earth. Until a shrieking, blinding snowstorm blew itself out, nothing moved in Rock Falls. Winter storms drove my mother almost to distraction. By contrast, my father was undisturbed by winter weather, if his valuable Angus cattle were safely sheltered. The worst thing to contemplate during a lot of the winter months was childrens' illnesses and the impossibility of getting a doctor -- or getting to one, within three or four days at best.

One of the happiest, most relieving moments of winter was an arrival of the county snowplow on a cold, brilliant sunny day following a heavy snowstorm. The sounds of the big truck, sounds that you had strained to hear for two or three days, brought people out-of-doors to watch and wave. Knowing that without the roads cleared, you wouldn't get a mile toward Mason City, even with a team of horses, over the immense snowdrifts along the country roads, that plow was a welcome sight. Seeing the big blade pushing through town, throwing snow right and left, was a thrilling experience. My mother would relax like a taut rubber band suddenly released. It was like watching her read the thermometer that she had poked into my mouth during a three-days fever and then hearing her say "98.6."

The best thing about winter for my father was the ice skating. None of that rough and dangerous ice hockey with crudely made sticks and rocks that substituted for proper sticks and pucks. No sir, R. V. was a figure skater and an exceptionally talented one. From the earliest times, a winter's day for us was spent working upstream at a reach of open water where the flow over riffles was so turbulent as to prevent the water freezing. We would try to get the water to flow over, rather than under, the downstream ice cover. The object was to spread a layer of water, like topping on a cake, to smooth out the often snowy and rough downstream ice surface, then wait for it to freeze solidly over night for a fine skating surface the next day.

The certain way to redirect the flow was partially to plug the area of open water flowing over the riffles with tree limbs, boxes, planks, or anything to raise the flows onto the ice cover. My father would be there the following morning with old-fashioned figure skates (none of those modern shoe skates for him). He would clamp on his skates, and limber up a bit, and then execute the most beautifully graceful figure eights and grapevines in the county, maybe in the entire State. The kids would actually gather and watch him...for a while. It was a great demonstration of skill, his one sports achievement, well worth any others.

Here again there were dangers, and my mother knew it. While the rivers often froze over to a thickness of a foot or more of ice cover where the waters flowed slowly in the pond-like reaches, the ice became very thin near riffles. Dogs and children were known to slip and break through ice at these places, to be washed downstream under the ice by the current's force, and perish. It was understandably a frightening prospect and a situation of extreme hazard. I shall remember forever that day when my brother Jerome did just what was most feared. He broke through to the fast-moving water. Fortunately, he clutched the thicker edge of ice cover, just below the riffles, before being carried under. I was there with Jerome and quickly grabbed a long tree branch, got it within his reach, and pulled him onto the thick ice. We didn't discuss the incident at home.

The winter's end was marked by one of the great, exciting seasonal events in town. It was when the ice went out, heralding arrival of spring. Sometimes it would take a while, requiring a heavy and warm rain on melting snow accumulations of the past winter. It was that combination which swept away the old mill dam and the iron bridge back in 1888. Often it would start in the night, after a warm and rainy spring-like day. I would rise at dawn to glance out the back porch window at a sight to behold. What the day before had been a frozen, motionless river was now a raging torrent of high water and enormous cakes of floating ice, sweeping down the main channel. Over the banks in the bottomland areas, chunks of ice two and three feet thick would be piled helter-skelter among the trees.

Again, danger. A swift current, very deep pools, and slipper ice so tempting to walk on, and snakes everywhere. It would be a month for the ice to melt and the river to subside. The only good thing about it was that, with an abundance of ice available, now would be ice-cream-making time -- home-made vanilla, chocolate, pineapple, and apricot ice cream and sherberts, produced in the buckets with the hand-cranked paddles. Fun to make and a great treat.

"TUNNEY WINS CHAMPIONSHIP, BEATS DEMPSEY IN 10
ROUNDS; OUTFIGHTS RIVAL ALL THE WAY, DECISION
NEVER IN DOUBT; 135,000 pay more than $2,000,000
TO SEE BOUT IN THE RAIN." (September 24, 1926)

With the ice melted, could fishing be far behind? Not very far, so it was time to organize my gear. First, I would cut a tree branch, thin but as long as it could be, perhaps 18 feet. Then, I would go to Bliem Brothers General Store, and Uncle Leonard would say "Well, Jack what will it be today?" He was the only person who ever called me Jack, and nothing but Jack. I would buy a roll of fish line, a cork or two, a few lead sinkers, and a few steel hooks. Back home, I would take the garden fork behind the house to dig angle worms.

With the equipment tied together, with a tin can half full of wet dirt and half full of angle worms, and with a bucket to put the catch in, I was ready. With Aunt Myrtle and Carolyn and Jerome and a dog or two, we would walk to the sand bar some 200 yards upstream. It was a sandy inlet formed by the currents, the best fishing hole around, and not so likely to be occupied by other fishermen, as it was not widely known. Often we packed a lunch and fished all day or until we became dangerously sunburned by the bright rays of an April sun. The mouth of the creek where Elijah Wiltfong had built his first dam 70 years earlier was good fishing too, as was Reed's bayou, but they were both three miles or more from home.

Early spring fishing yielded "chubbs" and "shiners," an occasional black bass, good frying fish for breakfasts, six to eight inches long and easy to clean. With perhaps 50 fish and a good sharp knife, I would cut off the heads, scrape out the guts, scrape off the scales, and wash them clean. What a feast the next morning with toast and fried potatoes. For some reasons, later spring fishing yielded mostly bullheads, a catfish-like species but darker colored, that needed to be skinned rather than scaled. They had sharp horns by the gills, and with one flip they could draw blood. Reed's bayou was the best place to catch them.

Spring promised another period of great enjoyments in the twenties. The family was dedicated to gardening. My mother was on at least ten seed companies' catalog mailing lists. Even before my father could thrust a fork into the fertile soil on Active Acres, we received our orders from Burpees, Parks, Kellys, and others, for peas, beans, carrots, beets, lettuce, cabbage, radishes, onions, spinach, sweet corn, squash, tomatoes, peppers, and herbs. About the only thing we didn't grow was mushrooms but Will Edgar kept us supplied from his crop, growing in the dark of his cellar.

Ever full of ideas, R. V. introduced us to the wonder of the hot bed. This was a frame surrounding a square hole dug into the ground on the sunny side of a retaining wall back of the house. The hole was filled with some loam and one part horse manure. Hot bed seeds were planted early under the glass of storm windows taken from the house. It kept plants out of danger of freezing. We moved them out to the garden about May 1. Other seeds were planted directly into a spaded, manured garden plot, first by putting two stakes in the soil at a measured distance, with string drawn between them, grooving the soil with a hoe along the string, dropping the seeds in, well spaced, covering with soil, tamping it down, and watering it. In a surprisingly short time, under the warm spring sun, a row of plants appeared. The garden on Active Acres was immensely productive...thank goodness.

In summer, the river flow declined and water temperatures rose. Fishing was over for the year but could swimming be far behind? The reach of flatwater and low current passing our home was the town swimming hole. It was reasonably deep, three to five feet in some reaches, with a solid, smooth ROCK BOTTOM. It was a fine swimming hole and acceptably clean in those days. As there were few towns upstream dumping sewage into the river (as Plymouth, like Rock Falls, had only the two and three-seat biffies or a rare indoor one with septic tank), and few livestock barns from which rains washed animal wastes, the river was safe for swimming. A flowing stream with moderate riffles and turbulence cleans itself by aeration of all pollutants in a seven-mile reach, so say biologists. At times, 20 or 30

Rock Falls main street from top of schoolhouse, 1911

John and Jane Wilkinson and their children, 1893

Henry and Anna Krug and their daughters, 1910

Rufus Verne Wilkinson, 1911

Edith Amelia (Krug) Wilkinson, 1912

R. V. and family, 1927

The Pool Hall, Oscar Morse, Tom Perrett, and Lou Zerbol, 1920

Rock Falls Schoolhouse, circa 1918

Rock Falls School Students, circa 1920

Harriett Perrett's Birthday Party, 1911

Rack Falls old stone church, constructed in 1867

Cerro Gordo County Courthouse, Mason City, 1901-1960

Shell Rock River flood of 1901

The old iron bridge into town, circa 1920

The Seven Passenger
Studebaker Touring
Car, 1918

Wilkinson Brothers Lumberyard Truck, circa 1920

The new bridge into town, 1929

The new schoolhouse, 1928

All four grades of Rock Falls High School, 1935

Main Street, R. V.'s bank, the tavern, the garage, and Bliem Brothers General Store, circa 1940

Entrance sign to Wilkinson Pioneer Park, 1962

Aerial view of Wilkinson Pioneer Park, the Shell Rock River, and Sundance Farm, Rock Falls, Iowa, 1962

of us were in the swimming hole, kids and grown-ups alike, but never R. V. and Edith. They seemed too dignified for that sort of thing.

There was little else for kids to do in the long, hot humid summer days during the twenties. A game of softball required at least 14 players, and there weren't that many boys and girls in town. Eight or nine was about the most that might be assembled at one time. I strolled around a lot, usually alone. Carolyn was busy with her young lady chums, all four or five years older than I was, Madalene, Dorothy, Levetta, Geraldine, Evelyn Snartz, Mary Jane and Jessie Bliem. Jerome was three years older than I and was usually off with his friends. Jerome was a good-looking, attractive, charismatic, gregarious, young fellow who knew everyone, was liked by everyone. He was a great talker, like his grandfather John, they had said. As a result, I really didn't say much at all until age 15 and Jerome had left town for college.

I would often stroll down or up the river. I walked across the bridge and down to the Rock Island Depot to see the big, long freight trains roll by, shaking the air and earth with their noise and weight. I liked watching the passenger trains, "63" northbound and "64" southbound. One time Bill Maher, a Rock Island engineer who lived with his wife Rose next to Delos and Sloane Stickney's business took me on a ride up and down the siding in the cab of his engine while he was spotting freight cars. What a thrill that was! Bill was a great, big, good-natured man and no mistaking his Irish origin. Rose was as sweet a woman as ever lived in Rock Falls. Too bad that people, including my father, held it against them for being Catholics. They were not always accepted into the predominantly protestant community. Such were the irrational times in the midwest.

"LINDBERGH DOES IT! TO PARIS IN 33 1/2 HOURS;
FLIES 1,000 MILES THROUGH SNOW AND SLEET; CHEER-
ING FRENCH CARRY HIM OFF FIELD." (May 22, 1927)

I often strolled over to Bert Olden's blacksmith shop to watch him shoe horses, and it was a fascinating scene. Whenever a farmer brought a team of large work horses for new shoes, Bert began by sizing up each of the two horses' hooves and selecting new shoes from his inventory, hanging by racks overhead. Placing a shoe in the forge, he worked his bellows on the big coke fire until the embers and shoe were red hot. With clamp in one hand and a big sledge in the other, Bert picked out the shoe and hammered it into just the size and shape, for the horse's foot. Then, he plunged the wrought shoe into a bucket of water to cool, causing steam to explode from the bucket. And finally, he grabbed a bunch of short, square nails from a pail, put them between his lips, took the shoe in one heavily gloved hand and a small hammer in the other, and he <u>backed</u> slowly against the rear legs of the horse. The teams were usually Belgians or Percheron breeds, descendants of the medieval "great horses" and weighing a ton or more. Fortunately, they were a placid, docile breed, excellent for draft animals and farm work.

Bert was a great muscular man, every inch the village smithy, but those horses were ten times bigger. While the farmer held the horse by the bridle strap and talked reassuringly to old Tom or Roy or Bess, Bert carefully grabbed hold of a rear leg, gently bent it backward at the knee, and gripped it between his legs. Then he quickly hammered onto the upturned underside of the bare hoof. What skill and daring! If the horse kicked, Bert disengaged, but as quickly returned to grip the horse's leg between his legs and hammer the nails into place. His finishing touch before releasing the horse's leg was to grasp a two-handled draw knife and scrape the edges of the hoof even with the shoe. The still warm iron shoes often singed the horses' hooves, giving off a peculiar, unforgettable smell. The job done, the farmer paid Bert a dollar or two and departed. Throughout this dangerous operation, Bert rarely said anything, but afterward he would kid with me for a bit and ask if I wanted to shoe the next team. Bert Olden was a big, powerful, gentle man, absolutely first class.

After July and August, signs forewarned of the end of the good old summer time, but a special event remained to be enjoyed. It was the harvesting of the results of all of those seeds that had been sown in the spring. The farm and town families seemed to plant much more than needed at harvest time, and several of R. V.'s banking customers and Edith's friends gave the surplus to us, not realizing that we too had a farm garden on Active Acres. And they often brought chickens, eggs, butter, cheese, milk, and cream as well. The garden produce kept us busy for many weeks of canning and pickling and preserving. "Waste not, want not," Edith reminded us. Early autumn heralded the arrival of apples from the orchard, and as my father would say, "The apples want peeling and pickling." To him, the lawns wanted mowing, trees wanted trimming, dogs wanted feeding and slop pails wanted emptying, potatoes wanted hoeing and so on in his world where inanimate things came to life.

The Number One event in late summertime of the 1920s was to attend the "greatest show on earth," the Ringling Brothers and Barnum and Bailey Circus. It was a fabulous extravaganza, and for the kids it was two equally entertaining events. The first began at daybreak, which meant awakening in the dark of the night and being driven to the Rock Island Depot in Mason City. There, the large crowds would be assembled, awaiting arrival of the circus train.

The entire process of unloading the immense array of

equipment, animal wagons, cages, and other trappings and setting it up in a nearby field was a marvel in precision, from the lumbering elephants, pulling and lifting, to the rhythmical driving of large tent stakes into the ground in machine-like order by a circle of five or six men and big sledges. The tent, sheltering some 10,000 seats, three rings, and five stages beneath the big top was pitched in place within three hours at most after the train had pulled into the rail station, whistles blowing and band playing and clowns acting up. The show itself, amusing as it was, was anti-climax to me. My favorite acts were the high flying trapeze artists, the fearless lion and tiger trainers, and the elephant routines in the rings. I did so enjoy watching those shapely women trapeze artists in their virtually naked attire.

And so the summer ended. The autumn was a pleasant change, the best season of the year in Iowa for weather. The oppressive heat, humidity, and frightening wind, hail, and electrical storms of spring and summer, storms that would send our family into the cellar on many nights, were behind us for another year. Winter's blizzards would come soon enough. The autumn months were cool, clear, crisp, dry and bright. The problem for pre-school boys, however, was that there was little to do in Rock Falls -- no fishing, no swimming, no harvesting, no canning, no gardening, no ball games. With older kids back in school, I was left to my customary diversions and observations: Bert Olden's blacksmith shop, Bliem Brothers General Store, the lumber yard, stockyards, and depot, to throwing stones at telephone poles, walking up and down the river, and climbing lots of trees.

"COOLIDGE DOES NOT CHOOSE TO RUN IN 1928;
STARTLES PARTY WITH 12-WORD MESSAGE; SOME
DOUBTERS, OTHERS SEE FIELD OPEN." (August 3, 1927)

In these quiet autumn days, I especially enjoyed the Bliem brothers store. Besides reading the labels on the dry, canned, and boxed goods, I could watch Uncle Valentine. Leonard's and Ferdinand's brother Val was a quiet, feeble, rapidly ageing, and very kindly man when I knew him. I was unaware of the tragedies in Uncle Val's life. He was married twice and both wives died in their twenties giving birth to a first child, and the children died also. A plasterer by trade, he became the Rock Falls Postmaster, receiving and sorting mail behind the pigeon-holed boxes in the back of the store -- mail that arrived twice daily at the depot. Uncle Val was also a partner in the store and a principal financer of the Farmers Savings Bank. He helped Uncle Leonard wait on customers. It was also his responsibility in the egg-for-groceries trading to sit for hours in the store "candling" eggs -- hundreds, or perhaps thousands of eggs a week.

Two strong memories remain of Uncle Val. One was his love of chewing tobacco. As he sorted the mail or candled eggs, the tobacco juice would build up in his mouth and leak out and onto his shirt. The other was his daily trip to the barber. Next door in the barber shop, in Zerbol's Pool Hall building, Uncle Val would stretch himself flat out in the chair, a steaming hot towel over his face, with only his nose showing. The barber would remove the towel, slap some lather over Uncle Val's face, and strop his long straight-edge razor, then scrape off the stubble. It appeared to me to be Uncle Val's best moment of the day.

I also observed activities at the lumber yard and the stock yard in those days before school changed everything. It was a special delight to follow a herd of cattle being driven through town to the cattle pens, then up the chute and into the railroad's cattle cars for shipment to market places. I had a good friend in Tom Perrett, cattle buyer and commission man, a large and jolly man, loved by everyone, with a large stomach and a slow, graceful, swinging stride. He was always quick with a joke, a widely-known raconteur, never failing to stop and have a word with me. He lived with his two sisters in the handsome white house at the top of Glover Street. I often watch Tom sauntering gracefully down the hill to the town center, whistling as he walked. One day, I was shocked to hear that Tom had put a shotgun to his head, pulled the trigger, and ended his life. Nobody ever figured out quite why.

There was a modest social calendar in the autumn days including one or two box socials, organized partly as fund raising events for worthy causes. They were held in the Modern Woodman and Royal Neighbor Hall, that long one-room structure with its kitchen equipment at one end across the street from Bert Olden's blacksmith shop. The idea was for females -- young, middle-aged, and old -- to bake cakes or pies to bring concealed in boxes to the social and for the males of comparable ages to bid on these delicacies in an auction. The exciting part was to see if some guy who was sweet on a gal could guess her box of cake or pie and buy it, so that they could then sit close together eating ice cream, pie or cake after the auction. There were plenty of leaks about whose cake was whose, and the bidding was very spirited. I was a casual observer until an age when that mysterious interest in women developed. Then, I did some bidding myself. What a riot!

In early autumn, I could look forward to my father's treat of bringing the family to the annual Cattle Congress at Waterloo. This offered an enjoyable ride in the Seven Passenger Studebaker Touring Car with the top down for the 90 miles down river from Rock Falls and for a return home after dark. The event meant walking through several barns looking at the rear end of hundreds of dairy and beef cattle, horses, sheep, and pigs as they stood in their stalls peacefully munching oats and hay, with prize ribbons hung beside them. It meant hot dogs and cold drinks and ferris wheel and merry-go-round rides, and throwing a softball at the black man's head sticking out from behind a curtain in an effort to win some worthless prize. Imagine that! The Cattle Congress was very much like the North Iowa Fair but for the fair's vegetable and flower exhibits, auto races, and sideshows. My mother didn't care a tinkers damn about attending the Cattle Congress, but she came along quietly, as it was a big, fun-filled day for Rufus.

Thanksgiving Day was another autumn occasion but of a purely family nature, a day for Americans to remember the pilgrims' escape from old world religious intolerances and give thanks for freedom and a bountiful new world harvest. As for the four Wilkinson families -- Mabel's, Theodore's, Wendell's, and Rufus's -- it was a day for each in turn to host the annual pig-out. It would begin at each separate home with elaborate preparations in the morning, cooking and baking. Families assembled at the host home at noon. Jerome and I would position ourselves well up front in the line with tray and plate to load up. It was always roast turkey and with enough stuffing, cranberry sauce, potatoes and gravies, beans, squash, carrots, salads, breads, pies, cakes, and ice cream to feed a battalion of infantry. The Wilkinson brothers and sister were never at all talkative, so after the weather had been thoroughly discussed before dinner and all had stuffed themselves, a silence settled over the husband contingent in the parlor, while the wives labored to do the cleaning up in the kitchen. Oh, those tireless wives! Enough leftover food was returned to the several relatives' homes to last for days.

What passed as a social occasion of sorts for some in late autumn was Halloween, on October's last night. It was reserved for young boy participation, not any girls, thank you. In later times, much later, this silly observance became a bland early evening boy-girl social hour of trick or treats with treats an obligatory formality, but not any tricks. But in Rock Falls in the twenties, it was serious business. We didn't bother with the knock at the door to bargain for a treat. It was just tricks only and we went straight for the targets, leveling every unanchored outhouse in town and moving on to anything else that could be moved. The crowning achievement of this event was reached in the year when a bunch of us managed somehow in putting a hay rake, a piece of equipment weighing over half a ton, on the roof of the Farmers Savings Bank overlooking main street. What a sight to behold the next morning!

That was about it for autumn's activities. My father loved the songs of Harry Lauder, the Scot who traveled the American show circuit in the late twenties. We had an old RCA record player, the one with the dog sitting there listening with one ear cocked at the Easter-lily-shaped horn.

We could crank this up and listen to Harry Lauder's earliest old records. When Harry came to town in person at the Cecil Theater right there facing the court house square in Mason City, my father sprang with tickets for the entire family. It was a good performance, I suppose, but personally I liked John Boles, Don Ameche, Nelson Eddy, Jannette MacDonald, and Al Jolson just as much.

The final high point of all seasons was at Christmas. Depression or no Depression you could just feel it coming. First, a heavy frost, then one or two snowfalls, then the river frozen solid and fit to skate on again, then Christmas season. Preparations at our house started well in advance. Suddenly the tree was there brought by Rufus from Mason City. Out came the boxes of ornaments from the back porch cupboard, that greatest receptacle for saved things. Wax candles were fastened to the tree branches, such that their flames would not set fire to the branches above them and to the whole house. The candles were set in the front windows, a wreath was hung over the front door, holly and pine boughs were spread around, candies were plentiful.

The value and quality of presents were unimportant -- just so there were a lot of small things, mostly home made to wrap. It was those other manifestations of Christmas that made it so special. There was the perennial reenactment of the baby Jesus manger service one evening at the church, with several children walking around in bathrobes acting like shepherds. There were people dropping by to exchange home made food presents. There were the Christmas carols on the radio (but never any community carolling that I recall). There was the open fireplace burning nonstop for three weeks. There was the BIG MEAL on Christmas Day, alternately served at our grandparents Henry and Anna Krug's and at our house. There was ice-skating and sledding, a school party to start a two-week holiday, and an evening Christmas program at the school. All in all, I was conditioned for a lifetime of living from one Christmas to the next, with unimportant happenings in between. So long ago, so far away, such happy times.

MAJOR EVENTS

"AMELIA EARHART FLIES ATLANTIC, FIRST WOMAN TO DO IT; TELLS HER OWN STORY OF PERILOUS 21-HOUR TRIP TO WALES; RADIO QUIT AND THEY FLEW BLIND OVER INVISIBLE OCEAN." (June 19, 1928)

As the twenties roared on for the industrialized regions, the agricultural economy continued its inexorable decline. Times in Rock Falls worsened because the plight of the township's farmers steadily worsened, and what was bad for the farmer was bad for the town. The sharp drop in prices following the close of World War I was followed by another slow, steady deterioration of prices, incomes, and land values. Farmers had learned how to produce more and more crops and livestock to aid the war effort. Now, they continued the pace in spite of a drastic drop in farm exports to Europe. From 1920 to 1930, the price per bushel of wheat slid from $2.14 to 63 cents, corn from 68 to 52 cents, oats from 58 to 35 cents, soybeans (the new crop) from $2.32 in 1924 to $1.66 in 1930, and hay from $11.80 to $7.30 per ton. For all farmers, those were very damaging declines. And as these bellwether crop prices eroded, farmers tried even harder to make up for income losses by producing more, only making matters worse.

Rufus and his brother Theodore dissolved their partnership in the lumber and implement business in 1922, for reasons never discussed. In their settlement of affairs, it was agreed that Theodore would take Edgewood Farm, the home place, and Rufus would become the sole CHIEF DEALER in lumber, machinery, feed, seed, coal, et. al. It must have been a sad occasion. Shortly, Theodore and his wife Blanche sold the farm and home place in Rock Falls and moved to Mason City where Theodore worked in the carpenter trade for many years. This uncle of mine, who I didn't know well, endured the tragedy of having his only son, Frank, suffer brain damage during a high fever at the age of two, which permanently retarded his mental development. He lived in Mason City for 65 years until his death in 1988, supported primarily by cousins Mary Jane and Jessie Bliem. Uncle Theodore died at age 88 from a fall from the roof of the house that he had no business shingling at that old age.

Soon after assuming sole proprietorship of the lumber business, R. V. was offered the new position of cashier and part owner of the Farmers Savings Bank. He accepted it in spite of -- or possibly because of -- evidence that the farm economy was deteriorating. He might have thought of selling the lumber yard, as trade declined toward the end of the decade. Retaining its management, he engaged Rudy Hansen at a very low salary to "wait on trade," what little of it there was to be. R. V. immediately assumed the full time job as the Rock Falls banker, the position which he came to enjoy despite its many headaches for him. I in turn became "the banker's son" to my playmates and later schoolmates, and as the Depression deepened, they often reminded me in derisive tones that I was the banker's son. Suddenly, a psychological barrier had been erected around our family which in subtle ways isolated us from the rest of the community. Thenceforth, while we heard some local news and gossip, none of us in the family every again knew what was really going on in town. We were sad about this, but not a word was said about it. Such was the silly and faint line of class distinction in a rural midwest hamlet.

Farming became steadily tougher, a losing enterprise. Most farming families adjusted, as they had been doing for generations, to high costs, low prices, and bad weather. There were few bankrupcies....yet. In earlier years of hard times, the inherently unorganizable farmers (unlike organized labor and business) tried repeatedly to band together for agricultural "equality" with urban workers by means of political action. It never seemed to work. The names applied to these sometimes partially successful, but mostly frustrating efforts came under the general terms of Agrarian Radicalism, a movement that was stifled at every turn in strongly conservative mid-America. There were the Granger Movement, an Anti-Monopoly Movement, Greenbackism, the Silver Problem, the Progressive Movement, and the Populist Movement. Political parties were formed, gaining a few seats in State and federal legislatures only to wither and die. Group marches on Des Moines and Washington provided scant relief to farmer frustrations.

There were some successes, notably against the most flagrant practices of the railroad and riverboat shippers, grain storage operators, and commission men, most of whom exacted their tolls from the farmer. The rate and produce shipping regulations by State governments and the Interstate Commerce Commission were landmark achievements. The monetary abuses by crooked politicians and greedy bankers lead to a flood of irredeemable greenbacks and over-abundant coinage of silver. This caused inflation, the time-honored means to repudiate debts, but the abuses were generally brought under some control....for a while.

Nonetheless an effective Farm Bloc remained an ephemeral thing, a will-o-the-wisp. And as R. V., an unalterable McKinley-Taft-Harding-Coolidge-Hoover republican, was to learn the banking business with help of fellow bankers in the Iowa Bankers' Association, he had no time for radicals and populists and Grangers and others of that ilk. Despite Iowa's claim to the most "Patrons of Husbandry," as Granger members called themselves, and with 1,999 local Granges and Grange Halls throughout the State's rural villages at the movement's height, their wasn't a Grange in Rock Falls, by George. Yes, young Rufus was a banker now. When he came home for the evening meal and we had slid into our places at the table, I could hear the exchange:

"Well, Rufus, how did it go today?"

"Another great day, Edith. New Deposits, new loans. Things are looking better all the time, by George."

But, of course, they weren't. And he must have known it from the bankers' association and from many newspapers and magazines. Bank failures were a measure of the severity of the looming crisis. In 1910, there were 58 suspensions; in 1914, 149; in 1915, 152; in 1920, 167, and in 1921, 505; and they plateaued at about 500 a year throughout the rest of the twenties. These were just State of

Iowa suspensions. Throughout the 13 heartland States, the annual number exceeded 6,000 closings.

Strangely, some major, positive events took place in the closing years of the twenties in this little farm-town community in the prairies. Despite a deepening Depression in the farm sector, R. V., now also on the Falls Township School Board, with a few of his merchant associates, including Leonard Bliem and fellow board members, persuaded a majority of the Board to vote on the proposition: "Shall the School Township of Falls issue bonds in the amount of $35,000 for the purpose of constructing and equipping a schoolhouse in sub-district No. 2." That sub-district was the 12-grade school with its ancient building at the east edge of town overlooking the Shell Rock. The vote carried and a whole new experience began to unfold before my eyes.

The old wooden structure had served the community for almost 33 years, having been constructed in 1893-1894, at a cost of only $2,777. At the time, it was intended for use as an eight-year grade school, but in 1912, the Township voted 175 to 35 to add the four high school classes, so by 1927 the building was overcrowded. Besides, it was a terrible fire trap. I attended school my first year in that old building. All that I recall is the frequent fire drills, always a pleasant interruption of work, a 15-minute morning and afternoon recess, and Marjorie Calvert, my first teacher, and a wonderful teacher she was.

The new building would be a very fine improvement for Rock Falls. It certainly did turn out to be a magnificently designed and constructed two-story facility. One major improvement was its all brick walls on concrete foundation and floors, reducing the fire hazard to nearly zero. The eight classrooms were bright and airy, with large windows in contrast to the dark, stuffy five rooms of the previous building. There were boys and girls showers for use following athletic contests. There were well-equipped manual training (carpentry) and home economics rooms, and kitchen facilities for serving meals at community functions, such as the Ladies Air Society church suppers. (The church had no such facility.) Long tables were set in the adjoining gymnasium, where meals were served, not on your individual plate, but in help-yourself style in large bowls and trays so that one could eat to his or her capacity, and most did just that or more, for only 35 cents a person. During the later, harder times, a hundred or more Mason City families drove the nine miles to these suppers and really feasted.

To me, the gymnasium was the greatest feature. Rock Falls now had the best high school gym in Cerro Gordo and Mitchell Counties, except for the large city gym in Mason City. I know that because I would have the fun of playing basketball in most of the surrounding towns, in Northwood, Fertile, Ventura, Meservey, Hanlontown, Manly, Rudd, Nora Springs, Mitchell, Plymouth, Grafton, Sheffield, Kensett, and Swaledale. Our gym was unique in being two stories high, floor to ceiling, with seating capacity for spectators, and a long, wide playing surface, larger than most. And there was a theatrical stage facing onto the gym from one side, with stage lighting, curtain, and dressing rooms back stage. Ben Henry, a Mason City architect, did a very thoughtful job of designing this building, and he brought the construction in nearly on budget as well. Final costs were $40,000, just over the bond issue floated at five per cent interest. (Please see accompanying school photos.)

At age seven, I derived more education from watching this building take shape than I did the next year occupying it as a student. All of my other duties and pastimes in the summer of 1927 were neglected. I was at the construction site every day, fascinated by the great skills of bricklayers, carpenters, plumbers, electricians, heating system installers, concrete mixers, roofers, glaziers, plasterers, and painters. And the black roofing tar that spilled here and there made nice chewing gum for Bill Dedina, Dave Edgar, and me. Most exciting was to watch that fabulous gymnasium take shape, with its polished hardwood flooring, high steel-girdered roofing supports, basketball backboards and nets at each end of the spacious room.

I was disappointed that nothing was done on the outside in the nature of athletic or recreational facilities. In the old school's grounds, the only play area facilities for recess time were three one-seated swings suspended between two trees, and two teeter-totters, hardly adequate to keep about one hundred students out of mischief. I had hoped for a softball and baseball diamond, tennis and volley ball courts, and similar features. I asked my father about that one time. I said, "Dad, why didn't they have some ball courts put in?" He replied that he had to take enough heat from town and farm taxpayers about the $40,000 spent on the building, and that I should be grateful for the gym. I was and said no more.

Still, there was plenty of space in the six acres behind the school building to provide at least some athletic facilities. It never came about, and with the Depression getting worse, in all the subsequent years when a baseball team of nine players could be gathered in the high school, which wasn't often, or when the "town team" was formed in the summers to play in the small-towns, Sunday afternoon, eight-team league, we had to play in Dave Gildner's pasture, but first clearing the diamond of cow pies and horse turds. Even so, outfielders had to field their positions with care in the knee-high weeds to avoid some unseen and slippery cow pies that could cause nasty, messy falls.

The excitement of the summer of 1927 would be a tough act to follow. I couldn't imagine another act that might take place in the community, so in the spring of 1928, I settled back into the routine of fishing, swimming, gardening, and throwing rocks at telephone poles. However, there was a brief flurry of excitement and activities that summer, if a poor second to the new school. It was the coming of electricity to town, with all that that implied.

Electric services to the public from power generated in large and centrally located, steam-electric, or distant hydro-electric plants and distributed to homes, stores and other consumers had been around since 1882. In that year, the first station went into service for a small section of London, England. Later that year, parts of New York City began to receive similar service. These were from coal-fired steam generating plants. The first hydro plant went into service at Niagara Falls in 1887 bringing electricity to Buffalo, 22 miles away. The technical problem was not generation, but long-distant transmission. Improvements were slow, but widespread low-voltage distribution served large cities by 1920, bringing power from more than 150 miles away. Small towns and farms were at the end of the line, the last to receive electric service.

The hey-day of electric utilities development and the rampant speculation in common stocks of companies came in the late 1920s. It was in those years that fierce competition developed over franchised service territories. Widespread mergers and consolidations occurred, made famous in the midwest by the electric utilities empire controlled by Samuel Insull of Chicago through his pyramid of 27 layered operating-company ownerships. Another was Foshay's empire centered in the Foshay Tower, that early landmark in downtown Minneapolis.

One such operating company, whether owned by Insull, Foshay, or other magnates is not known, was the Peoples Gas & Electric Company of Mason City. Why this company extended service all the way to Rock Falls as early as it did is surprising. Power companies everywhere were reluctant to service farms and small towns, as transmission distances were costly and power consumption was at low levels compared to that in cities. I suspect that R. V. may have been influential in persuading the PG&E to build to Rock Falls in 1928. Through his bank and lumber yard connections, he knew many Mason City businessmen, including Mr. Charles Strickland, president of PG&E. R. V. was even a member of the Mason City Chamber of Commerce and served as Secretary of the Mason City Saddle Club. (Charley Strickland had a beautiful daughter who I would someday admire, and from a distance, but that's another story.)

Bringing electric power to Rock Falls was not a major construction effort for the PG&E, just an automatic augur-type pole-hole digger, a crane or two to string the conductor from pole to pole, and a small insulator installing crew to shinny up the poles with claws strapped onto their boots. The whole effort of ten miles of transmission line and about two miles of the lower voltage distribution line around town to connect up with 30 or 40 houses and stores, plus some farm hook-ups, was done in a few weeks. Still, it was interesting to watch, and it was a blessing to the town to have that power. Our family could now put our old Delco battery plant out to pasture. Town-wide service was a vast improvement over the gas and kerosene lamps, and to have street lights right out there on a pole at every corner in town! Whatever next.

Well, next was electric stoves, refrigerators, washing machines, radios, reading lamps, toasters, vacuum cleaners, a fresh meats cooler in Bliem Brothers General Store, and another for Lou Zerbol's soda fountain and pool hall. Those were only the beginnings of a revolution in labor-saving devices and entertainment. I was glad to see our ancient and extremely flammable kerosene-fired kitchen stove replaced, and my mother was happier still to see the old wash tubs and scrub boards go. We bought a new radio, one that could bring in WGN Chicago, WHO Des Moines, and even KOA Denver, loud and clear. My father could get his livestock and grain prices quoted early every morning over WHO on trades for the big markets in Chicago, St. Louis, Kansas City, Omaha, and St. Paul.

Jerome and I could tune in late at night over WGN and listen to the great dance bands from the Aragon and Trianon ballroom and the Pump Room of the Edgewater Beach Hotel "in downtown Chicago on the beautiful shores of Lake Michigan," as the annoucer would proclaim. And we could also tune in Paul Whiteman, the King of Jazz, Wayne King, the Waltz King and young comedians Eddie Cantor, George Burns, and Jimmy Durante. And how about this for a list of the roaring twenties songs from popular broadway musicals like George White's <u>Scandals</u>, Ziegfield's <u>Follies</u>, Earl Carroll's <u>Vanities</u>, and somebody's <u>Blackbirds of 1928</u>:

       I'm Looking Over a Four-Leaf Clover
       Everybody Loves My Baby
       Clap Hands! Here Comes Charley
       Last Night on the Back Porch
       That Old Gang of Mine
       The Best Things in Life are Free
       Barney Google
       Mary Lou
       California Here I Come
       That's My Weakness Now
       If I Could Be With You One Hour Tonight
       Rose of Washington Square
       Sunny Side Up
       Diga Diga Doo

Ah, yes, those roaring twenties. What a landmark discovery was electricity! And now those new electric light poles, just waiting for you to throw rocks at all summer long.

"HOOVER WINS 407 TO 69; DOUBTFUL 55; SMITH LOSES STATE; SOUTH BROKEN; ROOSEVELT IS ELECTED GOVERNOR." (November 7, 1928)

Events of 1927 and 1928 would be difficult to emulate for a young lad's attention, but the summer of 1929 produced one that succeeded in doing so. In its 75-year history, the town had its north and south sides separated by the Shell Rock River, the two sides tenuously joined by a succession of five iron-framed and wooden-planked bridges. The demise of the first bridge, built in 1859, was caused by a spring flood that swept it far down the river valley. The reason for the demise of the second, erected in 1867, is unknown, probably another spring flood. In 1872, the third bridge had been built. It was washed out in 1875 by the big spring flood of that year. By November, a fourth bridge, spanning 152 feet and with an 18-foot-wide planked roadway was in service. This one lasted until 1888, when the great flood of April 4 took it a mile and a half downstream in a mass of twisted iron. By December, the fifth bridge was operating, and it lasted for 41 years.

In May of 1929, the Cerro Gordo County road maintenance officials decided that it was in the public interests to dismantle such a rusty old-timer. Its replacement remains to this day -- 64 years later, and despite many more floods -- a thing of beauty, and it was a lasting joy for me to watch it take shape. It is a 154-foot span of poured concrete beautifully proportioned and with graceful lines, supports, and railings along the sidewalks on either side. If its designer has not long since received a bridge design award, he or she certainly deserves one. The accompanying photo tells the story better than words can.

Construction work on the structure was clearly viewed from the back porch window of our house, a mere 100 yards upstream. First came the building of the foot bridge, a long, narrow, swaying suspension walkway spanning the valley some 165 feet long and 50 feet downstream of an alignment for the new bridge. It was quicker than a crossing by ferry but decidedly more hazardous.

Then came the supporting timbers to hold the abutment frames on either bank of the river. Then came the truckloads of sacked cement and lime and the loads of sand, and then a big concrete mixer on each side of the river. Gradually, pouring wet concrete mix into the forms that contained cleverly connected reinforcement bars of iron, the two sides of the arch grew slowly toward the middle, some 40 feet above the stream. What an operation, what a sight to see! Every day saw me inspecting the progress of that pouring. Finally, the poured concrete was joined in the middle and left to harden for several days before the wood forms were knocked away, leaving the graceful white arch in full view. Then came the concrete roadway, sidewalks, and four-foot-high concrete railings, prepoured and raised into place in sections, completing the great bridge.

On October 22, 1929, the bridge was dedicated with an all-day celebration, including speeches, dinner, and even a barnstorming airplane pilot giving rides off a makeshift runway in Dave Gildner's pasture. As the Historical Book Committee said, "It was a festive occasion for all." A dance was held on the bridge that evening. The dedication must have brought joy to the residents of Falls Township, and especially it must have been satisfying to my father, now the town Mayor. The decade of the twenties had been a tough one for this farm-town community. Now, what with a handsome new schoolhouse overlooking the river, a beautiful new bridge, and electric lights throughout the township giving a tremendous boast to the community's morale, this decade of agricultural depression was closing on a positive, upbeat note. With but nine more weeks until the decade of the thirties would begin, with prosperity everywhere (except in the rural heartland), surely this would be a turning point, things would surely be so much better ...next year. The thirties would surely bring a return of the good old days to Rock Falls and the farmers.

One week later, events of that next Tuesday, October 29, 1929, were reported by The New York Times in headlines and a lead paragraph as follows:

"STOCKS COLLAPSE IN 16,410,030-SHARE DAY BUT
RALLY AT CLOSE CHEERS BROKERS. BANKERS OP-
TIMISTIC, TO CONTINUE AID."

"Stock prices virtually collapsed yesterday
swept downward with gigantic losses in the most
disastrous trading day in the stock market's
history. Billions of dollars in open market
values were wiped out as prices crumbled under
the pressures of liquidation of securities which
had to be sold at any price." (October 29, 1930)

The radio was on in the bungalow on Mill Street along the Shell Rock River on that morning of October 30, 1929, and I was up and having a bowl of oatmeal and raisins with my father. The seven o'clock news was our first knowledge of events of the previous day in New York City. My father looked at me and said, "Judas Priest!" It was the nearest he could say to letting rip, as other men would have done, with an explosive "Jesus H. Christ!"

And so we have come to the final wild events ushering out the wild decade of the roaring twenties and heralding the arrival of the somber, desperate thirties. Yes, things would be different, all right, as my father warned me that morning at breakfast, far more so than he or anyone else could possibly have expected at the time.

CHAPTER VII

ROCK FALLS IN THE THIRTIES...
COPING

The handsome young banker, lumber yard and farm implement dealer, member of the Falls Township School Board, and Mayor of the Town of Rock Falls, surely must have seen the course of events in the autumn of 1928, a full year before the completion of the bridge, with some trepidation about them. He read the many newspapers and journals to which he subscribed, he had listened to the radio news, he talked frequently with other bankers, and he kept current on technological developments in industry and agriculture. Nonetheless, R. V. Wilkinson was a conservative republican whose political philosophy would agree with such expressions as "That government is best which governs least," "What's good for General Motors is good for America," and "The business of America is business," and other such gems from the Republican Party which were in part the cause of the ominous situation facing the American heartland. But if he was concerned, he hid his concerns well.

His observations and readings must have told him that the great war 12 years earlier had sparked incredible advances in technologies, such that production of more and more industrial goods and agricultural commodities turned out by fewer and fewer workers were piling up surpluses in excess of need. He must have known of the inordinate accumulation of foreigners' obligations to the United States both from still unpaid war debts, and from trade deficits incurred to buy more American goods than Americans bought from foreigners. He must have wondered about the republican administration policy of high tariffs to protect certain of American industrialists against foreign imports of competing goods. He must have sensed that this policy made it hard for other countries to earn dollars to pay their debts to Americans and to buy American goods and farm commodities, and that it would make foreigners retaliate by erecting trade barriers of their own against America, thus reducing demand for surplus American farm commodities.

As a banker, R. V. would have seen statistics on domestic debt: the United States government debts, the debt burdening States, Counties, and Cities, the astonishing rise of corporation and stock broker debt, and most ominous, the soaring debts of individuals. He would surely have seen how debt encouraged by liberal bank and industry credit policies enabled people to buy automobiles, a farm tractor, electrical appliances, and home furnishings for the mounting number of new postwar homes constructed, all "on time." He had to be acutely aware of ever lower farm land values and commodity prices, rising prices of industrial products and wild speculations in common stocks fueled by a bankers' willingness to finance speculators to the tune of 90 cents on the "invested" dollar in common stock.

Still, he may have felt, as so many others did, that agriculture could catch up with industry....next year, in the never-ending rise of prosperity. Herbert Hoover was a respected postwar food administrator, a sound businessman, and a successful mining engineer. In the Republican Party view, these qualities made him an excellent choice to carry into the future the policies of Harding and Coolidge. This ever optimistic Rock Falls banker had a safe, sound, small bank, so small in fact that he couldn't legally extend credit for large, risky farm real estate loans, and he was the conservative kind of banker to avoid that condition anyway. R. V. was also a merchant who would benefit from continued sound, conservative national leadership.

Reflecting on the approach of presidential elections day in early November, 1928, he might have wondered how he could share with the community the celebration of Hoover's coming victory over "that Irish Catholic Tammany Hall ward healer from New York City," as R. V. had characterized Al Smith. Besides, Hoover had grown up in West Branch, Iowa, a guarantee that he was of the right stuff and certain to carry the heartland and the minerals rich Western states.

I can almost hear him saying it: "By George, Edith, we'll invite everybody around to the house election night for oyster stew and crackers and to listen on our new radio to the returns as they come in." And Edith would have said, "All right, Rufus, if that's what you'd like to do."

So they did, and farmers and townspeople came, and there is little doubt in my mind that almost all of them rejoiced at the outcome. Hoover beat Smith badly in the electoral vote, 444 to 87 -- a landslide as it was called. Significantly, the popular vote was much closer than in the Harding and Coolidge elections of 1920 and 1924. In 1928, Hoover drew 21,391,000 votes; Al Smith drew a surprisingly large 15,016,000. Hoover campaigned about "The New Day." That it was, all right, October 29, 1929, and only eight months after he took the oath of office on the 4th of March, 1929.

THE STORM BREAKS

And so the gathering storm, forewarning for so long with its distant thunder, finally struck, and with an unexpected suddenness and fury. No more time to prepare for it, if preparations were possible. It was upon all of us. Silent Cal possibly had heard the thunder, for as early as August 2, 1927, he had issued his famous cryptic statement that "I do not choose to run for President in 1928." He then resumed his complacent presidential slumbers, indifferent to those speculative fevers rising to an excessive pitch as the sky blackened. Herbert Hoover, on the other hand, must have been one of those not listening.

Having already suffered nine years of Depression in the twenties, the agricultural communities of the nation were better prepared, or at least conditioned, for the onslaught to come. However, no human being could be prepared for the severity of economic, social, and psychological damage that would be inflicted with such indiscriminate disregard for race, color, creed, age, or breeding, position, or faith and belief in human rights and dignity. Yes, a few escaped any scars, very few indeed. Most survived, but they carried their memories for a lifetime and their scars to the grave.

What had happened? A thousand books have described it, why and how it had happened, and how it could have been prevented. It is not my purpose here to add analysis, rather to provide an account of how one small Iowa farming community and some of its inhabitants managed to suffer it and cope with the searing experiences of striving through nine years of economic and financial destitution in the thirties following nine years that were almost as tough in the twenties. There are sad and happy, tragic and comic, parts to my tale. But first, a bit of background.

The overall economy had not performed well for several months before the stock market crash. There were worrisome signs that, after seven years of uninterrupted industrial prosperity, the economy was faltering, but it was difficult to discern the trouble spots, what with government public relations and official hype to mask the true situation. A protective tariff act passed in the mid-1920s by the republican controlled U.S. Congress -- the Fordney-McCumber Act -- had begun the process of intergovernmental retaliation and a drying up of international trade. European nations were hardest hit by loss of American markets. The spiral of deflation that followed had melted away any significant exchanges of goods among all nations with the United States.

This destruction of trade brought on large-scale unemployment in western Europe. Europeans could not longer buy Henry Ford's automobiles, John Deere's tractors, and many other machines and tools, Westinghouse's electrical appliances and telephone instruments, and farmer Calvert's wheat, corn, soybeans, beef, and pork. Americans would no longer pay the protective import duties to buy the French wines and cheeses, Germany's cameras and industrial equipment, and England's fine woolens, cutlery, and chinaware. A sure way to destroy world prosperity was to destroy its trade among nations, but all of this didn't make good copy in newspapers and on the radio. The downward spiral was allowed to accelerate.

Another disturbing trend was mounting debt: national, State, local government, and corporate and individual debt as well. Greed, one of the seven deadly sins, struck its double whammy. Lenders of money craved a few percentage points more for hiring out their money. Borrowers of the money craved quick gains, hoping to repay in a cheapened, inflated dollar while pocketing a capital gain. Why did they lend and borrow so much? Greed. "If done to excess, money corrupts and destroys," said R. V., and Edith chimed in with, "Neither a borrower nor a lender be." Now, Rufus didn't agree with her entirely on that, so he tried to explain why, starting with, "Where would America be without good, sound banks?" I am sure that Edith had an answer by the look on her face, but she remained silent.

In the late twenties, money worked its magic on governments, businesses, and families alike. While the actual numbers do not seem large by the astronomical standard to which indebtedness would ascend in the 1990s, those in the shaky economy of the 1920s were frightening enough to cause concern. Between 1921 and 1929, short-term debt in the country rose from $102 to $150 billions, and long-term debt from $75 to $126 billions. Put in perspective, these rates of increase were three times those for national income over the same years.

Among the reasons were the decisions or the determination of the Federal Reserve Board to make use of its powers to expand money and credit in the banking system. It could do this in the blink of an eye through its open market purchases of federal securities and by lending to the banks at lower and lower interest rates, so that the banks could in turn lend to customers, including speculators in the stock market on margin accounts. Also, the introduction of the magic of installment loans was gleefully accepted by a public impatient with wartime frugality. The automobile industry was the active promoter and offerer of this new way of going into debt, and the Federal Reserve's Board of Governors followed a policy in the Roaring Twenties of opening wide the door to its money-creating system to feed the nation's borrowing frenzy.

By 1925, consumers' installment debt had grown to the unheard of sum for the times of $4,000,000,000 to finance buying of cars, radios, washing machines, sewing machines, furniture, even clothing. By 1925, the federal government debt had exploded from zero just before World War I to the almost incomprehensible sum of $8,440,000,000. Still, the consumers' debt level was a mere $35, and the federal government debt only $74 per United States inhabitant in that year. These miniscule amounts were only the beginning of America's great credit binge to astronomical heights: the $2,836,000,000,000 -- yes, trillion! -- of commercial bank loans outstanding and $4,002,000,000,000 -- yes, trillion! -- of federal government debt in 1992. Total private debt and federal government debt had mounted to $27,505 on each man, woman, and child in America, and it is still growing by nearly $2,000 per year!!!

Back in the Twenties, an alarming rise in real estate debts was caused by the rampant speculations in urban properties, exemplified by Florida's land boom. From 1922 to 1929 mortgage debt skyrocketed from $9.0 to $27.0 billion. As one writer put it, "...a more perfect device for inflation could hardly be imagined in this dazzling era." The future was surely over-sold, it was thought at that time. But another magical device for creating money....and debts was still to be wrought. It was that master generator of all money generators, the convenient, little plastic credit card, which would come to beguile another age.

The danger signals, the "weather watches" and tornado alerts, to carry on the analogy, became more numerous by the summer of 1929. I didn't notice it because of my preoccupation with the building of that magnificent concrete-arch bridge to span the Shell Rock, and my growing collection of empty pipe tobacco cans, but there were many clues to notice: construction of all single and multiple-family apartments exceeded by far the growth of population. Construction of stores, factories, and roads slowed dramatically in 1928. Automobile production tapered off, prelude to a later astonishing drop as more cars came off assembly lines than could possibly be sold. The count of freight-car loadings, an historic bellwether figure because of the dominance of the railroad systems, peaked and declined in June of 1928. Finally, farm commodity prices continued in their deep slide. Does it all sound a bit familiar?

Thus, that single one-week event of the October, 1929 stock market collapse was not the root cause of the oncoming Great Depression. It was merely a dramatic final manifestation of an underlying fragility in an economic system awash in debt, the final clap of thunder and bolt of lightning as the storm broke over the land. And it was damaging. Deflation replaced inflation. Virtually all of the economic indicators known to man declined rapidly. Factories soon closed to cut costs and avoid build-up of unsalable inventories. Workers were laid off by the millions, and without notice. Unemployment rates exceeded 25 percent of the work force before Hoover left office in 1932, leaving one out of four without work, and those other three had their wage cut to a subsistence level. International trade trickled to a halt. Mortgages on farmland and urban properties were foreclosed. Banks failed by the hundreds each day, and runs of depositors on surviving banks threatened total collapse of the banking system.

Back in Iowa, a "Farmers Holiday Association" movement under the leadership of Milo Reno (what a midwestern name!) gained momentum, and small wonder. The price of corn plummetted to 13 cents per bushel, hogs to three cents a pound, and cattle to five cents per pound. One thousand farmers, under Reno, picketed the deliveries of produce to markets, dumping milk and grains on the roads, as crop and livestock prices dropped to levels far below production costs. And in the face of this, President Hoover and his Secretary of the Treasury, Andrew Mellon (another banker), urged calm, optimism, and increased gifts to charities in this "temporary situation" because "Prosperity is just around the corner."

The numbers tell a story of alarming disintegration in American agriculture with the final precipitous collapse of prices from 1920 through 1932. From an immediate postwar I high in 1920, to one of the bleakest years of the early Depression period, wheat prices declined 85 percent, corn by 82 percent, oats by 81 percent, and soybeans by 70 percent, such was the devastation for the farming communities. Hard as it is to comprehend, during those same twelve years profits of industrial corporations <u>rose</u> by 83 percent. These kinds of disparities in the nation, never before so stark, could not last. The stock market was merely the trigger.

CRISIS POLITICS

<u>The New York Times</u> produced an outstanding historical and pictorial account of the Thirties, entitled <u>The Depression Years</u>, first copyrighted in late 1929, then reprinted with additions each year through 1939. It consists of some 300 reproductions, reduced in size by one-half, of the front pages of its newspapers issued between October 30, 1929 and November 3, 1939, interspersed with a hundred or more photo reproductions that appeared in its issues during the years. Many years later, the newspaper produced <u>Page One</u>, "Major Events 1920-1988 as Presented in <u>The New York Times</u>," which revised and updated its earlier publications with the same

style of front pages and photos.

With a few headlines and an occasional lead paragraph I have tried to broaden and enliven my own account of the Thirties with the headlines of the most newsworthy of the events beyond the American heartland, as reported by this, the world's leading, newspaper. These cryptic lines suggest that national leaders failed miserably to comprehend what was happening as conditions worsened during 1930 and 1931. In general, it seemed, either nothing was being done about them or the wrong things were being done. As noted earlier herein, all inset quotes are from The Times of the dates indicated.

"SENATORS DEMAND ACTION TO CHECK UNEMPLOYMENT. HOOVER'S STAND ATTACKED. SHARP DEBATE OVER JOBLESS.

"Washington, March 3, 1930. The existence of widespread unemployment in the nation was portrayed in the Senate today, coupled with an attack on the Administration, which was charged with seeking to 'divert' the country's attention from the situation....Prediction that American business activity would speed up to a normal rate within two months was made today by Secretary Lamont, who said that a slowing down in the last three months had not been as extensive as had been feared. 'My own opinion is that during the forepart of this year American industrial enterprise has had inevitably to slow down....that slowing down seems to be passing over, and with the usual increase of out-of-doors work....as weather conditions moderate, we are likely to find the country as a whole enjoying its wonted state of prosperity.'"

That same day's news reported on remarks by the well-known Republican Senator, Arthur Capper of rural Kansas, a sometimes loyal supporter of President Hoover, but not always, in view of his farm-belt constituency. Noting that it would be a year the next day since Hoover had taken the oath of office, Capper reckoned that this first year was one of "fact-finding by presidential commissions, of work on data and blueprints, of foundation laying." These, he said, were the marks of Hoover's engineering mind at work. He was so right but it was too late for that kind of leadership, too late for the engineering mind under the circumstances unfolding so rapidly. There seems to have been a peculiar unawareness and insensitivity to the gathering storm throughout the nation, an inexplicable ignorance of the desperate need for action, not more study.

"MORE WORK, SAYS HOOVER, AND DEPRESSION IS PASSING; 36 STATES ARE NOW NORMAL. President is optimistic, distress now confined mainly to 12 States, he says in statement." (March 8, 1930)

This news account stated that "...all evidence in the possession of the President indicated that the worst effects of the stock market slump on employment will have passed within sixty days." However, efforts of reporters to learn which were the 12 States in distress were fruitless. The Administration chose not to "single out these."

Actually, after the first shock waves of the week of October 23-29, 1929, the stock market stabilized and consolidated. Thereafter, it rose for six months to the extent of recovering about 35 percent of its steep losses in the first jolt. This was a snare and a delusion. It suddenly was hit by a series of after-shocks which began the dramatic decline over the next three long years. When it touched bottom in late 1932, a whopping two-thirds of the value of all listed securities had been wiped out.

> "SENATE VOTES $383,000,000 IN BILLS TO AID BUSINESS, PUSHING HOOVER PROGRAM. SWIFT ACTION PROJECTED.
>
> "It is the opinion of leaders of both parties that the long delay in passing the tariff has tended to retard restoration of prosperity." (March 26, 1930)

Throughout the first year following the crash, widespread views of business and political leaders revealed an astonishing misjudgment of the worsening situation and the needed remedies. First and foremost, enactment of a law that further <u>raised</u> protective tariff barriers to international trade over those already voted would almost surely cause further retaliation, inability of foreigners to buy American goods, hence even more unemployment in the U. S. and in all other nations. Second, complacent reassurances seemed to represent the only official policy theme. More than one thousand economists petitioned President Hoover not to sign the infamous Smoot-Hawley tariff measure voted by the Congress, but to no avail. Historian Schlesinger's <u>Crisis of the Old Order</u> quotes these business leaders:

> Robert Lamont, newly appointed Secretary of Commerce under Hoover: "There are present today none of the underlying factors which have been associated with or have preceded the declines in business in the past."
>
> Henry Ford, on November 4, 1929: "Things are better today than they were yesterday." (What a profound -- and utterly inane -- statement!)
>
> Charles Schwab, Chairman of the Board of Bethlehem Steel Corporation, on December 10, 1929: "Never before has American business been as firmly entrenched for prosperity as it is today."

George Roberts, Vice-president, National City Bank of New York: "There are no great business failures, nor are there likely to be. Conditions are more favorable for permanent prosperity than they have been in the past year."

John E. Edgerton, President, National Association of Manufacturers: "I can observe little on the horizon today to give us undue or great concern."

No wonder that R. V. Wilkinson, cashier of the Farmers Saving Bank of Rock Falls, Iowa, was such an eager optimist!

"WORST OF DEPRESSION OVER, SAYS HOOVER, WITH COOPERATION LESSENING DISTRESS; PLANS STUDY TO AVERT FUTURE CRISIS.

"Wise planning, based upon accurate data, can prevent a recurrence, he asserts." (May 2, 1930)

During the winter of 1930-1931, the situation became desperate. As historian Schlesinger writes of conditions in large cities: "With no money left for rent, unemployed men and their entire families began to build shacks where they could find unoccupied land. Along the railroad embankment, beside the garbage incinerator, in the city dump there appeared towns of tarpaper and tin, old packaging boxes and old car bodies. Some shanties were kept neatly scrubbed...others were squalid beyond belief...Symbols of the New Era, these communities quickly received their sardonic name: they were called Hoovervilles. And, indeed, it was in many cases only the fortunate who could find the Hoovervilles. The unfortunate spent their nights huddled together in doorways, in empty packing cases, in boxcars."

At the same time, President Hoover issued a statement giving his philosophy, saying: "If America meant anything, it meant the principles of individual and local responsibility and mutual self-help. If we break down these principles, we have struck at the roots of self-government. Should federal aid be the only alternative to starvation, then federal aid we must have, but I have faith in all the American people that such a day will not come."

It was clear, therefore, that federal government _fiscal policy_ would do nothing to stimulate the economy; indeed, it would be counter-productive, only exacerbating an acute deflationary spiral, adding to the ranks of the jobless. Adding further to the worst possible fiscal policy, the Federal Reserve Board, controlled by its member banks, initiated the worst possible _monetary policy_. It raised interest rates in its mistaken effort to keep foreign nations from withdrawing their U.S. bank deposits and to try to keep the U.S. on the gold standard, something the other nations had abandoned. Lower interest rates would act to stimulate the economy; raising them cut off credit, discouraged borrowing and investing, and further exacerbated the deflationary spiral and joblessness.

"DEMOCRATIC LANDSLIDE SWEEPS COUNTRY; REPUBLICANS MAY LOSE CONGRESS CONTROL." (Nov 5, 1930)

"HOUSE PASSES BONUS LOAN BILL 363 TO 39; SENATE PAVES WAY FOR SPEEDY ACTION; VETO BY THE PRESIDENT IS EXPECTED." (Feb 17, 1931)

"SENATE VOTES BONUS LOAN BILL, 72 TO 12; PRESIDENT SAYS HE WILL VETO IT AT ONCE. BOTH HOUSES PREPARED TO OVERRIDE HIM." (Feb 20, 1931)

"HOOVER URGES NATION TO BE STEADFAST IN THIS VALLEY FORGE OF DEPRESSION." (May 31, 1931)

"HOOVER DECRIES DEPRESSION PANACEAS; INDIANAPOLIS SPEECH HELD BID FOR 1932; PICTURES GLOWING FUTURE FOR NATION." (June 16, 1931)

"MELLON ASKS BROAD RISE IN INCOME TAX, ALSO LEVIES ON AUTOS, RADIOS, CHECKS; DEMOCRATS VOICE SHARP OPPOSITION." (December 10, 1931)

"POST AND GATTY END THEIR RECORD WORLD FLIGHT; CIRCLE GLOBE IN 8 DAYS, 15 HOURS, 51 MINUTES; 10,000 IN WILD DEMONSTRATION AT FIELD HERE." (July 2, 1931)

Aviation achievements were about the only reason for cheer, although there were some amusements to draw a laugh or two, jerk a few tears, and make you forget. Walt Disney was cartooning, James Cagney and Jean Harlow made the tears flow in <u>The Public Enemy</u>, Charlie Chaplin drew most of the laughs, and Boris Karloff (Frankenstein) and Lugosi (Dracula) scared you into forgetting for a while. Otherwise, the politicians continued to act in character, raise taxes, cut expenditures, balance the budget just at a time when nothing would be more certain than such policies for worsening the crisis. So passed 1931.

"BITTER FIGHT CERTAIN ON ECONOMY BILL OMITTING HOOVER'S 3-POINT PROGRAM; $613,000,000 TOTAL SAVING IS POSSIBLE." (April 25, 1932)

"SENATE PASSES $1,115,000,000 TAX BILL; BALANCES BUDGET AFTER HOOVER PLEA; $238,000,000 ECONOMY MEASURE REPORTED." (June 1, 1932)

"DEMOCRATS PLEDGE PARTY TO REPEAL OF THE DRY LAW AND QUICK MODIFICATION TO LEGALIZE BEER; PLANK AGAINST WAR DEBT CANCELLATION IS SUBMITTED." (June 30, 1932)

"ROOSEVELT PUTS ECONOMIC RECOVERY FIRST IN HIS ACCEPTANCE SPEECH AT CONVENTION; GARNER FOR VICE PRESIDENT BY ACCLAMATION." (July 3, 1932)

"TROOPS DRIVE VETERANS FROM CAPITAL; FIRE CAMPS THERE AND AT ANACOSTIA; 1 KILLED, SCORES HURT IN DAY OF STRIFE. Hoover orders evictions." (July 29, 1932)

"HOOVER SEES MAJOR CRISIS OVERCOME; CONFERENCE ADOPTS REVIVAL PROGRAM; BANK FORECLOSURES ON HOMES HALTED." (August 27, 1932)

"ROOSEVELT MAPS FARM RELIEF PROGRAM, PLEDGES TARIFF AID IN TOPEKA SPEECH; HOOVER POLICIES DECLARED A FAILURE." (September 15, 1932)

For a brief period before the elections of 1932, the country was mesmerized by the kidnaping and killing of the Lindberg baby, the rubout of gangster Jack (Legs) Diamond, and the conviction of Al Capone, Chicago's king of prohibition-days bootleggers and murderers. The battle for repeal of the prohibition law was forming, and the stage was set for the 1932 elections: Hoover and Curtis v. Roosevelt and Garner.

As is evident from the 1932 headlines, the approaching presidential election in November assumed enormous importance in the public mind. Hoover was the Republicans' choice for another four years; Roosevelt was the choice to unseat him. Economic conditions had dramatically worsened in America -- indeed, in the world. The desperation of the thousands of World War veterans gathered in tarpaper towns such as Anacostia Flats on the Potomac tidal basin area of Washington, D. C., exemplified alarming hardships nationwide. Unlike those large banking and industrial lobbyists in the nation's capital, those veterans could not afford a plush suite in the Willard Hotel in which to buttonhole a Senator or Congressman for favors. Those veterans got as close to Capital Hill as possible, but on orders from Mr. Hoover, the beautifully uniformed, ribbon-bedecked, young General Douglas MacArthur of the U. S. Army's Cavalry Division led his mounted forces in driving away the veterans with clubs, and putting their "homes" to the torch. Yes, things had got pretty bad, considering that the U.S.A. was supposed to be a democracy!

A slow, silent fear had set in. It was a new kind of mass fear, never before experienced on a national scale. It was a fear about losing everything -- jobs and savings, homes, farms, cars, children. Fear permeated the financial aspects of this crisis perhaps more than anything, because debt repayments were long overdue and unpaid, mortgages were foreclosed, depositors withdrew money to hoard it in the relative safety of mattresses, and banks failed.

Farm mortgage foreclosures ravaged the heartland, where in Iowa they made up one-half of the farm property transfered in 1932. Investors lost savings in stocks and bonds. The Chicago-based Samuel Insull electric utility empire crashed and disintegrated, wiping out millions of dollars worth of savings "invested" (surely no one had speculated)in the power company stocks. The terror spread from one State to another, forcing Governors to declare bank holidays.

Milo Reno, of the Farmers Holiday association, was a "hell-raiser" by local definition, schooled in the radical populist philosophies, and a preacher besides. He organozed a general strike for August 11, 1932. A few farmers in the western counties of Iowa couldn't wait. On April 27 at Primghar, a farm foreclosure sale at the county courthouse was broken up. The sheriff, his deputies, and an attorney for creditors were forced to kiss the flag. The group then headed for Plymouth County where they had heard of the pending foreclosure sale of a widow's property. The oft-told story of what happened next has many variations. However told, it was a sad and disgraceful incident.

The infuriated farmers first met at the widow's farm, swarmed around the insurance company's attorney (the mortgage holder), threatening to lynch him, and had the foreclosure proceedings called off. Then, the "mob," socalled at the time, met at the courthouse in Le Mars, strode into Judge C. C. Bradley's courtroom, where proceedings were in progress on another matter, and demanded that the 60-year-old judge not sign any more foreclosure orders. He refused and ordered the 100 or more farmers to remove their hats, (they wore hats, not caps, back then) and stop smoking.

At this, tempers flared. The poor judge was dragged from his bench to a truck, blindfolded, and taken into the country. His trousers were removed, he was smeared with axle grease, taunted, and threatened with mutilation and hanging. A rope was then drawn tightly around the judge's neck, and he was told to swear not to sign any more foreclosure decrees. The brave old judge refused, then fainted. Fortunately, the editor of the Le Mars Globe-Post, Mr. Rome F. Starzl (another great midwest name!), appeared on the scene and urged restraint upon the angry farmers. They smeared more grease over the dazed judge and departed.

That evening the county sheriff asked the Governor of Iowa for the State militia. That same day, another foreclosure sale on a place near Denison, in Crawford County, was disrupted by Milo Reno's Holiday farmers-ruffians, despite efforts of the sheriff and 50 of his deputies. This sheriff also called for the Governor's help. On the 28th, Governor Clyde L. Herring sent troops into both counties, restored order, and jailed many farmers. This brought the excesses to an end throughout the State....temporarily.

Back in Rock Falls, R. V. watched and waited, thinking of his traditional and increasingly active local banker role in the "clerking" of all farm sales. It was never a pleasant task, often a sad one, for the banker to record the pitifully low prices of the meager possessions knocked down at auction, then to collect the money from the lowest bidders. R. V. was indeed fortunate that his Farmers Savings Bank's capitalization of $10,000 was small enough to preclude, under Iowa banking law, the writing of long-term farm real estate loans. Such were for the bigger banks -- in Manly, Nora Springs, Osage, and Mason City. They would have to hire the attorneys and dispossess the frugal, hard working Falls Township farmers and their wives and little children.

However, R. V.'s bank had plenty of short-term credit outstanding to community farmers. These were production-type loans to buy tractors, farm implements, feeds, seeds, fertilizers, drain tiles, fencing, coal, out-buildings for pigs and cattle. The deposits had dropped at R. V.'s bank (well, not his bank, but rather the well-to-do Bliem brothers' and Ernie Stebbins' bank....R. V. just ran it) with the decline in farm prices and incomes. When the deposits drop and loans outstanding don't drop, any bank's balance sheet begins to look sick, whether it's the Farmers Savings Bank in Rock Falls or the National City Bank in New York City. It was a relief to Edith and Rufus that their community had faith in R. V.'s bank and had not started a depositors' run on it.

Despite these traumatic events, and hard as it is to believe, given his innate compassion for the less fortunate, my father had not lost his faith in Herbert Hoover. What's more, he had developed a passionate dislike of Mr. Franklin D. Roosevelt, a name which R. V. insisted on pronouncing with an accented Rooosss, as in rooster (which is really how it looked, rather than how it was pronounced... as in rose). As election night approached, my father began to mention to our family that oyster stew party at the house four years earlier and its happy outcome -- Hoover's 444 electoral votes while that Irish Catholic Tammany Hall ward-healing Al Smith received only 87 votes.

"By George," he said to Edith, "Let's provide another oyster stew party and listen to the returns come in on the Hoover-Rooosssvelt election." And Edith said, "All right, Rufus, if that's what you'd like to do." Rufus was absolutely convinced of the rightness of Hoover's policies and of his re-election with a sweeping majority. So, Rufus drove to Thompson-O'Neil's grocery store on North Federal in Mason City for the oysters (because Bliem Brothers did not carry oysters), and a general invitation went out by word of mouth to everybody in Rock Falls to come around to the house and listen to Hoover get re-elected.

"ROOSEVELT WINNER IN LANDSLIDE! DEMOCRATS CONTROL WET CONGRESS; LEHMAN GOVERNOR, O'BRIEN MAJOR." (November 9, 1932)

Well, it was all over quickly. It sounded great for Hoover at first because of six east coast States -- Maine, New Hampshire, Vermont, Connecticut, Delaware, and Pennsylvania -- with 59 electoral votes, going for Hoover. My father was beaming. But those were the only States that Hoover could carry. The other 42 States with 472 electoral votes (that's right, Alaska and Hawaii weren't yet States) opted for Roosevelt, the greatest landslide in the history of America's presidential elections. At 15 minutes after ten p.m. in the midwest, the Associated Press flashed the word from Hoover's Palo Alto, California, home: "Hoover concedes defeat." R. V.'s party was all over. The guests began to disperse quietly. Had there been a show of hands on who voted which way, I am certain that Roosevelt would have swept the Rock Falls crowd as well in that dark year.

THE LOCAL ECONOMY

In the four-months interval between the November 1932 overthrow of Hoover and the March 4, 1933, inauguration of Roosevelt, events intensified the nation's nearly chaotic economic and financial problems. As a lame-duck President, Hoover was powerless to salvage the wreckage of his plans. Still convinced of the rightness of his policies, his activities seemed directed to avoiding the blame for the debacle. At the same time, Roosevelt was hardly less difficult to deal with. Self-confident, even cocky over his victory, he was not about to cooperate in decisions of an outgoing Republican Administration which had wielded power for over a decade. He fancied the credit for the New Deal under Democratic Party rule.

Meanwhile, the banking crisis worsened, as a mountain of debts came due and more debtors became delinquent. In the heartland, 14 States filled the vacuum of the national leadership by declaring statewide bank holidays. Acting without partisanship, Iowa's outgoing Republican Governor and its elected Democratic Governor expedited through the General Assembly the measure enabling the State's Superintendent of Banking temporarily to take any or all troubled banks under a State trusteeship, to reopen under their old or new charters as the events permitted. In the first 12 days of 1933, while 13 of Iowa's 643 banks failed, an unacceptable rate, under the new State law, 135 banks were taken over by January 31. Many more were given a similar refuge in February.

The Farmers Savings Bank in Rock Falls was in the eye of the storm swirling around the Falls Township community. R. V. had quite a lively time in that small bank for a few years in the Thirties. There were the good and the bad aspects to running such a small bank in the farm country. It was good in the sense that he knew every bank customer so well that he could almost read and control their emotions about personal financial needs. A nameless, faceless big city banker couldn't do that. The flip side of this coin of intimacy was that it put an added strain on R. V. as he tried to assist farm friends more than he could or should. He had been by nature generous to a fault, but there was a limit to his unofficial banker's generosity. He stretched that limit many times. Many Rock Falls town and farm families told me in later years how R. V. had helped them at crucual times to keep them from going under. He must have had to do some explaining to the State bank examiners during their annual audits of the bank's operations.

This small country bank had its "correspondent" bank, as all banks not members of the Federal Reserve System had to have for purposes of clearing checks in any given geographic region. R. V. and his bank Board decided early on that they couldn't afford a small percentage (of deposits) fee to be a member bank of the System, as that percentage was the bank's thin margin of profit...if any. Also, as a State-regulated bank, it could do without the fed's minimum services. The Farmers Savings Bank correspondent bank was the Continental Illinois National Bank and Trust Company in Chicago. It was large, like the Chase Manhattan, Hanover, and Mellon big city banks, but big was not always better. Some 50 years later, the Continental was in big trouble over "nonperforming" loans to that Texas oil patch crowd, and the Federal Deposit Insurance Corporation had to bail it out with a five billion dollar subsidy at taxpayer expense. In the early 1930s, however, it was solid.

Every day, checks written anywhere in the midwest on R. V.'s customers' bank deposits would be mailed first to the Continental for "clearing." That is, the Continental would pay the several other country banks an amount which they had paid out to cash Rock Falls depositors' checking. The Continental would then wrap up these cancelled checks and send them off to R. V. along with a draft of the total amount to be reimbursed to the Continental. And when R.V. received them, he would have to remit to the Continental on the same day the amount of the draft. If he could not do so, of course, his bank was insolvent.

For months on end, my father hated to open that mail at Uncle Val's post office and see the size of that draft. He never knew whether he had enough in deposits and in the vault and till to cover the draft. Often he would ask me to get the mail for him to open and read the Continental's draft amount. As a 12- and 13-year-old, I couldn't fully appreciate the grave consequences and chain of events that would be set in motion if the Farmers Savings Bank was unable to cover those drafts, but we both knew that matters would be bad for the bank, our family, and the community if it happened. It never quite did, but it was close.

    My father had an effective means to reassure the community in the darkest days of the banking crisis. The row of only four commercial buildings in the town, except for Bert Olden's blacksmith shop and the lumberyard, lined the north side of main street, from east to west (see photo). These were the bank, the pool hall, the garage, and Bliem Brothers General Store. My father needed to walk from the bank to the rear of the general store, at Uncle Val's post office, at least twice a day to get the mail that had come to the depot on "63" northbound and "64" southbound. During the summer months, a gathering of men usually could be seen sitting on the steps and standing around in front of the pool hall. They were "loafing," as there was little else for them to do. They were the unemployed, the underemployed, the odd-jobs men of the town and the farmers who were caught up on field work and wanted a change of scenes or needed some misery company.

    In normal times, those few workers who lived in town held down jobs in Mason City, usually at the cement plant, packinghouse, sugar beet factory, or brick and tile plant. A few worked shifts for the railroad, and others worked on the County road maintenance crews. By 1932, many had been laid off or put on two or three-day per week shifts. They had time to loaf with the local odd-jobs men and farmers, talking crops, prices, jobs, and politics. My father made it a point while passing by this somewhat sullen and quiet group of men to whistle the whole way from the bank to the store and back again. And he often would stop and chat as well, but he told me that he never failed to whistle, and as loudly as he could. His idea was that, if the banker could whistle through those times, the men would perceive it as a sign that at least the bank was safe and sound and maybe things weren't all bad. He told me to whistle too.

    Spring, summer, and autumn in the Thirties would mark the appearance in town of some strangers nearly every day. My father called them hobos, bums, or tramps. Actually, they were for the most part not habitual transients at all but rather a few among the tens of thousands of unemployed Americans in those years who had taken to the road to look for work. They would hop onto open-doored, empty boxcars, cattle cars, and coal cars when freight trains were pulling out of stations, ride a few miles to another town, and hop off to look for work or beg for a bite of food or some money or perhaps some clothing.

    Again in normal times, R. V. believed that every man who really wanted to work could find a job, and those who didn't have jobs were lazy. He realized in the Thirties that his harsh view of this was very unfair, so he was no longer quite so hard-nosed about it. In fact, similar to railroad operators who first forced the transients off the rail cars, but later let them ride at will, my father was generous to these socalled hobos, bums, and tramps. They would hop out of the rail car near the depot, walk up the road to town, and head straight for the bank to ask for a coin to buy a loaf of bread. R. V. never failed to give.

Later, in about 1935, the pool hall succeeded in getting a license to sell bottled and draft beer, an argument over which R. V. had fought bitterly as Mayor, Councilman, and private citizen for years. Under the new ownership of Glen Kephart, who got the license and so remained a lifelong enemy of R. V.'s, it was no longer called a pool hall but became the Rock Falls Tavern. Thereafter, when an unwashed, weather-beaten, haggard man came into the bank and asked for money for a loaf of bread, my father would suspect him of wanting money for a beer, but he would rarely give him the option. R. V. would put aside his work, step around from behind the cashier's cage, and ask the man to come with him. They would walk together to Bliem Brothers General Store, R. V. hopping and skipping to stay in step with the man (and whistling), and R. V. would buy the fellow a loaf of bread.

Many times during the worst of days, my father would came home from a day at the bank, have supper, and say to me, "John, how about a ride with me into the country this evening?" So we would get into our old second-hand Chevy (not always reliable) and head out. By the way, the Seven Passenger Studebaker Touring Car had disappeared, I know not where or when, but I suspected the "why" of its disappearance. It was obviously not appropriate for the banker to propel so luxurious a liner around town and country in the depth of the Great Depression. Fine in the prosperous early Twenties for the prosperous lumberyard merchant and CHIEF DEALER, but no more. Actually, the failing lumberyard and farm implement businesses could no longer support such luxury, and certainly the banker's salary, reduce to $100 per month, wasn't enough.

In those evening rides, we paid brief calls on three or four farmers. Driving into an often rundown farmyard, typically one with a scattering of chickens, a skinny dog or two, and the pungent odor of livestock, my father would suggest that I wait in the car, as he walked to the house or found the farmer in a barn or shed or pen. They would have a quiet ten or 20 minutes conversation, first on one foot and then on the other, kicking a clod of dirt now and then or gently stroking a placid old horse or a milk cow.

With darkness coming on, we would drive back home. I asked my father what he and the farmers talked about during those still, seemingly tranquil evenings. He explained that the farmers were overdue on payments on a loan to the bank, and he would try to get a small payment from them or rewrite the loan, with the interest due being added to the new loan or just to chat a bit about how they and the families were getting along, what they needed, how he might help them, so that they could avoid selling out and giving up the farm. It was merely an act of reassurance to longtime friends and bank customers who faced hard times.

A few days before Roosevelt took the president's oath of office on March 4, 1933, financial panic struck the nation. The Rock Falls bank was one of nine or ten banks in the entire State which had not already closed doors under State protection to avoid depositors' "runs" on the little money they had left. The new President acted promptly with an emergency Proclamation. Again, from <u>The Times</u>:

> "ROOSEVELT INAUGURATED, ACTS TO END THE NATIONAL CRISIS QUICKLY; WILL ASK WARTIME POWERS IF NEEDED." (March 5, 1933)

> "ROOSEVELT ORDERS 4-DAY BANK HOLIDAY, PUTS EMBARGO ON GOLD, CALLS CONGRESS." (March 6, 1933)

After this national moratorium on all banking, all of the Iowa banks came under protection of the State banking department. None could reopen without the Superintendent's authorization.

As a practical matter, the local Falls Township economy had been operating somewhat like a barter economy for some time. Most folks did without money, the age-old medium of exchange. They began to exchange things, not money, with each other, trading the essential food, clothing, and shelter to survive. Farmers butchered their cattle, hogs, and sheep rather than sell them for pennies a pound. They stopped selling milk and then butchered all the milk cows not needed to produce for family milk, cream, cheese, and butter. They raised chickens for the meat and eggs. They planted big gardens, usually with seeds saved from year to year. Bliem Brothers General Store took poultry and eggs "in trade," for dry goods and non-food essentials, such as canning jars and lids, soap, and toiletries, and they were more than generous in extending credit to farmers and town families for canned and packaged food. Many people shared houses to save on fuel and electricity. People sewed and patched and exchanged clothing and handed it down over and over again. A vivid memory of mine is that of my mother, sitting quietly almost every evening, darning socks for my father, my brother, and me. Somehow, basic essentials of living were reused and spread around among families, such that everyone managed to survive.

The declared national bank holiday served to make the barter economy official for a time, and of course it was a barter economy all over the nation. In those last trying months under Hoover, a chaotic situation came frightfully close to anarchy. Roosevelt's inauguration speech ("the only thing we have to fear is fear itself...") and subsequent decisive emergency actions saved the day. The bank holiday proclamation had been announced on Sunday, March 5 to be effective from Monday the sixth through Thursday the ninth. R. V. was as confused and puzzled as everyone else about the new banking rules to follow, as nothing had been disseminated in writing from the Roosevelt government. If Iowa had not closed all the State banks, R. V. could have accepted deposits but could not have permitted withdrawals and he had none of the script money to be issued by Washington. Because of some complexities in the new banking law passed in seven hours by the reconvened Congress, the President found he could not reopen the banks quickly.

"ROOSEVELT EXTENDS THE NATIONAL BANKING HOLIDAY; CONGRESS EMPOWERS HIM TO REOPEN SOUND INSTITUTIONS; HALF BILLION BUDGET CUT NEXT."
(March 10, 1933)

However, by the following Monday, March 13:

"MANY BANKS IN THE CITY AND NATION REOPEN TODAY FOR NORMAL OPERATIONS, BUT HOARDING BARRED; ROOSEVELT APPEALS ON THE RADIO FOR FULL CONFIDENCE." (March 13, 1933)

In Iowa, 211 banks were freed from State trusteeship, reopening within days. As soon as federal law permitted, 48 more followed. Ten were liquidated. The remaining 359, including the Farmers Savings Bank, were continued under a State closure until the banking superintendent's ruling on them. Of these, 245 were reopened in due time, 114 were either liquidated or recapitalized and sold.

The precise technicalities of having the Farmers Savings Bank reopen are unclear to me. I know that R. V. was champing at the bit to return the bank to operation at the earliest moment. One evening, in mid-March, he said to me "John, how would you like to ride to Des Moines with me in the morning?" I was surprised and delighted with the prospect. First, it meant a long ride in our new Dodge pickup. How we could afford a new Dodge pickup in early 1933, I never figured out, but we had one. It was not one of the monsters later to come into vogue, with their high-wheeled base, four-wheeled drive, stereo system and tape deck, and everything but color TV. It was a simple little six cylinder, no frills, miniature truck with a three passenger cab and a 6- x 10-foot bed. Probable cost was about $600 then, it was a handy run-about, useful at our lumberyard and a family car as well. However, I still missed the old Seven Passenger Studebaker Touring Car.

The next morning at an early hour, we were off to the State Capital, the big city of Des Moines. Edith had put up a sandwich lunch for her Rufus and me to eat on the way

-- 130 miles due south on highway 65. We arrived there by about eleven a.m., and my father soon found the State Department of Banking. Two outer-room secretaries were very kind to me with candy and chit-chat while R. V. was in the inner office doing what he had to do. Shortly, he emerged, face beaming, with a piece of paper waving in his hand and saying "The bank will be open tomorrow." To celebrate, we crossed the street to the magnificent capitol building and climbed a circular stairway all the way to the dome. We stood outside atop the iron-railed walkway until my father looked down and became sick, so we hastened inside, rushed down the stairway, into the pickup, and pointed the little Dodge-em north toward Rock Falls.

I was not to learn the exact technicalities essential to the bank's reopening for more than half a century, and only then from cousin, Mary Jane (Bliem) Maxon, our Uncle Leonard Bliem's daughter. At the time in 1933, Uncle Val, Leonard's brother and the postmaster, was also the Farmers Savings Bank's president. Ernie Stebbens, a local farmer, was vice president, and Uncle Leonard, the grocer/drygoods merchant, was one of the Directors. The State banking department considered the Rock Falls bank's outstanding loan portfolio, mainly loans to destitute farmers, as "worthless paper," which had to be "offset" on the bank's books by an equal amount of Certificates of Deposits, before the bank could open. The Bliem brothers and Stebbins came to the rescue with the required "CDs," in effect "buying" the worthless loan paper. So far as the borrowers knew, those loans remained on the bank's books, and as collections in whole or in part were made by the bank, they were credited to the Bliems and Stebbins. They, not my father, were the little bank's saviors. A fair deal for all concerned.

Other prospects for the local economy were no rosier than those of the bank. The lumber and farm implement business was dying. Farmers simply had no money, except for seeds, feeds, and other farming essentials. Farmers occasionally needed machinery such as a mower, hayrake, baler, manure spreader, discs, or harrows. For R. V., the banker, the problem was granting a risky loan, and for R. V., the merchant, having to take some no-good used machine in on the trade and then trying to resell it. He lost rather than gained on most such deals. I often had the uninspiring task of cleaning and repainting the old trade-ins, but they would still look old and no good. We couldn't carry tractors because we couldn't compete with the big dealers in Mason City (who were also going broke), and we couldn't afford to carry the inventory.

The coal business dried up too, except for the school coal, because everyone burned wood or corn cobs, even the whole ear of fine corn, when the price went to ten cents a bushel. The harness business was obsolete with the coming of the tractor, dead as the buggy whip business. We did sell a few sacks of livestock feeds, a few blocks of salt for cows to lick, quite a bit of binder twine during harvest season, some nails, some steel and wood fence posts, woven wire and barbed wire, a little grain seed, some lime and baling wire. Any profits made on such sales were not enough to pay Rudy Hansen's pitifully low wages to run the place, which he did faithfully from 1928 to 1936.

Rudy was loyal to my father, staying with him for as long as he could, but the time came when Rudy just had to leave for a better job. He was a nice man. I spent hours talking with Rudy at the lumberyard in those quiet summer days when no customers came. One day, my father occupied Rudy building small pigs farrowing houses with lumber that we couldn't sell any other way, but the pigs houses didn't sell either. Jerome and I had the job of unloading an occasional carload of coal into the bins along the siding, the dirtiest and physically hardest job I could imagine at the time. The railroad charged "demurrage" on a rail car spotted on the siding to be unloaded, if not emptied for its use elsewhere by the railroad within three days. There were a few close calls, but we managed to avoid a charge.

Thinking back, I am amazed at my father's entrepreneurial flair, considering this farm-town's setting and the times. With the economy plunging in the summer of 1930, he bought the horse pasture opposite the main street's row of stores, paying a few dollars for this choicest one-acre location. Before I knew it, a fine new gas station began taking shape on that corner, with two DX gas pumps, a big underground gasoline storage tank, compressed airhoses for filling tires, a mens' and a womens' toilet out back, and a concrete-lined grease pit over which cars could drive to have an oil change and grease job. What a great addition to the town. The gas pumps were interesting. After draining ten or less gallons from a glass-contained upper tank of the tall pump, where levels for one through ten gallons were marked, you pumped a handle vigorously back and forth to force gasoline back into the glass chamber. When filled to ten gallons, a pipe drained off the excess back to the storage tank. Hence the expression "pumping gas."

I pumped plenty of gas that summer, both before and after R. V. sold the new station to Chuck Chehock in 1931. R. V. kept it for a year, but it needed an owner-operator. One of my first steady jobs was at the DX station from six to seven each evening, while Chuck went to supper. Chuck paid me ten cents an hour, 15 cents if he came back late. Chuck watched every penny, and we didn't get along so well but I stuck at it because I wanted a bicycle. After I had saved 150 dimes, I quite the job and went to Mason City to buy the used bike that I had spotted for $15.00.

The supper hour at the station was quiet, often spent pitching horseshoes with Dave Edgar and Bill Dedina. I had driven stakes in shallow sand boxes behind the station by the grease pit, and before long it was an all-day attraction in town. As many folks missed the joys of horseshoe pitching (but not President George Bush), I shall describe the game. The two stakes are set 40 feet apart (30 feet for women), each in a six-foot-square box of sand covering dirt. Two or four may play. If two play, each pitches two shoes from one stake to the other, then walks to the other stake and pitches his two shoes back. If four play, there are two partners, each pitching in one direction only. You then score one point for each shoe pitched closer to the stake than the opponent's pitch, but a shoe must be within the width of a shoe to the stake, or it doesn't score. If you pitch a shoe around the stake, it's a wringer, scoring three points. If your opponent pitches a wringer over the one you pitched, he wipes out your three points. Well, at least it was something to do.

In earliest times, shoes were real used ones from the horses' hooves. Later, shoes were designed by the National Horseshoe Pitching Association, incorporated in 1921 as the sport's governing body. It specified shoes weighing two and one-half pounds, seven and five-eighths inches in length, seven inches wide at the greatest width and with a three and one-half inch space or opening between the calks or toes of the shoe. How about that? All you ever wanted to know about this serious game, all except that Ted Allen holds the U.S. record of 72 consecutive wringers in tournament play. Yes sir. Yes sir.

An added attraction for me was that Oscar Morse lived in the old Morse Hotel right next to the gas station along main street. He would limp over and talk to me frequently. Oscar was Bert Morse's brother. Bert was the highly respected landowner-farmer on the west border of town and for many years Deacon of the Methodist Church in Rock Falls. They were sons of George O. Morse, an early leading tycoon of Rock Falls and farmer who acquired and worked the largest holding in the township -- 840 acres. It was said of George O. Morse that, in early times, he served as walking banker of the community. Whenever someone needed a loan, he would go to George O., where a deal could be struck on the spot.

Unlike brother Bert or the wealthy father, Oscar was the pre-eminent social drop-out to which the word "bum" is the most fitting. It was said that he spent his youth as a cowboy in the West. Most people thought that Oscar was off his rocker, as they say, because of his strange lifestyle, his conversations, and his utterly filthy attire and unwashed, unshaven stubble. As sole occupant, he had turned the fine old Morse Hotel into a disgracefully, unbelievably dirty dwelling. On the contrary, I believed Oscar was much smarter than most folks gave him credit for being, that he had simply opted out of anything requiring a semblance of responsibility or conventional living. He was the ultimate cynic; he heard a different drummer. And he had not worked a day in his life to my knowledge unless as a young cowhand; still, he kept current on events, not just in Rock Falls, but in Washington, D. C., and throughout the world. He must have read many newspapers and magazines, probably given to him by brother Bert.

Oscar had no teeth, his eyes watered continually, he was always scratching himself. He frightened most children without meaning to, but I came to enjoy talking with him. I'm sure that Oscar was not a boozer, my father's term for anybody who had ever taken one drink, nor did he smoke or chew tobacco. Often he started a conversation with me by saying, "Boy, whataya think of this fellow Rooosssvelt (he pronounced it as did my father) down in that there White House?" or "Boy, what's Governor Herring goin to do next?" or "Boy, what's Rufus up to these days?" He always called me boy. He discussed politics with me at length, always a twinkle in his eye and the tone of a complete cynic. On more than one occasion, he said to me, "Do you know, Boy, the only difference 'tween me and brother Bert is that I'm crazy and I know it, Bert's crazy, and he don't know it." That was Oscar (See pool hall photo herein.)

> "PRESIDENT SIGNS BILL FOR LEGAL BEER; EFFECTIVE HERE AT 12:01 A.M. APRIL 7; HOUSE APPROVES FARM RELIEF 315 TO 98.
>
> "Bottling to start now. Regulations are issued for permits and posting of Brewery Inspectors. Racketeers are barred. Licenses will be issued only to those who show a reputable past. Drys map an early fight." (March 23, 1933)

As the Depression deepened, the local economy gave up two of its commercial enterprises and gained one. Sad to say, Bert Olden gave up his blacksmithing career, a victim of the farm tractor that replaced the old work horse. The automobile repair garage on main street was next to fail. If a car needed repairing, you fixed it yourself or junked it. However, the conservative, dry State of Iowa legalized beer by a vote of 377,275 to 249,943 in a statewide referendum on July 10, 1933. Glen Kephart was ready with his application for a beer license. Soon, the Rock Falls Tavern was in business. Glen kept the pool hall going, as well as the ice cream counter and barber shop, but draught beer was the center of interest, good times and bad, much to my father's dismay. And he was soon to be proven right. There were a few in the community who just couldn't handle it. One was my father's Prairie Farm "herdsman," as R. V. called his hired man on the stationery marking R. V.'s entry into the elite circle of purebred Aberdeen Angus cattle breeders.

My father had purchased the Prairie Farm in the early Thirties, probably for a low price. It was the farm originally owned by his father John Wilkinson, but later sold by one of the family. It became home for a small herd of black angus cattle, R. V.'s favorite pastime. It kept him busy while he wasn't running the bank, the lumberyard, the gas station, the School Board, and the Town, as its Mayor. The herdsman drank too much beer, spent a lot of his time in the tavern, neglected his family and the cattle, thus had to be replaced. A few others had what might be called a drinking problem, but very few. One sad case, however, ended tragically in suicide.

Drinking seemed not to be the big problem during the Depression years that it was during Prohibition, possibly due to the persistence of the IOGF, International Order of Good Templars, over the previous decades. I liked Kephart because he ran a clean and orderly tavern but even more as he organized a summertime baseball "town team," with uniforms, equipment, and everything. For a few of the townspeople and farmers, a beer or two at the end of the day's work...or worry was a nice relaxing treat. A case in point was Ed and Paul Hansen, brothers and railroad workers who lived as batchelors with their two unmarried sisters Annie and Tillie in the house across the tracks near the depot. Their evening ritual six days each week was to walk to the tavern for one pint of beer and walk back home again without uttering a word. There are few finer social institutions than the English pub, but it takes five centuries or more for a nation to appreciate its amenities. America is still too young.

"PROHIBITION REPEAL IS RATIFIED AT 5:32 P.M.; ROOSEVELT ASKS NATION TO BAR THE SALOON; NEW YORK CELEBRATES WITH QUIET RESTRAINT.

"President Proclaims the Nation's New Policy as Utah Ratifies." (The 36th State to do so, December 6, 1933)

Bliem Brothers General Store survived and thrived on its virtually Depression-proof business, not the least of which was the egg trade. Uncle Leonard was the consummate merchant, possessing the valuable German traits of thrift and astuteness in all dealings. He wisely accumulated the best farmland he could buy during the worst farming years. Unlike my father, Uncle Leonard always rented his farms on shares, traditionally two-thirds of the grain crops to the tenant, one-third to the landowner. And no fussing around with livestock.

Renting on shares was a clean arrangement which also provided an incentive to the tenants to maximize net crop values. By contrast, R. V. -- autocrat that he was -- always tried to run his farms by managing a hired man or his herdsman at the modest wage of hired help. This arrangement offered no incentive to the hired hand, and it showed in most results, first at Active Acres, then Timberline, then The Prairie Farm, then Sundance. And he wanted livestock because he liked livestock, particularly those purebred black angus, and never you mind whether the hired man liked livestock. This meant low crop yields, high costs of operations, more responsibilities caring for live animals. Uncle Leonard never named his farms, but they all made him rich; R. V.'s farms kept him poor. Still, perhaps R. V. had more fun with his livestock than he would have enjoyed with grain farms.

Summertime seemed the worst season to endure in the Thirties. It was so hot, humid, windy, and quiet. As the folks were out-of-doors more, you noticed how disconsolate and tense and worried they seemed. There wasn't the usual smiling, laughing, and joking any more. As well as pumping gas, I mowed the lawns for the Bliems and the church for nickels and dimes and worked in the lumberyard without any pay. For a few weeks one summer my father banished Jerome and me to Timberline, one of his briefly run farms, to hoe the morning glory vines out of the corn fields. It seemed R. V.'s idea of keeping us occupied, out of mischief. It was the worst assignment of my early years, far, far worse than unloading the carloads of coal. We were taken to the field, miles from anywhere, in early morning, each with a hoe, a sack of lunch, and drinking water, and we would hoe and pull those ever-loving morning glories in the hot sun for eight or nine hours until someone came in the Dodge-em pickup and took us home. I hated it. You could hoe, and you could pull all day, and you could see no visible progress in that 60-acre cornfield.

After the morning glory episode, I got work from the County under its weed control program, thanks to Ray Edgar who worked with the County Highway Department. This work was cutting thistles with an old-fashioned scythe from the cow pastures where thistles seemed to thrive and where the cow-pies abounded. The $4.00 a day pay was the best ever for me. I worked with Dave Edgar and Bill Dedina. But it was too good to last. The County ran out of funds.

Then there was that summer when Jerome and I decided we should go into the potato business. We rented, or more precisely were given the use of, ten acres of land on our father's Active Acres. In the spring, we cut into pieces what had to be thousands of seed potatoes, and we planted them in long rows on those ten acres, dropping the pieces, each with one eye or more, into about 200 rows. As they sprouted and formed into healthy plants, we began to have dreams of profits. Then the potato bugs located our field and started chewing. We sprayed, but with limited effect, so we debugged by hand. In late summer, when the surviving plants had formed nice new potatoes in the ground, we borrowed a horse-drawn digger and were all set to harvest. Then the rains came in torrents, and we couldn't get into the water-logged field to work. Finally, when the ground had drained and dried out, many potatoes had rotted. However, we managed to harvest about 200 bushels.

Jerome, with his popularity with the city folks, plus his born-salesman personality, was designated as the chief of marketing, and I was field production manager, i.e. the digger. We loaded the pickup high with sacks of potatoes, and Jerome headed for Mason City to sell them. He was but partially successful, as so many people raised potatoes in their own backyards in those hard times. We might better have raised ten acres of brussels sprouts or broccoli, or anything but a root or tuber vegetable in a wet field of a kind that everyone else raised. We had many unsold spuds at the end, and spoilage was high. I was glad to see next year's school term about to start.

So much for the local economy of Falls Township as it was seen by an emerging teenager in the early Thirties. It wasn't all bad, I suppose, when you stop to think about it in a relative sense. Still, if things had not yet reached rock bottom, they were pretty near to it.

SCHOOL DAYS, SCHOOL DAYS

"...dear old golden rule days." To the 20,000 little farm-town communities of the American heartland the school was more than a place where you learned reading, writing, and 'rithmetic. It was the center of social, cultural and sometimes political activities, the place where the farm families and the townspeople met, had picnics and parties, held meetings, enjoyed their children's athletic contests, voted, planned, watched school plays and debates, and much more. The school system and its school houses in the town and country were primary forces in keeping the communities glued together during the Depression when other and larger forces were beginning to tear them apart or destroy them.

An educational experience in Falls Township School at Rock Falls was...what shall I say...something else. It all started in the primary room where, under guidance of only one teacher, some 40 kids were assembled into four grades, all in the same one room and one teacher. After 68 years, the mind grows dim about those formative years. My first teacher was Marjorie Calvert, a lovely lady, then dear old Aunt Myrtle for the next two years. In the autumn of 1929 skipping fourth grade, I was advanced to a secondary room upstairs for grades five through eight under Dolores Finnell, another fine teacher and lady. The somewhat more exciting four years began in the summer of 1933, in the high school -- five rooms, basketball, and girls.

Those early years in the lower grades were generally carefree years. My parents put me on a long leash, allowing me to learn at my own pace. My customary attire during the summer months was a single piece, blue denim, bib-fronted, shoulder-strapped pair of overalls, and that was it -- no shirt, no underpants, no socks, no shoes. I disliked the return of autumn. It meant wearing shoes again. In high school, life began to take a more dignified turn. In addition to the varied curriculum, including such awful things as alegbra and geometry and chemistry, there was a grim determination on the part of the administration and a group of four teachers to engage us in all kinds of extracurricular activities. These included stage plays, declamatory contests, marching band, orchestra, field trips, and if enough players could be mustered, team sports.

A marked improvement over the earlier grades was that high school students had the use of five classrooms: a big assembly room, where all four-year students had individual desks and in which some classes and the spelling bees were held, the typing room, the south classroom, the chemistry room, and the manual training room. Happy were the hours spent in the manual training room, turning the high speed lathes and saws, and producing useful pieces of furniture. The typing room offered happy times as well. It was here that Mrs. Lucille Usher taught me one of the most valuable and practical skills of my lifetime; it was to speed-type accurately. Once acquired, this skill was as natural as breathing for the next 60 years.

The south classroom was small, but one I particularly liked, because it was there that a very attractive, young blond Scandinavian tried her hardest to teach me the mysteries of algebra and geometry, with limited success. It was largely the distraction of her attractiveness and only partly my basic mental incapacity. I was unable to grasp the simplest mathematics.

Another small room on the second level was reserved for the teaching of chemistry. The Falls Township School was required to offer a broad curriculum, including chemistry, to maintain its accreditation with the State's Education Board. Otherwise, the school would be required to consolidate with a nearby school district that offered the requisite curriculum. This was a very touchy subject. Just as every little soul must shine, so too every little town must have its very own high school, so that boys and girls could go to school where they were with parents, and where town identity was not lost for lack of a high school. My father fought tooth and nail for half of his life to keep the Rock Falls school from being consolidated with another town. "Lose the high school, and the town will die," said Rufus, and a prescient statement it was.

The problem with a broad curriculum was that it cost money, and this was worsened by another virtual necessity of small-town life. Every high school, however small it was, had to have a marching band, so that (in Cerro Gordo County, for example), it could march up Federal Avenue in Mason City at the annual music festival and be a source of pride to Rock Falls. Those two requirements, the marching band and broad curriculum, were hard to fulfill with a 44-student high school enrollment and a small-town tax base.

What to do? In the summer of 1934 or 1935, when the teachers were being hired for the upcoming year, the local Board decided that the time to hire a fulltime music teacher had arrived. They hired Mr. Borup. He was a nice man who played a mean hot saxophone in an itinerant night club dance band. To solve the curriculum problem, they advised Mr. Borup that he would be the new chemistry instructor as well. It was soon clear that no student would become the great Rock Falls chemist. Not only did Mr. Borup not know litmus paper from newspaper, he had no disciplinary attributes. As a result, our chemistry class was a riot. Bill Dedina, who was a bit the bully and was larger than Borup, made life miserable for the poor man, and he soon departed to the probably more congenial life of a tenor sax in the night club circuit.

Field trips were a pleasant change of scene from the classroom. Each year, two, three or all high school grades at one time were taken to a industrial plant in Mason City for an educational tour of facilities. Without variation, the expedition each year was to the cement plant, the meat packing plant, and then the sugar beet factory. These were dirty and smelly tours, particularly to Jacob E. Decker & Sons slaughterhouse. They did reveal to us the industrial genius of making machines that mass produced goods, while making men labor in the most unhealthy and dangerous conditions at low wages and for long hours. After a century of struggle, the labor movement was still not well-organized in the mid-1930s, barely two years into the Roosevelt presidency and with a Democratic Congress.

The air in the cement plant was thick with fine lime dust. It spread out across the countryside, all the way to Rock Falls, nine miles away, on days when the wind came out of the southwest. The Decker meat packing operation, awful enough in the plant, could be smelled in Rock Falls under similar wind conditions. That plant converted live cattle and hogs into some 25 products, from beefsteaks and chops to dog and cat foods. The sugar beet factory converted field grown beets into white sugar. It was free of dust and odor. Not explained to our students was that the sugar beet plant produced at full tilt because of the high American tariff and quota on imported cane sugar from Central American countries, so they couldn't sell to us. This kept retailers sugar prices artificially high and American sugar processors richer (and consumers poorer). That bit of knowledge was not a part of the educational tour.

If field days were fun, declamatory contests and the school stage plays were pure hell. The contests were designed by parents to make children miserable. The format was that each year the schools would enter County competitions with a three-person team, presenting three rhetorical discourses before an audience of admiring and nervous parents. The three subjects were oratorical, the serious stuff, dramatic, the heavy stuff, and humorous, the funny stuff. Winners at County level would advance to district, regional, and finally State competitions in Des Moines. A panel of judges in each subject rated first, second, third and last place winners.

I was painfully shy as a kid. Jerome was just the opposite. He was also a great talker, which is why I did not really learn to talk until Jerome went to college. Nonetheless, I was expected to compete in declamatory events. Carolyn was our family's dramatic contestant, and Jerome was our oratorical contestant. He could make a commendable address on any looming issue of the times. I was told to be humorous. In my senior year, I found a humorous piece of writing involving a preacher giving a spell-binder of a sermon. It suddenly was great fun for me, and I swept the County and district competitions. Then came the regionals, and I was confident. However, to my dismay and misfortune, one of the judges was a preacher. He didn't take my spoof of a sermon at all well. He gave me the lowest marks. My father was furious of course, but we had to accept defeat. After that episode, religion became even less of a factor in our family than before.

Stage plays were as bad for bashful kids but at least you had company in your misery. Again, in our family, it wasn't a question of whether to enter. We entered. It was easy to get a part, as there were usually more parts than candidates. In fact, some times an actor had two parts. Practice was during after school hours, an annoyance, as I had more entertaining things to do after school. Also, I hated leading roles as a lover or something silly. It was not that I minded kissing the heroine in the final scene. I just didn't like doing it in front of an audience. One play, "Mulligan's Magic," had me as Mulligan, a tent-show barker and patent medicine man, a part somewhat like that of Meredith Wilson's "Music Man." I even had to sing!

The worst exposure was when I had to deliver the valedictory address at the senior class's graduation ceremonies. Not only did this involve delivering the speech; it involved writing it. When the night arrived, I was desperately nervous. Standing in front of those faces, with the class motto, "Success Crowns Effort," hanging above my head, I made a botch of it. I couldn't control my voice and I talked too fast to be understood. I was awful.

We had some interesting teachers. Mr. Borup was destined to suffer as much trouble with the band as with his chemistry class. Without disciplinary skills, he couldn't get any of us 15 more or less to practice and learn how to play instruments, let alone play together to an audience. Learning trombone wasn't a high priority for me. The band died one night. We were all ready to play a number or two in the gym before a class play began. Lots of people were seated in the gym when Mr. Borup raised his baton and tapped on the music stand. We started the rousing march well enough, but something happened to mess it up. We got out of timing with each other and with the drummer. First one and then another instrument faltered, and then the drummer quit, and finally the whole band sputtered to an embarrassing, deafening silence. Mr. Borup started us again, and we died again. I could have cried for him.

Mrs. Usher was more than just a good typing teacher. She was a strict disciplinarian. She brooked no nonsense from anyone -- not even the School Board. In the end, she was fired by the Board when she got too pushy and thought that she had become indispensable. She worked her way up from teacher to principal and superintendent, ruling with an iron fist for years, the best teacher Rock Falls hired but she pushed too hard and finally had to go. I was forever grateful for her typing instructions.

Another teacher, Mr. Hoadley, was a huge strong man, an ex-boxer and a good manual training teacher, but that's about it. He had trouble actually reading from the printed page. He did try to teach me how to fight with the two pair of boxing gloves that Jerome had somewhere acquired. During one lesson, Hoadley hit me so hard, not intentionally, that everything went shiny and black for a few seconds. That took care of my urge to learn how to box. The janitor, Charles M. "Pappy" Lee, was also an ex-boxer and a character as well. I thought that he must have sustained a severe blow to the head during his younger days. He was our faithful and efficient janitor from 1927 through 1936. In his sixties then, he had operated a groceries and meat market in Mason City, then was the city public safety commissioner for several years. Pappy was often a bit cranky with kids. He maintained the school building as clean as a whistle, but he got to thinking it belonged to him rather than to the public. Eventually he had to retire.

Except for three attractive young high school ladies, my entire attention was riveted on basketball. It was the only team sport we had, due to a scarcity of students. The basketball team required only five players and a couple of substitutes. Baseball required nine, football eleven, and hockey and swimming were out of the question for want of a pool or rink. And nobody had heard of golf then. Most of the small towns had the same problems, so it evened out. The basketball season started in early autumn and ended in late spring. We competed with some 20 towns, once a week throughout the winter. Monday through Thursday from three to five was practice time preparing for Friday night games with other towns. The school bought uniforms, but we had to buy our own socks and shoes. We often had to furnish a family car for trips to other towns. On one such trip, I drove (at age 16) for five of us, and coming home late at night through Mason City, I was ticketed for speeding. My father made me pay the $5.00 fine in court.

Monte Duncan, another teacher, was our coach for two seasons. He had to teach history, geography, and something else as well. He was a good coach but terribly temperamental. We had a good won-lost record with him. Donald Dunton played center, Bill Dedina, Russ Edgar, and Cliff "Red" Senneff alternated as guards, Lee Usher, Truman Motland, and I alternated as forwards. Duncan invited us to his house (the teacherage) where his wife promised us cake and ice cream after every victory, so we proceeded to win 19 games in a row. When we lost the 20th and last contest, they didn't invite us in for the treat, which seemed to us was pretty stupid of them.

At the end of each season there was a district tournament among small Class B schools. In my senior year, we had another hot team. The district tournament (to be followed by regional and State meets for the winners) was in the big Class A Mason City field house gym. After winning two games, things went wrong in the final game. The pressure got to us and we lost. It was the end of high school basketball for most of us. The Rock Falls girls had many excellent teams thanks to Wilma Brown, Arlene and Virginia Rodrain, Lorraine Hansen, Olive Jensen, Mildred Navratil, Molly Napoletano, and Helen Heinrichsen.

Well, everything considered, the small-town community school in the American heartland may have lacked for great teachers and elaborate facilities during the dark days of the Great Depression, but it was a pillar, an anchor, and a safety valve for students and parents alike. In most ways, it outperformed the church, open in most towns for a couple of hours a week. The school was always open, so it seemed, and always a community communications center. I know that we in Rock Falls, as families in other hamlets in the County, were aware of the magnificent educational plant in Mason City, with its auditorium, swimming pool, track and field house, football and baseball fields, basketball court, tennis courts, school libraries, and maybe 50 or more teachers. But when it came to local pride and loyalty, effort and <u>esprit de corps</u>, you couldn't beat the small-town schools out there in the country.

ENTERTAINMENT

Apart from the entertaining aspects of those years in

high school, there were other events to come, and at surprisingly low cost. That was one good thing about the Depression years. Entertainment, at least what passes for that in the entertainment industry, had not yet become the expensive trash that lay in store for America.

Free movies night in Rock Falls was an example of how communities brought a little joy to nearly everyone during an otherwise grim period. Some fellow in Mason City came upon the idea of showing old film either from his own collection or by renting from a film library. He drove a little van, and mounted in the back of it were the necessary camera and sound equipment. Wednesday evenings were Rock Falls's turn for the movie man to come. Shortly before the darkness settled, he arrived in the schoolyard and backed his van around so that the back end was pointed at the two story brick wall of the north side of the school building. Somehow, he (or Pappy Lee) got onto the roof of the building and draped a big white bed-sheet, or more likely four sheets sewed together, over the side wall. By this time, three or four dozen people, mostly kids, had gathered in chairs set on the lawn by Pappy Lee. When darkness came, the camera rolled, the picture was projected onto the bed-sheet(s), and a rich variety of cops and robbers, cowboys, indians, and heavy romance was offered, all for free.

During the brief intermissions for a change of reels, advertisements by local merchants, all hand printed, were focussed on the bed sheet(s), such as Farmers Savings Bank for all of your banking needs; the Bliem Brothers General Store for groceries and dry goods; Chehock Filling Station for gas, oil, grease jobs, and tires; Kephart's Tavern and Pool Hall; R. V. Wilkinson, the CHIEF DEALER, for all your lumber, coal, and farm supply and machinery needs. Then, back to the film, the white hats and black hats shoot out, and home to bed.

The Rock Falls baseball club offered more low budget summertime entertainment. Under Glen Kephart's leadership and support, the community put together nine players, ages 16 through 46 years. Jerome hustled money from those merchants who sponsored the free movies, plus a few individual contributors, to purchase nine uniforms with shirt and pants only. We bought our own spiked shoes, socks, glove, and cap. Balls and bats were financed by passing the hat at games. With an eight-team league, a game was scheduled every Sunday afternoon, with a neighboring town. On Sunday mornings after church, we went to Dave Gildner's pasture cum ball park to shovel the cow pies and horse turds from the baseball diamond, drag or rake the dirt surfaces smooth, and spread out the lime lines marking the batters' box and the baselines from home plate to first and third bases. We were then ready to play ball.

The team had some very good baseball players. Lillard

Nicholas, husband of Will Edgar's daughter Levetta, was a very fine shortstop. Jerome was an excellent first baseman. Bill Dedina made a great catcher, Dave Edgar was a small and a hard-working second baseman, Glen Brown was a fine pitcher, and Gus Yost, our large and powerful stonemason and the oldest player, was our best hitter. Milly and Forey Jones covered third base and left field. Gilbert Wegener usually came by to umpire. I was a mediocre lefthanded pitcher with a real sharp breaking curve ball, but my trouble was control. I was wild as a March hare on the mound, walking so many batters that I would last about two or three innings. No doubt about it, I was good at basket ball but a lousy base ball pitcher. I couldn't hit worth a damn either.

In the summers of 1934 and 1935, I was fortunate in having two remarkable experiences which I would certainly call great entertainment. Both were very heady events for a 14-year-old and 15-year-old. The first was a trip to the World's Fair in Chicago, the second a trip to California.

The World's Fair, opened in the summer of 1933, was held over a second summer by popular demand. It was providing a great sense of national pride, a glimmer of hope, and a spark of joy to the whole country during the Depression. By one means or another, everyone attended who possibly could manage the time and money. Jerome was allowed to go in the summer of 1933 while still a high school student. My sister Carolyn, graduating from high school in 1931, had gone to Mason City Junior College for two years and then on to Iowa State Teachers College in Cedar Falls. Now home for the summer and without work, she wanted to go to the fair. The Bliem girls, Mary Jane and Jessie, who had graduated from high school in 1930 and 1934, respectively, were also home from college, working in the store.

The three women decided that it would be great fun to take in the fair together. They persuaded the parents that they were mature enough to undertake the journey. As usual there were family friends to shelter them, this time in a suburb of Chicago where the women were promised free lodgings. Nobody went anywhere in those days without the help of their family friends. One just didn't incur the costs of staying in a hotel, and it was before the days of the ubiquitous motel. In this instance, it was the Percy Stark family. Mable Stark was Art Wetter's sister, and Art and Lottie Wetter were prominent Falls Township farmers. They were good friends of Rufus, Edith, Leonard, and Mabel.

Now enter Aunt Myrtle, who was still teaching school. She wanted to go to the fair, and everyone agreed that it would be nice for her to come too. Mary Jane had secured the use of her parent's car for the drive of 350 miles to Chicago with the pledge that they would never travel over 40 miles per hour. Now enter John-boy, who also wanted to go, since his brother had been and his sister and Aunt and cousins were going. And there you have it.

The journey to Chicago seemed endless at that limited speed, but it was completed from dawn to dusk of a single long day in July. The five of us were put up at the Stark home as promised, at what must have been a great inconvenience to them. As Percy was on the verge of unemployment, we insisted on paying a room rent. We parked the car and travelled by streetcar each day to the fairgrounds on Lake Michigan's downtown Chicago shoreline. I enjoyed the fair immensely, particularly exhibitions, new machines, inventions, pavilions of foreign nations, and a lavish array of rides and side shows. I wanted to see Sally Rand's famous fan dances and strip tease shows, but the box office folks wouldn't sell me a ticket.

I was petrified by the big city. My worst fear was of being separated from the four ladies on our tour, getting lost, and never being heard from again. I was most uneasy about going through the suburb of Cicero on the way to and from Stark's house, as I knew that Cicero was the hangout of Al Capone with his bunch of prohibition-days gangsters. After all, it was near the time and place of the gangland execution called the St. Valentines Day Massacre of the 17 mobsters in a Cicero garage. That week in the windy city was some experience.

The Chicago trip must have given me some self-confidence. The next summer I found myself requesting permission of my parents to travel to California. The occasion was a visit to Rock Falls by Glen Edgar and his son and daughter with Glen's brothers Will and Ray. Glen had sought better opportunities than our town for his wife and seven children in the 1920s, moving to El Centro, California, in Imperial Valley to work for a Ford dealership. He had come through Rock Falls on his way to pick up a new Ford at the factory in Detroit for an El Centro customer. While getting the new car, he left his son and daughter with their cousins, and I was invited to ride to El Centro with them.

To my astonishment, I was granted permission to go. It was remarkable that I was allowed to take this journey, considering the nature of the times, the cost, my age, and the distance involved. I can't imagine how my parents had brought themselves to let me go. The deal was that another passenger, Elmer Christiansen, and I would buy all the gas and oil for the ride out and back to Rock Falls, when Glen returned for a second car that summer. (At seven gallons for a dollar, the total gas bill was no more than $25.00.) Elmer was a young local farmer and a friend of our family, having dated Carolyn for a <u>long</u> time. He needed a change of scene about that time, so it was nice for him to come.

We headed west one fine morning in the new Ford. Not being able to afford an overnight accomodation in a hotel, we drove the whole 3,300 miles without a night's stopover, and I must say that got tiresome for all of us. Still, no one complained, we were a good-natured bunch, and we saw many interesting sights along the way: the drought-ridden dust bowl of the Great Plains through Nebraska, the Rocky Mountains through Colorado, a bit of the Grand Canyon, and a small wide spot in the road called Las Vegas in Nevada's desert. Finally, we crossed Death Valley at night to avoid the 115-degree daytime heat, and were in the orange groves of San Bernardino, California, early the next morning.

We took leave of an already homesick Elmer at a hotel where he was to meet friends, and I agreed to meet him at that spot in two weeks. We would wait there to meet Glen Edgar, ready to start back for Iowa. I was going on to El Centro, 150 miles to the south, to stay with Glen Edgar's family. Then, I would take a 700-mile side trip to northern California for a visit with the Henry Weitzes and then back to San Bernardino.

The Imperial Valley in July is incredibly hot, but my stay with the hospitable and friendly Edgars was enjoyable because they took such good care of me, showing me the irrigation fields, driving me to the Mexican border and city of Mexicali. They were as hard up as everyone else during those years, surviving on their vegetable and fruit crops. Annie Edgar, Glen's wife, was lean and tall and about the nicest woman I had met outside our home, and the six sons and daughter Mary were the finest young folks imaginable.

The six sons had some odd jobs and were constantly in search of steady work that summer. They were lanky young men, all of them six feet three inches to six feet eight inches tall. They showed me the intricate irrigation systems for the fields of vegetable crops grown in the valley -- lettuce, tomatoes, peppers, spinach, melons, grapes and fruits by the thousands of acres. The water was being brought all the way from the Colorado River through an immense concrete-lined canal. Some water was siphoned aside to make the desert bloom; some flowed on to the great metropolitan centers of Los Angeles and San Diego. Without water, the desert was blowing sand; with water, fabulous fruits and vegetables were grown.

I had little pocket money to carry me through my west coast travels, because R. V. took a salary cut at the bank that summer pending improved economic conditions, but Aunt Myrtle chipped in to help me from her teaching salary. So, after six nice days in El Centro, I bought a Greyhound bus ticket (dirt cheap as was the gas) for the 700-mile travel up the coast and back to meet Elmer. I travelled through cities, across San Francisco Bay by ferry beneath the unfinished Oakland Bay bridge, and on through the Sacramento Valley to a place near Red Bluff. My parents had arranged for me to be put up with the Weitzes, another among those Rock Falls community farming friends who had fled from the farm depression of the heartland in the 1920s to try their luck in California with a peach orchard and a fine chicken hatchery. Henry's wife Georgina, was another of Art Wetter's sisters. The orchards and hatchery were on a small acreage near Gerber, a little hamlet off the bus line. To get there, I had to be let off the bus on the main highway in the dead of night to walk five miles over to the Weitze place. I was not only frightened in that darkest of moonless nights, I was also becoming quite homesick.

The Weitzes were great hosts, friendly and generous, just like Annie and Glen Edgar. I arrived in time to help pick an enormous crop of big juicy peaches. They were all over the place, bending the tree branches, on the ground, in sacks and boxes, on trucks, far more than could pickers pick, pack and eat. How different from Rock Falls! Their oldest son, Roger, a student at the prestigious University of California in Berkeley, was home for the summer. After a few days in the orchard, Roger took me on a tour to the west coast at Eureka. On the way, we walked to the top of the high and actively volcanic Mount Lassen, no minor feat in a day's time. Beyond Eureka, we drove south all of the way through the famous redwood forests, then to San Francisco and to the university across the bay.

The Greyhound people saw to it that I made a non-stop bus trip from Berkeley to the rendezvous with Elmer in San Bernardino, avoiding a costly overnight stop. Shortly after arriving, Glen Edgar appeared, bless his heart, and we headed east across the desert toward the midwest. A fascinating diversion to the Boulder (then called Hoover) Dam, being built across the Colorado River close by Las Vegas, was most enjoyable before a non-stop run for home. What a journey! Thanks to great family friends, the trip set me back less than $100.00. A great education and a good dose of needed self-confidence.

Here ends a brief account of life and times in -- and at times well beyond -- small-town Iowa during some of the bad Depression years, the first half of the Thirties. Not too bad, you say? No, they weren't too bad for many of us in the heartland's cornbelt, not as bad as for the "Okies" of Steinbeck's tale, "The Grapes of Wrath." And why not? Maybe because in the cornbelt more food was grown in backyards, and less of many things was needed to survive than in other times. And why was that? Maybe because in those days there was _more_ of some things -- more strength to endure hardship, _more_ self reliance, self help, more helping others, more sharing, more grit, guts, pluck, faith, hope, and charity, and not so much of other things, not so much waste, fraud, and greed.

CHAPTER VIII

ROCK FALLS IN THE THIRTIES...
HOPING

Midway through the decade of the Thirties, the farm-town community of Rock Falls had settled into a period of quiet desperation. The barter economy continued. People tried things, failed, and tried again. The garage and repair shop was bought and sold four times. Finally, it was closed. Delos Stickney closed his little variety store, sold the old stone house, and moved away. The blacksmith shop had folded even earlier. Business at the lumberyard worsened, with money lost every day it remained open. The once great Bliem Brothers General Store extended credit as long as possible but only so much produce from farms could be taken in trades for groceries before a profit turned to a loss. The DX gas station was lucky to sell 50 gallons of gas a day, and the three cents a gallon profit hardly was enough to cover Chehock's electric light bill.

On the farms, long established, hard working, skilled farmers lost almost everything and moved away. Prices of hogs bottomed at $2.30 per hundred pounds. Imagine, less than 2½ cents a pound for Iowa's largest farm productions. Corn at ten cents a bushel was not worth feeding to hogs. Those golden ears became farmhouse fuel. Eggs at seven to nine cents a dozen had little value in trade. The herd of milk cows didn't pay. One cow for family needs was enough.

A strategy soon developed among farmers to help those facing foreclosures to survive liquidation by the banks or insurance companies that held mortgages and other loans on land, livestock, and machinery. At foreclosure sales, all farmers agreed to bid a few cents, a nickel or dime, for machinery put on the auction block and a dollar or two for the land and livestock. When all items had been knocked down to the highest bidders, they sold it all back to the farmer for the same few dollars and cents. Everybody then went home, leaving the lenders to contemplate the write-off of the loan as a total loss. Under such circumstances, lenders were reluctant to advance any new credit.

MORE POLITICS -- LOCAL TO GLOBAL

Following the 1932 election, President Roosevelt took immediate steps to turn things around. Farm, job, railroad, food relief, and public works programs to pump money into a stagnant economy were launched. In the first four years under the New Deal, dozens of national programs and laws were tried quickly in an effort to prevent a complete social and economic collapse. New laws were enacted, new regulations promulgated, new programs implemented governing food and shelter relief, job insurance, unemployment compensation, social security pensions, drought relief, health care and medical services, stock market, transportation, labor, banking, farming activities. Depending upon one's political persuasions, reactions to FDR's first-term rule ranged from wildly exhilarating to grimly unsettling.

One highly visible program to farmers was drought relief. A natural calamity of growing proportions demanded more and more federal attention. All or parts of at least 15 western and midwestern States, nearly one third of the nation's land area, were in the grip of an unprecedented drought. During the worst summers, the sky over Iowa, a State not devastated as some were by the drought, was dark at noon with the dust clouds blown eastward from the baked High Plains of Kansas, Nebraska, and the Dakotas.

> "RELIEF BILL GIVES PRESIDENT FUNDS NETTING $6,000,000,000; HE ACTS AT ONCE ON DROUGHT. Will Speed Relief Bill. House to Pass Measure Under Suspension of the Rules. $1,172,000,000 Allocated. But More Than $5,000,000,000 Would Go to Roosevelt From RFC and PWA Programs." (June 3, 1934)

PWA stood for Public Works Administration. It was a centerpiece of the Roosevelt presidency's efforts to bring quick relief in the form of jobs nation-wide for repairing and improving the sadly deteriorated infrastructure -- for roads, bridges, dams, waterways, sewers, water supply systems, anything involving public service. The idea was to bring useful employment to hamlets and cities all over the nation. It was intended to provide visible results of progress and achievements to communities, and (not least) to gain lots of political mileage.

As could be imagined, a program of this magnitude inevitably provided some juicy political plums to pick. How it happened that Rock Falls qualified for a plum from the County Democratic Party members that were running the program was hard to understand...or was it? The decision was made to build a dam across the Shell Rock River! Did Rock Falls need a dam across the Shell Rock River? It certainly did back in the 1880s, when the old stone mill and the bridges were washed down the river by spring floods nearly every other year. Now, in 1935, the valley had been swept clean by repeated floods, and local folks knew better than to build in the floodplain. It would seem hard to justify a dam for flood control. A new grist mill would have been nice 50 years ago, but no more. Surrounding lands were not level enough to irrigate with water impounded above a dam. The river didn't provide enough flow and head for a hydroelectric power dam. Fishing was better in a moving stream, than it was in a still pond.

Never you mind, the decision-makers in the courthouse dispatched an engineering survey party to situate the best place for a dam. Wouldn't you know? They would settle on one of the most scenic reaches along the Shell Rock to mar its beauty. The site chosen was one hundred yards upstream from the old mill-dam site and the famous shell rock falls found by Elijah Wiltfong nearly a century earlier. The dam would despoil a wide sweep of the old mill pond, in every respect the worst imaginable site selection from an engineering, economic, environmental, and esthetic standpoint. Had there been and environmental movement in the 1930s, as in the 1970s and 1980s, the site surveyors would have been run out of the county.

Townspeople had no warning about this PWA project, as they had not been told a thing, and there were no locally unemployed laborers called to work on it. One fine morning in the summer of 1935, a big bulldozer appeared at the site, along the southwest bank of the river (see Map III), near its confluence with the little creek from the south. Some trucks followed, loaded with large boulders. These were dumped at the shoreline and the bulldozer pushed them into the river in a line about 30 feet wide. More trucks appeared with more boulders, crushed rocks, and gravel until these obstructions, perhaps seven feet higher than the water surface, jutted halfway across the river. And then, mysteriously, all work stopped, whether for lack of funds or other infrastructure priorities or political priorities is not known. Nothing more was done to either finish that dam or to undo the damage.

The Town of Rock Falls, poor as a church mouse, could have used a lot of public improvements about that time, a small centralized water supply system with water treatment plant, to replace the wells that pumped less than pure and safe water to houses, a centralized sewerage treating and disposal system to replace the hazardous two-holers in the town's backyards. The raw sewage was far more of a health hazard than the river was a flood hazard. The town could have used a nice little library to encourage adult education and reading for pleasure. The town could have used a street improvement and sidewalk construction program, or a fire truck and firehouse to replace the useless voluntary brigade equipment. The town needed a post office building, a town hall, better street lighting, better telephone service, public playgrounds and parks facilities and equipment, better county roads connecting to Mason City, a good emergency medical facility staffed with a part time nurse, a school lunch program, even a part time policeman, and a baseball field free of cow pies and horse turds. The town needed that one-half a dam like it needed smallpox. R. V. was livid with rage when work on the dam started. He was more than outraged when it was suspended.

Federal relief to the farmer was first a confusion of ineffective and irrational programs. Under the new Secretary of Agriculture, Henry Wallace, a brilliant son of the founder of Iowa's popular Wallaces Farmer magazine, effort was made to restore commodity prices to levels that would give the farmer a fair profit. Within Roosevelt's famous first 100 days, a method was advanced by Wallace to drastically curtail production, even while people were starving and without shelter in the cities. Sadly, the Agricultural Adjustment Act (AAA) of May 22, 1933, became law just too late to forestall spring farrowing of the 1933 pig crop and spring cotton planting, so Wallace issued the infamous order: the farmer was paid to kill his pigs and plow under his cotton plants to cut production and raise farm prices!

Imagine R. V.'s reaction to that. He never forgave Roosevelt and Wallace for the farm program and that unfinished dam in the middle of the river. He became convinced that the aristocratic Roosevelt from Hyde Park on the Hudson was insane and that Wallace was a communist (long before he was proven to be one), and that everyone else in the Democratic Administration was either a communist, or a crook, or a boozer.

Gradually, a complicated, two-pronged, voluntary farm program emerged and has lasted for five decades with mixed and unintended results. In simplest terms, the first prong was intended to curtail production of all food and fiber crops. The farmers who signed up at the U. S. Agriculture Stabilization and Conservation Service (ASCS) offices -- there was one in every county -- agreed to accept an acreage "allotment." Agreeing to plant fewer alloted acres, they would be paid outright and generously at so much per acre for land idled. Variants of this socalled conservation program, preserved by tinkering and scheming politicians, remain in effect today, nearly 60 years later.

The second prong was intended to assure "equality of agriculture" with labor and industry by a farm price support program. Equality was a vague word, so it was soon replaced by "parity." even vaguer. Parity meant equality of purchasing power for farmers with other segments of the economy. Parity would prevail for farmers whenever a fair ratio was established between prices of crops farmers sold and things which they bought, using a base period of known farmers' and urban wage-earners' prosperity as the standard for comparison. The base period chosen by the feds was 1910-1914, the socalled Golden Age of Agriculture.

Price supports worked as follows. Those ubiquitous party decision-makers decided that Art Wetter for example, a hard-working and highly efficient producer who farmed over 400 acres of excellent land just south of Rock Falls, could raise as much corn as he wanted to raise, or he also could choose to sign up to curtail his production by participating in the allotment program. If Art signed up, then no matter what the prevailing market price of corn was, an ASCS office would set a "support price" for Art's corn of so much per bushel, estimated at a level to assure Art the magic parity.

When Art harvested his corn in the autumn, and he did not want to sell it on the market right away at a low market price, say $1.00 per bushel, he could store it in big cribs on his farm. He would have the federal ASCS employee inspect the stored corn, give him an equivalent of a warehouse receipt for it, and pay him a storage fee. Then Art would take this receipt to the Farmers Savings Bank, and R. V. would be required by law to give him a loan on every bushel of Art's corn at the fixed support price, say $2.00 a bushel. Art now had his cash to pay expenses and realize a profit, R. V.'s bank had its loan on which interest (then about three percent) was paid, and the loan, usually for six to 12 months duration, was guaranteed by the feds, in this case the U. S. Commodity Credit Corporation.

Suppose the going price of corn rose to $2.50 a bushel. Art could unload his corn-cribs, sell his corn on the market, take the cash to the Farmers Savings Bank, pay off his $2.00 a bushel loan with interest, and pocket the difference as profit. Suppose the market price of corn stayed at $1.00 a bushel during the loan period. When the bank loan came due, Art could telephone the feds at the courthouse and say, "Come and get your corn and pay off my loan at the bank." The United States would thereupon take the corn off his hands, sell it on the market, and pay R. V.'s bank for the full loan amount plus interest, and Art would keep his $2.00 a bushel received when he originally borrowed on the stored corn in his "warehouse."

Neither the bank nor Art could lose on this kind of a deal. The government could lose and usually did. For the next 50 years, it paid every participating farmer over the country a guaranteed price for grain crops harvested. And where did the money come from? Income taxes levied on the urban folks mainly. If Uncle Sam did not want to or could not take the corn off Art's hands right away, Art continued to store it on his farm and receive 25 cents a bushel from the government as a storage fee.

These programs are available for other crops as well -- for wheat, barley, rye, oats, flax, soybeans, and milo. Midwestern farmers and western wheat ranchers soon became strictly grain producers and large warehousers. Sometimes four and five years of crops were stored (and rotting) on the farms and ranches, with storage costs paid by taxpayers. Farmers gave up raising cattle, hogs, sheep, chickens. Enormous 100,000-head cattle and hog feedlots developed in the High Plains. Not a living thing moved on midwest farms anymore, except for an occasional pheasant, and even it had a hard time surviving, as farmers cultivated fence row to fence row, in order to offset lost production on idled land, leaving no cover for game birds. The farmers also applied more pounds of fertilizer on the alloted crop lands to offset lost production on idled land, thereby defeating the purpose of the allotment program.

The only noise in the countryside came in the spring, when tractors appeared to plant the crops, and in the autumn when they reappeared to harvest the crops. Otherwise, it was dead silent. The rest of the year the farmers were at northern Minnesota fishing resorts or on Florida's golf courses or deep-sea fishing launches, spending the government's largesse. Fifty years after the Depression, in the mid-1980s, farming in the midwest was referred to as the "corn-soybeans-and-Florida syndrome." Clearly, farm programs of the Depression years, coupled with the vastly improved technologies and farming practices, encourage overproduction, with total disregard for market demand, making big mechanized farmers a new, well-heeled welfare class.

As one may have guessed, my father never once participated in a government farm production-control program for the four farms that he operated at various periods during the Thirties. In a way, I admired him for it. He was so anti-Roosevelt and was so convinced that the programs were fundamentally wrong for Americans, that he denied himself the financial benefits of them year after year. Whether a direct price-support subsidy or an allotment plan to idle land, R. V. said, "I won't have them government dummies on my place, telling me what to raise and how to use my land. I'll keep my freedom and my self-respect." And so he did, losing money all the while in the cash grain markets or by feeding his grains to those beloved Aberdeen Angus cattle. He simply refused to sign up, and he was a happier man for it. Hurray for R. V., the last of a kind!

"ROOSEVELT SWEEPS THE NATION; HIS ELECTORAL VOTE EXCEEDS 500; POLL SETS RECORD. Roosevelt Electoral Vote of 519 Seen as a Minimum. No Swing to Bolters. Landon Concedes Defeat." (November 4, 1936)

There was never a doubt about the outcome of the 1936 elections. Roosevelt was nominated by acclamation at the Convention. He was a popular, colorful leader. In the campaign, he appealed for more time to get the country toward stability and prosperity. The Republicans chose Alf M. Landon, Governor of Kansas, wealthy from oil and gas holdings, but otherwise as different from FDR as one could be. He was a good man, a decent man, with good ideas for sound programs, not an immovable Republican of the Harding-Coolidge-Hoover variety. But he had a flat voice and a flatter personality. He simply had no chance, and my father must have sensed it, as we did not have an oyster stew election night party at our house in 1936.

"DILLINGER SLAIN IN CHICAGO; SHOT DEAD BY FEDERAL MEN IN FRONT OF MOVIE THEATER. Reached for his Gun. Outlaw's Move Met by Four Shots. Had Lifted his Face. Desperado Had Also Treated Finger Tips With Acid to Defeat Prints. Two Women Wounded..." (July 23, 1934)

There was another public figure in the 1930s, one who caused nearly as much excitement, entertainment, and headlines as did Roosevelt. He was a cheap thug and murderer who came from out of nowhere during the Depression years, along with Pretty-Boy Floyd, Baby-Face Nelson, Clyde Barrow, Bonnie Parker, and lesser dregs of humanity, staging a series of audacious broad-daylight bank robberies in the midwest. If they hadn't been so trigger happy, they might have become true folk heros (as a movie tried to make Bonnie and Clyde later) because it was almost amusing to read of the gang's exploits in obtaining large amounts of money from a number of banks so easily without harming anyone.

But they were not modern-day Robin Hoods. John Dillinger had been jailed in Crown Point, Indiana, near Chicago, for bank robbery. In March 1934, he and an accomplice locked up 30 guards and inmates at the point of a wooden pistol carved out and smuggled to Dillinger by his "moll." They escaped with two machine guns and the sheriff's car. You've got to admire someone who can pull that off. Dillinger put together a gang of five henchmen and set off on a reign of terror, with frequent heists of the banks within small cities. One was the First National Bank of Mason City. They hit it at noon on the busiest corner and time in the city, right out there facing the Courthouse Square, walking away calmly with $60,000. They were not seen again until, one by one, they were trapped and slain. They were the springboard to fame for the young J. Edgar Hoover, who was Director of the Federal Bureau of Investigations for about 50 years longer than he should have been.

And finally in those exciting times around the world, there was another thug and murderer on the loose in another country, but he was more skilled than was Mr Dillinger. As a result, he lasted longer and he inflicted vastly more damage. It can not be said that the world had no advance warning, such as these <u>New York Times</u> headlines:

"HITLERITES BATTLE FOES IN BRUNSWICK STREETS. Thousands of Herr Hitler's followers thundered down the streets here to the accompaniment of martial music as a curtain-raiser event." (October 18, 1931)

"NAZI LEAD IN FOUR STATES; WIN 162 SEATS IN PRUSSIA; LIBERALS NOW IN MINORITY. Hitlerites Gain Heavily. Finish Second in Bavaria." (April 25, 1932)

"VICTORY FOR HITLER IS EXPECTED TODAY. Repression of Opponents Held to Make Election Triumph For Regime Inevitable. Fires Blaze on Borders. Nazis Light Them as Sign of 'Reawakening.'" (Mar 5, 1933)

"HITLER BLOC WINS A REICH MAJORITY; RULES IN PRUSSIA. Nazis Roll Up 17,300,000 Votes. Get 44% of Total Poll and Even Wrest Control of Bavaria From Catholics." (March 6, 1933)

"HINDENBURG DROPS FLAG OF REPUBLIC; NAZIS CARRY CITIES. President Orders Black-White-Red of Empire and Swastika Banner Flown Side by Side. Fascists Win in Prussia." (March 13, 1933)

"HITLER CABINET GETS POWER TO RULE AS A DICTATORSHIP; REICHSTAG QUITS SINE DIE. Hindenburg Less Active. Hitler to Issue Decrees, With More Authority Than Predecessors." (March 24, 1933)

"HITLER CRUSHES REVOLT BY NAZI RADICALS; VON SCHLEICHER IS SLAIN, ROEHM A SUICIDE; LOYAL FORCES HOLD BERLIN IN AN IRON GRIP. Police fill the Streets. Goering's Forces Keep Curious Throngs on Constant Move. Machine Guns Mounted. Storm Troop Chiefs Die. Reactionaries also Hit. July 1, 1934)

"VON HINDENBURG DIES AT 86 AFTER A DAY UNCONSCIOUS; HITLER TAKES PRESIDENCY. Hitler Consults Cabinet in Secret. New Election Possible." (August 2, 1934)

"HITLER FORECASTS NO REICH OVERTURN IN NEXT 1000 YEARS. Proclamation to Nazi Congress Says Movement Won't Yield no Matter What Happens." (Sept 6, 1934)

"SAAR GOES GERMAN BY 90%; LEAGUE DELIBERATES TODAY; ANTI-NAZIS ALREADY FLEEING." (January 15, 1935)

"GERMANY BEGINS A DRIVE TO END NON-NAZI PRESS. 'Dictator' May Dismiss Editors and Suppress Newspapers. Religious Organs to Go. Owners Must Prove 'Aryan' Descent." (April 26, 1935)

"HITLER SENDS GERMAN TROOPS INTO RHINELAND; OFFERS PARIS 25-YEAR NON-AGGRESSION PACT; FRANCE MANS HER FORTS, BRITAIN STUDIES MOVE. Versailles Curbs Broken. Army Marches as Hitler Speaks." (March 6, 1936)

"HITLER DEMANDS RIGHT OF SELF-DETERMINATION FOR GERMANS IN AUSTRIA AND CZECHOSLOVAKIA. EDEN RESIGNS IN CRISIS. HITLER ASSUMES CONTROL OF ARMY" (Feb 21, 1938)

And so the the storm clouds thickened again, as the greatest nation in the western hemisphere, crippled by the Depression of its own making and pre-occupied with its own problems of relief and recover, unwittingly helped to unleash a monster upon the world. What a price it would pay for political hesitation and indecision!

IOWA'S SKIES BRIGHTEN...BRIEFLY

Massive infusions of cash and credit into the American economy began to have an effect upon heartland farmers as early as 1935. Aided by recoveries in foreign nations, and Roosevelt's sharp devaluation of the dollar <u>vis-a-vie</u> gold, farm product exports improved...temporarily. Further, aided by the prolonged High Plains drought, the Iowa farmers saw crop surpluses vanish, shortages appear, and prices rebound...temporarily. In 1934, farm product prices were still 45 percent below the record levels of 1929, but by 1935, prices had improved to only 30 percent below 1929 levels, and by April 1937 to only 12 percent below. Business was picking up too. Unemployment nationwide was cut from eleven to five million between 1934 and 1937, and New York Stock Exchange stock values recovered to four times the 1932 lows. It looked like happy days were here again.

With brightened prospects for Falls Township farmers, prospects brightened for Rock Falls, its banker-merchant, and his family as well. R. V.'s salary at the bank, down to $100 per month in 1933, was restored to $125 in 1935. Wow! Lumberyard trade improved, as community farmers who had remained loyal to R. V. began spending on feeds, fertilizers, long-deferred fencing, and out-building repairs and new machinery purchases. (The disloyal, and R. V. knew who they were, "by George," could "trade in Mason City if that's the way they wanted to act." Also, the grain and cattle from his farm brought a slightly better price, and he was able to sell a little more fire and life insurance. Then there were always a few sales to clerk.

R. V. was forever on the lookout for a few extra dollars, and clerking a sale helped out. Every farm sale had to be clerked, as things on sale were collateral for loans in many cases. Normally, for a percentage fee, a bank was the official clerk and its employee sat by the auctioneer, clipboard, pencil, and paper in hand, listening and watching carefully to record the purchaser and purchase prices of all items sold. Since R. V. had sustained a salary cut the bank's Board members let him keep the modest fees for himself. After all, clerking meant much after hours work.

So, when Jack Dorsey, the area's number one auctioneer, knocked down an old manure spreader for $200, R. V. made about three dollars. There were many items, and most sales lasted all day. With at least a sale every month to clerk, he made about as much at that as the bank's salary. The additional work came in collecting the money from each buyer after the sale, taking it to the bank, adding things up, and paying off the sold-out farmer. R. V. would carry blank promissory notes from the bank to these sales, handy if a buyer was just a bit short but a good credit risk. If so, R. V. could advance him a loan on the spot. Everybody knew R. V., and he knew everybody, and they knew that he could write loans on the spot, so he was a favorite to be clerk, and it often meant a bit of business for the bank.

After Rock Falls High School, then Mason City Junior College, my sister Carolyn went on to Iowa State Teachers College in Cedar Falls. With summer school sessions, she soon had her degree and teacher's certificate. She started a teaching career at age 19 in 1933 in the one-room, country schoolhouse, Falls Township District No. 6. She had to walk the 2½ miles to work from Rock Falls every day, with lunch bucket in hand, to teach 16 students, little five-year-olds and big 13-year-olds, spread over eight grades.

For this she was paid $55.00 a month plus $5.00 each month for being school janitor. In bad winter's weather, she stayed nights at Martin Hinrichsen's nearby farmhouse. Students' families were poor, judging from Carolyn's only description of the lunches, grain sorghum mush between the slices of homemade bread, brought by children of Mexican aliens, seasonal laborers in Martin's sugar beet farmland. For a year and a semester, Carolyn paid her father $10.00 of her meager wages for board and room at home. Happily, she found a better position in 1935 at the Orange Township School near Waterloo, married Ken Hoffman, moved to Hudson and became an able school administrator in the fine school system serving Waterloo.

My brother Jerome, Rock Falls School graduating class of 1934, created quite a stir in the family. He put in a year at Mason City Junior College, enjoying new-found companions, lady friends he took out late dancing and a bunch of guys who sat around half the night in Mason City's bus depot coffee shop drinking cokes. Most of his new friends were Irish Catholics, which didn't please R. V. one bit. He also enjoyed being in drama productions, which required evening rehearsals. He developed rather liberal political ideas, possibly from his new friends. During two summers, Jerome worked full time at the Standard Oil gas station on the corner of Courthouse Square and part time at the YMCA. He even took a room there during the winter. He was well known and well liked. Everyone called him Jerry. We did not see much of him after he left home for Mason City.

Jerome's activities necessitated heavy demands on the family's car and modest but frequent demands for spending money. As a teenager, he developed some characteristics that made life difficult at home. He had a seemingly morbid desire to tease Carolyn and me mercilessly, something I could take but Carolyn couldn't, and he liked to precipitate arguments with my father on any subject at any time, except when he slept until noon after his nights out.

His arguments centered on politics and religion. As a skilled debater, Jerome was to the <u>left</u> of Roosevelt politically, while my father was to the <u>right</u> of Hoover. For the sake of debate, Jerome defended <u>Irish</u> Catholic positions and questioned Protestantism, making for some white hot arguments. He would needle, taunt, and trap my father relentlessly. On more occasions than I care to remember, a supper meal would end without dessert with my father declaring, "I'm going back to the bank to work," Aunt Myrtle crying, "I'm going to bed," and my mother laughing, "I'm going to my safety valve, the flower garden." I would go outside and throw rocks at telephone poles until dark, and Jerome would go off to Mason City in the family car.

Soon Jerome left home for good, as Carolyn had done. My father drove him to the Milwaukee Depot in Mason City, in early autumn of 1935, for the train ride to Chicago and on to the University of Michigan at Ann Arbor. My father came back to the house, sat down, and cried and cried. He said that he probably had failed to understand Jerome. He did suffer from a horrible case of acne which did not responded to any treatment, was a constant irritation to him, and scarred him for life. He became an artillery major in World War II, earned a post-war doctorate at Michigan, and became a distinguished professor at Knox College in Galesburg, Illinois. At age 44, Jerome died of a brain tumor.

Suddenly, it was a lonely time for me in Rock Falls, as even Aunt Myrtle, a permanent fixture in our household, took a teaching job in Rockford, 20 miles away, and came home only on weekends. R. V. would drive her to Rockford every Sunday night and back every Friday, year after year, when he certainly had many more things to do. He was very kind to Myrtle for decades, but she returned it by giving most of her meager teaching salary to help the family.

Despite improved farming conditions, it was tough for a 15-year-old to find work. Twice in the summer of 1935, I was surprised by the words from my father, "John, there is a carload of cement on the siding that wants unloading in 24 hours," and "John there's a carload of lumber on the sidetrack that wants unloading in 48 hours." Business was picking up at the lumberyard. Jerome helped some each time after his work at the Mason City gas station, and between us we cleared out the cars just in time to avoid demurrage charges. Those 94-pound sacks of cement became heavier and dustier as the day progressed, as did the larger planks of dimension lumber.

About that same time, I was really surprised by these words from my father: "Well, now, how would you like a job with a threshing crew?" I was not a farm boy. I had had no experience threshing grain. I wasn't as strong as farm boys and men. What kind of a job, I wondered, but I said, "Let's go. When and Where?" He had lined up a real job helping a farmer friend of his.

Midwest farming was historically, and remained during the Thirties, primarily corn-and-hog farming. The three major crops were corn, oats, and hay. Corn was marketed through hogs as pork on the hoof, except for small amounts sold as grain for cash. Oats were a cash grain crop, sold for meal or consumed on the farm by horses before tractors took over. Hay was also horse feed or for the few remaining dairy herds of the midwest. All wheat and most barley were grown in the High Plains States to the west. A few beef cattle herds were pastured in Iowa in summer and fed out to market size in winter. So it was before soybeans.

In this three-crop culture, harvesting meant threshing oats, picking corn, and making hay. Harvesting began with the first of two cuts of alfalfa or red clover hay in May and June. Corn picking did not begin until late September. In between was the exciting, even sociable, season for threshing. Over its 100-year history, threshing became as much of a social as an economic event. Typically, the season began in July, when farmers cut their ripened fields of oats with binders. The grain binder automatically binds bundles of cut grain with twine and kicks them to the side at intervals to lie in the stubble for a few days of drying out. Then come the shockers to stack the bundles into shocks of ten or 12 bundles carefully formed to allow further drying of grain heads. When grain heads and straw stems are dry, it is time to thresh.

One or two farmers would have invested in a threshing machine and a steam engine, two massive pieces of equipment called "the rig." Sometimes the rig was owned jointly by 15 or 20 farmers. In Falls Township there were perhaps four or five rigs serving the annual requirements of some 100 farms, 20 or 25 per rig. The rig would be spotted at a farmer's place, close by the barn and out-buildings, on the day before threshing at that place. The next morning, before daylight, the rig owner who knew the most about the steam engine, arrived to start up the coal-fired boiler for a head of steam by five or six a.m. With a long snouted oil can, he also oiled dozens of gears, sprockets, wheels, chains, and assorted apertures in the magnificent threshing machine wherein grain would be tossed about vigorously until separated from chaff and straw.

Meanwhile, as dawn broke, pairs of neighborhood farmers began silently appearing in the farmyard driving their teams of horses for pulling a hay rack or grain wagon. No more than a terse greeting was heard as the men proceeded to their assigned duties. Quickly, those pairs with hay racks, one a "pitcher" and one a "stacker," fanned out and across the field of shocked grain. Working on the stubbled ground, one man began stabbing the shocks of bundles with his pitch fork and tossing two or three bundles at a swing into the rack, where the stacker began carefully distributing a balanced load. When racks were loaded to a dizzying height, the teams of horses would be directed back to the barnyard, where the load stopped on either side of the threshing machine.

Now the noise started. When a long, thick, blackened belt joined to a big pulley hubbed to the steam engine was engaged to another big pulley hubbed to the threshing machine, it seemed like all hell broke loose. The engine belched black coal smoke, hissed steam, and grumbled, and every wheel, sprocket, and chain on the threshing machine began to clatter. Men pitched bundles of oats onto a conveyor belt which disappeared into the bowels of the thumping, shaking machine. Dust rose everywhere. Grain heads started pouring out of a pipe at one side of the machine. Chaff and straw were blown out the end of a long, flexible pipe that could be swung around to shape the straw stack.

The pandemonium continued non-stop until noon. Then, suddenly everything went dead silent, except for a gentle chugging from the steam engine. It was dinner time for 20 or more very hungry farmers. Wives had been cooking up a storm in the farm's kitchen all morning, jabbering all the while, and a massive spread was ready at the long table in the house or yard. Little was said for the next hour, but huge quantities of meat, potatoes, vegetables, bread and butter, milk, cakes, pies, and coffee were consumed.

Promptly at one o'clock, the men strode to their hay racks, wagons, and machines, and the noise began again, to continue until the work at that farm was done. If it was a big crop, threshing might go on without stop until darkness fell, at which time another massive meal was served. Then, as quietly as they had arrived, the men would depart for home and a short night's sleep. At dawn they would be at the next neighbor's place for another day of threshing. This went on seven days a week for a month or longer, only interrupted by rain, until the last farmer in the crew had had his crop threshed.

The morning when my father dropped me off in Art Wetter's farmyard at dawn was the beginning of an experience. I discovered that I was to be a pitcher on the handle end of a three-pronged pitch fork hoisting bundles onto an ascending rackload of stacked grain bundles. I was concerned but determined. I would say little, take the teasing, eat everything in sight, and never, ever show fatigue. After all, I was not just the kid from town, I was the banker's son, and I was not about to let R. V. down.

The great institution of threshing was all over within two or three years of my job as a bundle pitcher. The newly developed, tractor-drawn field combine did all tasks from cutting the ripened crop to sending streams of separated grain (to a wagon) and straw (to a windrow) from the combine as it moved across the field. No more horses, no straw stacks, no group dinners, no group suppers, no community of effort. Soon the tractor and combine became one monstrous $125,000 machine. The same thing happened to the cooperative corn-picking by hand, when the tractor-driven, $125,000 picker/sheller/chopper came. The same thing happened to haymaking from field to barn loft, when the field baler came. And who needed a crop of oats with no horses nor milk cows to feed, when dairying came to be considered a nuisance because cows had to be milked twice a day. Less and less hand labor, more and more machines. Not that progress in agriculture was all bad, mind you, but the community became vastly different when the corn-soybeans-and-Florida syndrome set in.

Changing times were slow to change the famous North Iowa Fair in those days. When threshing was done and the second cut of hay was in the mow, the late August fair was scheduled before corn-picking time arrived with the first frost that matured the crop and just before the new school year began. There was the more famous, annual Iowa State Fair (and one in every other State as well), but not every one could go that distance, and few could afford the cost of a night's lodgings in far off Des Moines.

In the beginning, fairs were intended as markets, for buyers and sellers to gather and trade wares. They would be organized to promote trade by offering opportunities to demonstrate skills and crafts, as well as for the exchange of ideas and the bartering of goods. Fairs date at least from Roman times, when frequent fairs were held throughout the Empire. Agricultural fairs in America also descended from a desire to improve agriculture by transplanting the European agricultural revolution to the new nation. They became an enormously popular and successful institution to promote educational improvements in farm and home life, as well as an entertainment spectacular.

During most of two decades, our family looked forward eagerly to its annual visits to the North Iowa Fair on the near south side of Mason City. It was a well attended regional event in good times and bad for some 15 surrounding Counties. The 1935 fair seemed an especially happy, large, and successful one, benefiting as it must have been by the strong recovery in the farm economy. Our family, including Aunt Myrtle, usually stayed together through the confusion of barns and open air exhibits, but that year was a first for me, receiving a few dollars and freedom to roam alone.

I was impressed by the big outdoor and tented exhibit of new farm machinery, the rubber-tired tractor, combines, corn-pickers, manure spreaders, discs, harrows, mowing machines, and more. I enjoyed the food hall with its prize winning plates and baskets of garden and orchard products, and its displays of flowers. I liked the demonstrations of 4-H (Head, Heart, Hands, and Health) activities, so widely known for its work as one of America's enduring organizations for the good of young farm folks throughout the decades. I particularly favored the livestock barns, displaying those great Percheron and Belgian horses, the Jersey, Guernsey, Holstein, and Ayrshire milk cows, the Hereford, Shorthorn, and Angus beef cattle breeds, the Duroc, Hampshire, Yorkshire, Berkshire, Poland China, and Chester White hogs, Suffock, Shropshire, and Columbia sheep, even some chickens, the Plymouth Rock, Rhode Island Red, Buff Orpington, and Leghorn. I was amazed to see those incredibly large, muscular dairy bulls, the fiercest of all the livestock breeds.

Having taken in the good stuff, I slipped off for the shadier aspects to which modern fairs had succumbed. I do not refer to the harness races, auto races, and evening's extravaganzas. They were great entertainment. I mean the cheap, tawdry, midway sideshows. In full swing from noon until midnight, these sleazy hangouts of the tattoes con-artists, pick-pockets, and pimps could -- and often did -- separate the rural Iowa hayseed from his hard-earned money quicker than you could blink.

It was amusing to watch such slippery characters work the crowd. One could place a wager on every kind of roulette wheel, target shoot, slight-of-hand game, or gambling device ever dreamed up. One could attempt to throw a hoop over a post on which a seven-carat diamond ring (of glass) hung, with a million to one chance of success. There was a girlie show as well, with a couple of faded, jaded roses out front to entice the crowds into the tent. One could witness the promotion of a boxing match between the show's resident muscleman and a planted local hick.

I blew 50 cents one time on the boxers. After hurling mild obscenities and insults at one another on a stage in front of the crowd, the two men went into the tent, and the show barker sold tickets to a pumped up crowd. If unsold seating remained, the two boxers reappeared, now in boxing trunks and gloves, to hurl more insults before returning inside the tent. More tickets were sold. Inside, after two rounds of feinting and ducking, the hick took a slightly glancing blow to the cheek, and collapsed for the count of ten. Soon, they were out front again, the hick claiming foul and asking for a rematch. More tickets sold, another fake fall, on it went. So much for the 1935 fair. For six days and nights, it drew over 30,000 folks a year.

Local citizens would agree that the year 1936 marked <u>rock bottom</u> for most heartland farmers. Besides persistently disappointing crop and livestock prices, remaining far below levels in the Twenties, and a false start toward recovery in 1935, weather struck a one-two punch, one that knocked out the best of farmers. Excerpts from a diary of Boon County farmer Elmer Powers in a 1936 issue of the <u>Des Moines Sunday Register</u> describe hardships wrought by worse weather than had ever been experienced.

It started in early January with 20-degree below temperatures, strong winds, and heavy snows. With such harsh weather, the phone lines out, and impassable roads, a flue epidemic struck, taking many lives, young and old. Back-to-back blizzards on February 4th and 8th left farm families in total isolation. The snow plows came through on some roads by the 15th, needing the help of farmers with shovels to penetrate the deepest drifts. Another blizzard called "...the worst of the season," swept across the land on February 26th.

A heat wave struck on May 16th. The diary says: "today was a bad day in the fields. The weather was hot, and the wind blowing almost a gale and clouds of dust...filled the sky." On June 16th, "...a storm gathered...but it passed" without rain, and the wind and heat were destroying small grain crops. By June 25th, "Grasshoppers...reported to be very thick" nearby. By July 4th "...a 20-acre field of oats...devoured by grasshoppers during one day's time." On July 14th "...the twelfth consecutive day above 100 degrees, reaching 108 this afternoon."

By late July, the damage was done, almost total destruction of the crops, and pastures burned dead. By August 4th "...many farms have passed into the hands of banks and insurance companies..." On November 10th, "We finished husking today" with the corn yields "...between 12 and 15 bushels per acre." (Seventy to 80 bushels to the acre were normal.) With grain in short supply, grain prices soared. On December 10th, "another letter...today from the county treasurer about my delinquent taxes." And finally, on the

20th of December "the happenings of 1936...made a deep and lasting impression...still close in their minds." It was one year to remember, all right. The Des Moines Register for July 16, 1936, reported 317 deaths from Iowa's 13-day heat wave and 3,848 deaths from the same heat wave over 10 States of the midwestern region.

Sadly, 1937 brought a sudden and severe economic contraction. Inexplicably, unemployment doubled, manufactured production slumped to 1934 levels, prices collapsed, particularly farm prices, with a return of abundant crops. The New York Stock Exchange lost $20 billion in values of securities. How could this happen? Culprits were sought: too rapid a rise in wages with growing power of the unions under Roosevelt; a mere temporary stimulus from soldiers' bonus paid the year before, just a quick shot in the arm; heavy losses on farms and ranches, due to the devastating drought; too much caution by the bankers, a contraction of credit. Whatever it was, previous efforts had failed to lay a sound basis for recovery, leading to massive frustration among the populace.

The nation and Falls Township settled back into a recession, a new term coined in 1937 to distinguish conditions from those of depression. For the farmer, it was more of the same over the past 17 years. In late spring, I was putting together a few words for my valedictory address at the class graduation ceremony in the local gym, an effort made difficult by my growing cynicism. How could one subscribe to the notion of a class motto that "SUCCESS CROWNS EFFORT," considering the miserable state of affairs every where? To parents seated in the folding chairs placed in neat rows by Pappy Lee on the basketball court, that motto seemed ludicrous for the times.

With farm-town communities, so intimately tied to the fortunes of agriculture, little had changed since the 1929 crash, except that many old established families had given up the corn-hog approach to farming in the midwest to join the great exodus to California. In 1937, with another hot summer, scant rainfall, high winds, and another decline in farm produce prices, the feeling of futility was near its peak. The severe drought in the Great Plains crept closer to Iowa's normally humid region. With little to leave behind, the Iowa farmers joined those from Oklahoma, Kansas, Nebraska, and the Dakotas in seeking to start anew in the irrigated valleys of the west. A popular song of the day was Al Jolson's "California Here I Come." A widely read novel was The Grapes of Wrath.

I was restless. Knowing that I would be off to college soon, I could hardly wait. Thanks to the Mason City Public Library, I began reading more and more books during that year, mostly biographies and foreign classics of literature. During the 20 years of agricultural depression, our family subscribed to the Des Moines Register and Tribune, a highly regarded daily that brought the rest of the world closer to Rock Falls. Columnist O. O. McIntryre, a contributor on New York City social and political matters, with his urbane, sophisticated style, attracted me to seek a career in journalism, as did Walter Lippman, who covered the Washington scene, its politics, and foreign and domestic policy. And there was that great political cartoonist J. N. "Ding" Darling, on the newspapers staff.

Radio provided such entertainment as that fellow with WHO-Des Moines who sat at a microphone every summer afternoon, receiving play-by-play telegraphic reports of baseball games of the Chicago Cubs from Wrigley Field, and the Chicago White Sox from Comiskey Park. He made it sound as though he was in the ball park calling plays with exciting voice and background sound effects. He was off to a quick start on a career of deception and make-believe. His name was Ronald Reagan.

TRANSITION

The day following the evening of 1937 graduation ceremonies was a day for the annual Rock Falls school picnic. In the morning, Pappy Lee set out long tables and folding chairs in the grove of oak trees behind the school building. Shortly before noon, families began to arrive laden with dishes -- potato salad, cooked beans, peas, carrots, onions, fried chicken, pork dishes, beef dishes, baloney, spaghetti, hot dogs, hamburgers, meat loaf, sausages, cake and jello, rolls and buns and butter, cookies, and pies, pies, pies. The School Board furnished ice cream and lemonade. No question about it, the Falls Township housewife could turn out a feed that would nourish a regiment, Great Depression or no Great Depression. For those able to rise after the meal, there were games and prizes -- tug of war, sack races, foot races, horseshoe pitching, and softball. It was a truly festive day, the end of another year, and a beginning of summer, those lazy, hazy days of summer.

There was never a question about where I would begin college in the autumn. Despite some summer odd-jobs, the pay wasn't going to allow me into Harvard or Yale. It was all R. V. could manage to keep Jerome in the University of Michigan, even with Jerome working for his board and room. I would go to Mason City Junior College and live at home. This meant having to use the family car, an old Oldsmobile of marginal quality, five days a week, but we still owned the Dodge pickup. It also meant packing a sandwich lunch in the car at noon with Bill Dedina. He also entered the junior college, riding back and forth with me and helping out on the gas, but he liked college even less than high school, so he didn't finish his first year. Too bad, because he was such a bright fellow.

During those rock bottom years, it was surprising how many local young peole went off to college. The two Bliem sisters attended the University of Iowa, the Edgar sisters Dorothy and Madalene, Ray and Josie's daughters, and Levetta and Geraldine, Will's daughters, went to Iowa State Teachers College. Marvin Calvert, Elmer Christiansen and others attended the two-year Hamilton Business School, located on the floor above Woolworths overlooking the Courthouse Square in Mason City. Many more attended other colleges that I was not aware of. It was not always for lack of funds that many more didn't go on to college; rather it was parents' needs to have their children on some payroll, or that they were needed to help with farm work. Somehow, I had managed to save $45.00 for the first term's tuition, and living at home saved on expenses.

It was my intent to take courses leading to a degree in journalism, but first year requirements limited choice. One took the foundation courses for a general educational background and these were English Composition, one foreign language (French or German), Speech, and two electives, a course in American government, history, or economics, and a course in Biology, Chemistry, or Mathematics.

Mason City Junior College was a first class operation with a first class faculty. It opened in the autumn of the year 1918, offering six two-year programs in Liberal Arts, Engineering, Pre-commerce, Pre-medical, Pre-dentistry, and Education. The college was located on the third floor of the splendid Mason City High School building on East State Street, next to the Public Library and YMCA and two blocks east of the city's center, a fine urban setting when compared to Rock Falls. One of about 20 such two-year institutions in Iowa, it was accredited with most universities and four-year colleges.

Each State had a large, public, State university and a State agricultural university. To advance to either of these, the junior college grades had to be acceptable, "C" or better within a range from "F" through "A." My teachers were Grace Ellis Burke Titus for English, Ida Iversen for Biology, the extremely attractive young Myrtle Oulman for Speech, Dan Herrick for Government, and Laura Kampmeier for French, all excellent teachers. Other faculty members were S. L. Rugland, L. L. Minor, O. A. George, Luela Carlton, Eleanor Hazlett, Harold Palmer, and Guy Crosen. The football coach was J. A. "Judge" Grimsley, also the coach for high school basketball, and Clayton "Chick" Sutherland with whom I would become well acquainted.

I was eager for the basketball season to begin. First came football, an eight-game schedule once a week through September and October, played on Friday nights at the high school stadium under lights. Despite no experience in the game, I tried out and made the team. Surprisingly, at the season's end, I received the traditional college letter to be sewn on a sweater, although I had played but a few minutes in a few games. I was a bench-warmer.

More than ready for basketball, I tried my hardest to make the starting line-up in the five-man team. I remember it well -- long hours practicing, then the first game, and I was not selected to start, nor in the second either. But in the third game I was put in to substitute at center in the second half. I started sinking shots from all over the court, carrying the team from defeat to victory. From then on, for 20 some games of that memorable season, I was the starting center. We had two great coaches, head coach Clayton "Chick" Sutherland, and assistant, Lonnie Hansen, two very fine gentlemen.

What a year! The two starting forwards were Everett "Sonny" Fletcher and Ken Banning; the two starting guards, Henry "Hun" Hert and Jim Woodhouse; with Lloyd Woodhouse alternating with me at center, and Lee Huff or George Gitz at the guard positions. (The fine Woodhouse brothers came from Plymouth.) The eight of us played as a single, coordinated unit, a rare achievement in basketball games. We played a game or two every week all around the State, and on February 17, 18, and 19, 1938 came the big 22-team Iowa State Junior College Basketball Tournament in Des Moines. It was a grueling three-day affair in the huge basketball court at the Drake University field house. We eliminated Muscatine on Thursday, Red Oak on Friday afternoon, Washington on Friday evening, Esterville on Saturday afternoon and beat Burlington in the final game on Saturday evening. We were State champions. Sonny Fletcher was named the All State forward on the All Star team, Henry Hert named the All State guard, and I was named the All State center. We also led in individual scoring, Fletcher first with a 55-point total, I was second with 52 points. A great team.

"HITLER ENTERS AUSTRIA IN TRIUMPHAL PARADE;
VIENNA PREPARES FOR UNION, VOIDS TREATY BAN;
FRANCE MANS BORDER; BRITAIN STUDIES MOVES;
65,000 TROOPS MOVE INTO AUSTRIA...Himmler
Rounds Up Nazis' Foes." (March 13, 1938)

I had come to Like Mason City in that school year of 1937-1938. It was a clean, lively, friendly prairie city of 27,000 residents, and I became acquainted with many of its people. I had seen little of the city on those annual visits to Dr. Hardy F. Pool, the tough old dentist at his office on East State Street, visits usually followed by a movies treat at the Cecil Theater, as Dr. Pool considered novocain unnecessary before drilling anyone's teeth.

I took to roaming Mason City's business district when a spare hour or two permitted. The typical stroll took me from the junior college westward past the public library next door, past the <u>Globe Gazette</u> building and Dr. Pool's office in the big <u>professional</u> building in the next block. With an introduction from R. V. I was escorted through the newspaper's plant one day by W. Earl Hall, who told me of the joys and headaches of journalism. At East State and Federal, I would turn north past the First National Bank, and close by on its north side, the most venerable Gildner Brothers haberdashery, facing west on Courthouse Square. Further northward, I passed Woolworthes (beneath Hamiltons Business College), and in the next block the city's leading department store, Damon-Igous. I then passed the well-known Green Mill Cafe, owned and operated by the Pappas brothers, then Thompson-O'Neil's meat market, and a block beyond, facing Third Street, the imposing Hanford Hotel.

Turning toward South Federal, I would pass Courthouse Square, and then several small retail shops, such as the Abel and Sons clothiers, a small bank, Yonkers department store, and Sam Raizes and Sons (Milt was a fellow student of mine). On the west side of South Federal was the Palace Theater, not so fine as the Cecil but with good movies shown, much better than at the really cheap movie house on to the south, amid some wholesale houses, and semi-industrial shops ending at the entrances to the North Iowa Fair Grounds.

Facing Courthouse Square on the south stood the small Park Hotel, designed by Frank Lloyd Wright. On to the west I would come to Bob Chamber's Standard Oil station, where Jerome had worked. Much further west and across the railroad, was the large Mercy Hospital. The city's other hospital, the Park Hospital (where I had left my tonsils back in 1932), was a small, three-story facility at the northwest corner of Courthouse Square.

Just across from the Park Hospital, facing south onto the square, stood one of the most magnificent of all of Iowa's -- perhaps all of America's -- early courthouses, one of the handsomest examples of early American architectural style. (See photograph herein.) This was the Cerro Gordo County Courthouse, built of native stone in 1901, in service for over half a century, and bulldozed and smashed to extinction in 1960.

It stretches the extremes of incredulity to believe that such a monstrous, outrageous assault could have been allowed on such a priceless landmark, such a perfect gem of structural grace and beauty. It is hard to fathom the stupidity, crass commercialism, or whatever it was, to see such a shocking wrong, such a senseless act of extravagant vandalism, inflicted upon Mason City's only real claim to a semblance of historical attractiveness. It is said that city and county employees disliked working in it and wanted to get rid of it. But what an alternative they and the city got! A tawdry brick and glass box, utterly devoid of character, hidden a block or two away -- as well it should be -- while the handsome old courthouse became just another parking lot. It really does defy belief.

To my complete surprise, I was asked in early June to consider a transfer to the University of Minnesota in the autumn. This proposition came from one Al de Buhr, a Mason City resident, student at the University of Minnesota, and socalled BMOC -- Big Man on Campus, up there in Minnesota. Among his many extra-curricular accomplishments he was the editor-in-chief of the reputable students' newspaper, the <u>Minnesota Daily</u> and, as expected, a student in journalism. He was in Mason City scouting for basketball talent to add to the Minnesota Big Ten roster. The Big Ten was a long-standing athletic association of the midwestern State universities formed to promote their academic interests among prospective students and to provide competitive sports and other events throughout the year. Successful participation in any Big Ten sport was becoming big-time stuff, a stepping stone to professional status and big money, and good teams were good publicity for universities as well.

Al de Buhr's proposition was a two-hour-a-day, five-day-a-week job in the cafeteria of the Student Union, the university's activities center. Thus, I could earn meals and an allowance for room rent. Those were the times before huge subsidies, sometimes proven illegal, to attract seven-foot-tall basketball players and similar giants for other sports. The Big Ten did not need to offer much in the way of generous enticements at that time. Things have since changed a bit.

What I was being offered sounded attractive, and not just because of my interests in journalism. The job seemed like a non-job job, and room and meal costs at an out-of-town school were the big items of expense. Tuition at Minnesota for out-of-state students was only $195 a year. Basically, that would be about all of the cash outlay, if I played basketball and worked the ten hours in each week. However, the 19,000-student enrollment made Minnesota an enormous education factory, decidedly intimidating to the young man from Rock Falls, Still, it might open doors to the world of journalism, and being a successful jock there put you close to a career in big time sports. I was awestruck by the size of the place, just from reading about it in Al de Buhr's student Year Books. But it was attractive, and Al was a smooth talker. R. V. had his doubts, but Edith said, "Go for it," and so did Chick Sutherland.

Then, to complicate matters there appeared from somewhere someone from Grinnell College. Grinnell was an 800-student, four-year, liberal arts college in central Iowa with an excellent scholastic reputation. In return for my basketball skills, I was offered not only a board and room non-job job there for the next year, but summer employment beginning as soon as the school term for the current year ended. Summer's work would involve campus grounds-keeping and would pay for next year's tuition. This was an expensive private school, so it was good pay. I needed to look into that, as I certainly needed the summer job, and there were no prospects in Rock Falls. Before I could do so, Al de Buhr took me up to Minneapolis for a look around and to meet the head basketball coach of the Gophers, Dave McMillan. I was impressed with everything except McMillan, a mean, tough, bully of a man. Back in Iowa, I went down to Grinnell and the summer gardening and lawn tending labors, free meals, and lodgings in the college dormitory.

Within the first week of settling into this new situation, two things served to alter matters. First, I did not like the scene at Grinnell. It seemed so small, quiet, and uninteresting in contrast to Minnesota's twin cities. It was located in a slumbering little town off the beaten path in the middle of Iowa's corn fields. I had had enough of that. And then of more importance, the setting was not made more attractive by the presence of large cockroaches that shared my dormitory room with me. I quickly and decisively concluded that Grinnell was not for me and that I couldn't endure the summer there. I called Al de Buhr and told him that. Admittedly, I could not have picked a better small college for scholastic reasons, but I had begun to think bigger. The second thing was, I met this girl.

ODETTE

It was an evening in early July at Grinnell College. A supper dance was in progress for several prospective new students for the autumn term starting in September. It was a social occasion as conclusion to a full day's program of orientation, interviews, and talks by faculty members and administrators of the College, acquainting prospects with Grinnell's curriculum, amenities, and costs. Young folks had come there from around the State and beyond. It was a standard practice in small colleges during the mutual selection process. There were no SAT scores to be sick about at the time, just face-to-face talk, exchanges of letters, brochures to examine, and a submittal of grade records. I surmised that the dance would offer a little entertainment during an otherwise tedious existence, so I put on a clean shirt and trousers and joined the crowd.

Some time during the evening I suddenly realized that I was seated at a table with an extraordinarily attractive young woman. We smiled and exchanged a few pleasantries. As others were dancing, I felt that I should ask her for a dance. She must have sensed this because to my astonishment, she said, "Let's dance." And I said, "I don't know how." She replied, "Let's give it a try." We got along surprisingly well after a few missteps, but soon we agreed that it would be nice to leave the warm dance parlor for a walk in the night air. That did it. It was a beautiful summer night -- moon, stars, everything. We walked and we talked late into the evening. This sudden encounter with a stranger of the opposite sex was a decidedly new experience for me, and I believe it was for Odette as well.

One point of common interest was that Odette lived in Mason City, and she had just finished a year at the junior college, as I had. We had not met before, largely because I was not a great communicator, painfully shy, and I had neither the time nor the money for extra-curricular activities. My day was always to arrive early from Rock Falls, go to morning classes, eat my brown-bag lunch in the car, go to the afternoon classes, then head for the football or basketball practices in the stadium or gymnasium, and then head for Rock Falls.

Odette was a classic beauty with the trim and shapely figure of a goddess, and she had a gorgeous head of hair. It wasn't red, but somewhat sandy-orange, which she called British tan, and that was O.K. with me. Besides, Odette was lively and bright, she had a quick, keen intellect, a great sense of humor, and an engaging smile and laugh. She had it all, almost more than I could handle under the circumstances, what with the July moon, the stars, the smell of flowers and her perfume. I stumbled around through the evening quite inarticulately.

We discussed the looming subjects of where to attend college and what to study. Odette was interested in music, sang in the college chorus, and was an accomplished pianist. The course offerings, teaching talents, and outside activities at Mason City Junior College seemed inadequate for her interests. She hoped to go away, and she had been considering several colleges. I mentioned my proposition from Minnesota and learned that Odette's sister Yvonne had been a recent graduate of the U. of M. We didn't return to dance that night, parting very late, and agreeing to meet again back in Mason City. I returned to my cockroach infested dormitory and started to pack. Odette told me that she had decided against Grinnell. That was all I needed to know.

Back in Rock Falls, I needed to play up the cockroach problem rather forcibly with my father and talk up the Al de Buhr proposition more and more. Fortunately, R. V. and his bride Edith, had honeymooned in Minneapolis nearly 25 years earlier, remembering it as a very lively, historic, and attractive city, which it certainly was. My mother had particularly agreed with me, that the twin cities of Minneapolis and St. Paul had more to offer to a college student than did Grinnell in the middle of Iowa's corn fields. I guess that she felt, without expressing it to my father, that the bigger the change from Rock Falls, the better for me as a challenging learning experience in and out of the classrooms. In the end, my father reckoned that, if I was going to be a great basketball star, the chances for fame and fortune were better at Minnesota than at Grinnell.

With my parental clearance nailed down, I quickly arranged with Al de Buhr for another journey to Minneapolis. While strolling around the huge athletic plant -- football and baseball stadiums, track field, basketball and indoor field house -- we had a chance encounter with head basketball coach McMillan. He was still the bully as before, but after a brief chat, he gave his blessings to my coming for a chance to play Golden Gophers basketball, with the parting warning to "...be prepared to work your ass off."

My self-appointed agent Al de Buhr, then drove me to the Student Union cafeteria to sign for the two-hour-a-day clean-up job. This done, I went to the administration offices, presented my year's credits from Mason City Junior College, had them accepted for transfer in full toward the degree from Minnesota, and made sure of the acceptance for admission. This done, I returned to Iowa with the single thought in mind of seeing Odette again.

For the rest of that summer of 1938 -- July, August, and early September, Odette and I had lots of fun together despite the 19-mile separation between Rock Falls and the Stoddard family's large lake shore "cottage" on Clear Lake where Odette spent her summers. I needed to ask my father for the Dodge pickup and a couple of dollars quite often. Still, you could buy seven gallons of gas for a dollar.

J. C. Stoddard, called "Jace," and his wife Camille, Odette's parents, were genuinely great persons. They were as kind and friendly and thoughtful to me at all times and places as I could possibly imagine anyone being. They had understood the difference involving their daughter and me, but it didn't seem to matter to them at all. My background was the quiet hamlet and Odette's the bustling city, mine the English-German and Odette's the French-Irish heritage, my Protestant and Odette's Catholic upbringings. I always received a warm welcome at their home and cottage, despite my chronic lack of spending money.

Sailing with Odette in her very own sailboat, dancing to two or three Big Band one-night stands at the Surf, and a movie now and then, and the summer passed quickly. When autumn came, we parted, Odette to attend Colorado College, a small liberal arts college in Colorado Springs, and I to enter the huge University of Minnesota. Odette's parents, bless their hearts, asked me if I would like to chauffeur Odette to Des Moines in one of their Buicks and put her on the train to Denver. What fine parents they were. It was so nice of them. I accepted and brought the Buick back to safely to the Stoddard home.

CHAPTER IX

ANOTHER STORM, ANOTHER WORLD, A FINAL SUMMER

Despite its charms for some, the summer of 1938 would bring a bittersweet event into the life and times of R. V. Wilkinson, CHIEF DEALER in lumber, coal, feed, seed, farm machinery, harness, and hardware. For over 28 years, since 1910, through the golden age of agriculture and the agricultural depression, R. V. had persisted in this business, from the top to the bottom of fortune. Finally, without a moment of hesitation, when a buyer came along, R. V. was ready. He sold out -- lock, stock, and barrel.

The time to sell it was long overdue. In fact, there was not much left to sell except the land and five buildings. The inventory of stock in trade had been drawn down severely as the recession of 1937-1938 worsened. While a very hesitant recovery, aided by large crop yields and a massive program of government outlays, brought moderately better times for small-town merchants through the remainder of the decade, farming continued an uncertain venture at best, and the competition from big-city merchants became fierce. Labor and production costs remained too high, farm product prices too low, and even in 1940, more than eight million unemployed men and women continued to stress the need for something besides the New Deal to release the country from the grip of the Great Depression.

R. V. was philosophical about selling his lumberyard. "It was fun while it lasted," he said one evening at supper. "Now, I've got some other fish to fry." None of us knew quite what my father had in mind or what was intended by that remark, but it seemed that something was brewing.

BRIGHT LIGHTS

The Mississippi River charts a crooked course through 25 miles of the twin cities, flowing over the Falls of St. Anthony and beneath the Hennepin Avenue bridge in downtown Minneapolis, then between high bluffs southeasterly toward the ancient frontier outpost of Fort Snelling, on its path to St. Paul's downtown State capital area and then on into America's heartland. Things had changed by 1939 from when Father Hennepin first set eyes on the place. High on the river's east bluff and a few hundred yards below the Falls stood the immense cluster of commanding structures of the University of Minnesota, third largest university in the nation in that year. Its centerpiece was the magnificent Mall, at the upper end of which was the beautiful Northrup Auditorium, facing the Mississippi, and at the lower end the sprawling new Student Union. On either side, in matching architectural character, were the graceful library and the Schools of Chemistry, Physics, Engineering, and Business Administration. Other buildings extended far and wide over the campus grounds, including the huge athletic field house, the 60,000-seat football stadium, and the baseball and track fields. A separate School of Agriculture in St. Paul was among the finest "Aggie" colleges in America.

My $7.00 ticket on the Rock Island enabled me in less than two hours to ride the fancy new streamlined Rocket on the Rock Island's main line all the way into the Milwaukee Depot in downtown Minneapolis. On the approach through St. Paul, past the tall grain elevators and flour mills, and into Minneapolis, I became quite frightened. It was that whole new world feeling. Detraining in the handsome Milwaukee station, I carried my light paperboard suitcase on the short stroll through the red-light district, where the world's oldest profession still thrived, past the Nicollet Hotel, on to the curb of Hennepin Avenue. At this point I boarded the "University Ave SE" trolley by courtesy of the Minneapolis Street Railway Company. Over the river bridge near the Falls, a turn to the right, and in five minutes I was at the entrance to the university.

Needless to say, the transition from the 250-student Mason City Junior College to the 19,000-student University of Minnesota was traumatic, as was the change from living at home in the 130-resident quiet of Rock Falls to the big city bustle of Minneapolis. And it was all so immediate! D-day was September 26, 1938, starting with that six a.m. cafeteria clean-up job, then the day's classes, and off to practice basketball. As though the early morning job and late afternoon jock-work weren't enough, I had signed for a heavy load of courses: Journalism, Advance Writing, English Literature, and psychology, 14 credit hours altogether, when 12 were considered the normal load. A leisurely meal was out of the question, and I had to scramble to buy my first set of textbooks. Oh well, I had asked for it.

I quickly learned that I had undertaken an almost impossible threefold task: one, to work at the Student Union job from six to eight in the morning; two, to attend class and course lectures for six hours, with lunch at the Union squeezed in; three, to practice for the Big Ten basketball competitions from three to six in the afternoon. Those 12 hours left me exhausted. The work seemed easy enough, but the time of day was awful. Etched in my mind is the sight of those flashing yellow traffic lights as I walked the 12 blocks from my room at the Roach's house over to the Union before daybreak, sometimes in very cold weather. I took my breakfast at the Union, then mopped floors and cleaned the tables, chairs, and toilets.

My problem was in trying to be both a student, taking worthwhile courses of study, and being a Jock as well. The Jocks took "pipe" courses in "Phys ed" leading to coaching careers. I had other things in mind. After supper at the Union and return to my room, I was too tired to study for the next day's course assignments. I still have nightmares about coming to classes unprepared. It was impossible, but I stuck with it for three long months, the first term.

My scholastic record forewarned of an early dismissal from the university -- a B, a C, a D, and one last minute cancellation with no credits, which a kind, sweet lady instructor permitted to avoid my taking an F. Still, I was permitted to sign on for the second term beginning in January 1939. I continued the arduous basketball practices, but fortunately I was soon able to quit my cafeteria work. Good fortune had smiled again, this time in the person of Bill King, a classmate I had come to know.

Bill was a pleasant Norwegian. He had a slight Nordic accent, nothing uncommon in the twin cities. He lived in Minneapolis and was working his way through the university by a part-time lumberyard job, full time for the summers. He was a member of a social fraternity, and he asked if I would like to consider joining it. I made it clear that I had to support myself through college, that a fraternity was out of the question.

Furthermore, when I left Rock Falls for those bright lights in those big cities, I knew next to nothing about college fraternities and sororities. What little I heard about them was from Jerome, and he had no kind words about them, based upon his University of Michigan observations. He was not alone in this regard. College fraternities had a dismal reputation for being the exclusive preserves for the well-to-do snobs and playboys, discriminating in their unspoken membership policies against blacks, Jews, and assorted bad people. They were also famous for their overzealous hazing rituals to test the characters of "pledges" before admitting them to full membership. And because they used Greek letter names and symbols for identification, it was suspected that they were sort of secret societies.

Despite such impressions, Bill King sparked my curiosity enough for me to accept his repeated invitations to a lunch at the Alpha Delta Phi chapter house, where I hoped to find out for myself something about fraternities. My observation did confirm what was partially true, and obvious, that most members came from well-to-do families, and that most chapters indeed denied memberships to blacks and Jews. On the other hand, the Alpha Delt members struck me as being geniunely decent, honest, friendly, studious, and unpretentious young gentlemen. I learned that joining was strictly a social matter, that there was nothing secretive or sinister, that it was likely not for everyone, rich or poor, and that members were expected to be congenial and gentlemanly and to evidence high standards of scholarship and conduct. If that was being a snob, then I was a snob.

Bill King was persistent with his invitations. I came to know and like many other Alpha Delts, particularly Bill Lycan, a university swim team member, Fred Anderson, basketball player, Harold Van Every, star football quarterback and the four Molander brothers, all from Bemidji, Minnesota. As out-of-towners, they were residents of the house on University Avenue near the stadium. Other house residents were from Duluth, Detroit Lakes, and Owatonna, and our house president Frank Watts, was from Des Moines. Many other fine young fellows were Ev Sherman, Charles Parsons, Enir Johnson, Joe Atkins, Ken Crawford, Lowell Daniels, E. Roger Muir, Charley Harris, Bob Dougan, Bill Mahoney, John and Don Scroggins, Arney Ueland, Kyle Fossum, Jim Otness, and many more. They were all townies, living at homes in the twin cities.

One autumn day as the quarter's end approached, Bill described a situation which he thought might appeal to me. All fraternities had dining rooms for members at which all meals were served to the out-of-town house residents, and only week-day lunches to the townies. The Alpha Delts had an arrangement for the exchange of help with another fraternity three doors down the "Row" of some 20 houses lining University Avenue. Each house furnished a waiter cum dish washer to the other, thus avoiding a working member having to serve meals to his fellow members. The pay was all your meals; the disadvantage, you ate them where you worked. I pledged immediately, and few of my lifetime decisions have proven wiser and happier ones.

>"ROOSEVELT OFFERS $9,000,000,000 BUDGET,
>WITH NEW RECORD TOTALS FOR DEFENSE; ALSO
>ASKS $875,000,000 FOR RELIEF NOW."
>(January 6, 1939)

When the autumn term ended in December 1939, I ended my cafeteria job and my stay with the Roach family. I was soon back in Rock Falls for two weeks of Christmas holiday time, with a free ride from Frank Watts on his way to Des Moines. Returning for the winter term, I would move into the Alpha Delta Phi chapter house as a resident pledge. I would take my meals at a kitchen table in the Sigma Alpha Epsilon house with five fellow waiters. What a relief no longer to walk to work in the dark of early morning, particularly with the onset of a Minnesota winter. And my only cost with the Alpha Delts was $8.00 a month membership fee and $25.00 a month room rent. This and the $65.00 for the tuition per term I borrowed from the Farmers Savings Bank. I was fortunate to be supporting my college year away from home by working and thanks to a small loan.

I was able to get a full-time, ten-day job as a sales clerk at the Gildners' clothing store on North Federal in Mason City. It was a typical old-fashioned haberdashery, 30 feet wide and 150 feet long from street front to alley, offering everything in mens wear from hats to shoes. The Wilkinsons had patronized it for generations, favoring it over the nearby and more up-market trendy Abel & Sons. My introduction to the job was, not surprisingly, my brother Jerome, thanks to his network of Mason City friends. My friend and a classmate from junior college days, Bob Major of the funeral parlor Majors, was also a temporary sales clerk. The pay was good, and I could spend some of it in the store at discount prices for Christmas presents.

The holidays passed all to quickly, and I was back at college. In the kitchen at the SAE house, the dishwasher-waiter job was a great experience. The six of us exchange workers made a smooth team, and this was essential, as we had to serve several meals and wash many dishes, pots, and pans, all by hand and quickly. We alternated so that each performed the same total hours per week but at a different time. Breakfasts and dinners were served to only some 20 house resident members, while lunch was served to some 85 townies as well. We all worked the lunch shift in finely tuned coordination and eating on the run in order to make it to our two o'clock classes. Only two of us were needed for the breakfast and dinner shifts, but these two served the other four in the kitchen. The house employed a husband and wife cooking team, the husband absolutely useless while his tiny wife did all the work. She was a dear woman and so kind to us, making sure that we had the finest of the foods, often some extras not served to the dining room SAE crowd. She was a sweet little scottish lady.

This new work enabled me to survive the rigors of the basketball season through winter quarter, so that I earned my Golden Gopher "numeral" sweater, evident of successful completion of that freshman year of Big Ten basketball. I was actually a sophomore, but the first year for all jocks in the Big Ten in all sports had to be as a freshman. The heavy woolen, gold colored Gopher sweater had "39" sewn on the chest and the gopher insignia sewn on a sleeve. I also survived scholastically, but just barely, and enrolled for the spring term, thanks to the substantial help with some course work from new-found fraternity brothers, and to the library room in the chapter house, available for quiet and undisturbed study. The house was only minutes away from my job and classes, so I saved much time as well. Indeed, I was a fortunate young student.

DECISIONS, DECISIONS

The regular autumn-winter basketball season ended in late March. To be ready for the coming season, coach Dave McMillan laid on a five-weeks spring term practice period for his slaves, allegedly to keep us in shape for the following year. With my grade level marginal at best, I decided I must choose at once between basketball and scholarship. Not wishing to be the perennial jock, I opted out, didn't show for spring practice, and never played basketball again. Would that all decisions were that easy!

In the spring of 1939, things seemed to be looking up for me after a daunting autumn and winter in the new world away from home. I had shed the jock attractions with all that that implied. No more sweaty gymnasiums, sweaty uniforms, athletes foot, the shower rooms crowded with other naked jocks, hard labor, exhaustion. I could see the light at the end of the tunnel of odd jobs in farms, cafeterias, and kitchens. So many people had been good to me over the years: parents, brother, sister, Aunt Myrtle, junior college faculty, the Stoddard family, the university faculty, members of the fraternity, the cook and my fellow waiters, and....not the least, Odette.

My undistinguished grade record showed a bare C average and for only 80 credits, short of the number constituting two full years of college. I was barely surviving. This prompted the decision about my major course of study, that henceforth it would not be journalism, in which I had lost interest and had no talent for, but rather economics and finance. Behind this decision were vague notions about someday possibly teaming up with my father in some new and different place, maybe in California, maybe in a new bank. a lumberyard, or a cattle-feeding operation when and if we could get this Depression behind us.

"PRESIDENT OPENS FAIR AS A SYMBOL OF PEACE; VAST SPECTACLE OF COLOR AND WORLD PROGRESS THRILLS ENTHUSIASTIC CROWDS ON FIRST DAY." (May 1, 1939)

"AXIS POWERS SIGN TEN-YEAR ALLIANCE TO RE-MAKE EUROPE. Pact is Sweeping." (May 23, 1939)

"ROOSEVELT ASKS CONGRESS TO CHANGE NEUTRALITY ACT; OPPONENTS AWAIT REACTION." (July 15, 1939)

"GERMANY AND RUSSIA SIGN 10-YEAR NON-AGGRESSION PACT; BIND EACH OTHER NOT TO AID OPPONENTS IN WAR ACTS; HITLER REBUFFS LONDON; BRITAIN AND FRANCE MOBILIZE." (August 24, 1939)

The summer of 1939 began for Odette and me as the repeat of 1938. Odette was back at the Clear Lake cottage, I was at home in Rock Falls. It was also a summer in which I had an opportunity to assist my father in a significant way for a change. As a result of his gregarious involvement in everything that he could find time for, and of his varied and frequent contacts with the banking, commercial, and agricultural communities in Cerro Gordo County, R. V. had many friends and acquaintances in many organizations. It transpired that the North Iowa Fair Board which directed the operations of the annual agricultural fair in Mason City through a Secretary-General Manager, found itself in early 1939 with that important position vacant. My father had heard about this vacancy when he sold the lumberyard, back in 1938. Now, he "had those other fish to fry."

He applied for the job, despite his two farms, clerking sales, selling insurance, and trying to keep the Farmers Savings Bank afloat in the still depressed days of the late Thirties. Still, with his background, he was the perfect choice to run the fair. He was a member of the Cerro Gordo County Board of Education, the Cerro Gordo County Rural Library Board, the Cerro Gordo County Farm Bureau, the Iowa Bankers Association, Belgian Draft Horse Corporation of America, American Aberdeen Angus Association, and President of the Rock Falls Garden Club. And what's more, R. V. was a committeeman for both the Boy Scouts and the 4-H clubs, he was organizer and secretary of the Uniform Livestock Improvement Association. In addition he had been President of the Mason City Commercial Club for six years. Whatever else! He was offered the fair job, he accepted, and he was ready to go.

My return from college for the summer gave me the opportunity to offer to relieve my father of routine banking chores, allowing him more time for the new fair job. He seemed tremendously interested and enthusiastic about the fair as a place for promotion of the fine work of the 4-H organization of young farm boys, to show high quality farm animals, and to show the latest in farm machinery and farm management practices. So a deal was struck. For spending money, but no salary, I would spend time at the bank as a "acting assistant cashier" whenever he was out of town for fair business, which turned out to be almost every day in the three months before the September fair event. He received a much better salary from the Fair Board than from the bank, which helped immensely, and he loved every minute of this year-around, part-time, almost full-time job.

The position was a demanding one. It included selling exhibition spaces to businesses and organizations all over northern Iowa, urging livestock breeders to show animals, allocating show barn spaces, lining up show business performance companies for the Grand Stand programs, arranging auto and harness races, booking a midway carnival company, advertising the fair, talking it up, giving speeches, preparing items for the press, attending countless meetings, keeping the books, and all with one clerical assistant. I thought that he tried doing too much of it himself, as he was not good at delegating work. Still, he and his Board of Directors certainly put on a successful fair in 1939.

I enjoyed going into the little bank on the corner of main street every day, becoming reacquainted with farmers around the township who had accounts there. I learned all about small scale operations of commercial banking, which were not unlike those of large city banks, except for the sheer size differences. At age 19, I was not empowered to make loans to farmers asking for credit. Rather, I would tell my father at the end of the day that, say, Tony Napaletano had come into the bank, saying "Tell Rufus I need some mon for da pock," that was Italian for "money for the pocket." My father would then get Tony on the telephone, agree with him on the amount and terms of a loan, so that Tony could come to the bank the next day, and I could have him sign a note and give him the cash. It worked out fine. Although we had Erna Kramer working full-time as secretary and bookkeeper, I learned to close and balance ledgers at the end of the day. Some experience.

All in all, it was a most pleasant summer, this last one of the Thirties, pleasant except for one very sad day in the fading days of August. By mutual agreement, Odette and I ended our love affair. Why? Well, several reasons seemed to demand it. We really were from two totally different economic, social, cultural, and religious environments. Whatever the combination of real or imagined differences or incompatibilities -- money, religion, personality conflicts, uncertain futures in a world at war, both of us agreed that there was little prospect for a compatible future together. In Cole Porter's lyrics, his lilting refrain of the time, "It was just one of those things" that wasn't meant to be.

THE DISTANT THUNDER

As summer turned into autumn, the threat of war worsened with frightening speed. Those momentous, shattering events of September 1939, unprecedented in the history of mankind, would alter forever the lives of tens of millions of people throughout the civilized...and uncivilized world in ways impossible to foretell.

"BRITISH MOBILIZING. Navy Raised to Its Full
Strength, Army and Air Reserves Called Up;
Parliament Is Convoked." (September 1, 1939)

"HOSTILITIES BEGUN. Warsaw Reports German Offensive Moving on Three Objectives. Roosevelt
Warns Navy." (September 1, 1939)

"HITLER GIVES WORD. In A Proclamation He Accuses Warsaw of Appeal to Arms. Hitler Tells
the Reichstag 'Bomb Will Be Met by Bomb'"
(September 1, 1939)

"BRITAIN AND FRANCE SEND ULTIMATUMS; WARSAW
CALLS ALLIES; ITALY NEUTRAL; GERMANS ATTACK
POLES ON 4 FRONTS." (September 2, 1939)

"BRITAIN AND FRANCE IN WAR AT 6 A.M.; HITLER
WON'T HALT ATTACK ON POLES; CHAMBERLAIN CALLS
EMPIRE TO FIGHT." (September 3, 1939)

Despite the catastrophic development in Europe, America's Great Depression persisted through the early autumn, largely because America clung to neutrality. In rural communities like Rock Falls, little happened to alter the remorseless perpetuation of hard times that had endured for so long, since the early 1920s. The vast sums of Federal money spread across the country in useful public works and relief programs, or in make-work schemes, had not trickled down to Rock Falls since that half-completed rock-fill dam to cross the Shell Rock River had been abandonned in midstream in 1933. Unemployment remained high, new work opportunities off the farm were scarce, land values continued to drop. Farm commodity prices recovered only slightly, remaining far below those in the early post-World War years. Corn sold at 50 cents a bushel, wheat at 64 cents, oats at 30 cents, soybeans at 95 cents -- hardly enough to cover production costs. Falls Township farmers stayed on the government welfare rolls by virtue of price supports, enough to avoid bankrupcy, not enough to prosper. The Town of Rock Falls languished and withered.

"HOUSE DOOMS ARMS EMBARGO, 243-181; $1,000,000,000
IN WAR ORDERS EXPECTED; BERLIN SEES U.S. TAKING
SIDE OF ALLIES." (November 3, 1939)

An event that marked the beginning of the end of the Great Depression occurred in November 1939. In that month the United States Congress amended the Neutrality Act to permit sale of arms to foreign belligerent Nations if on a cash-and-carry basis. Until then, the isolationist element in America, a hangover of World War I, had been strong in the United States Senate, where conservative Republicans had always succeeded, with a coalition of southern Democrats, in carrying every vote on the no-more-foreign-wars issue. But Hitler's Nazi rampage and the imminent fall of France, Holland, Belguim, Poland, and Norway, as well as a mounting danger to Great Britain, finally brought the Senators to their senses.

Immediately following this amendment, orders from the Europeans poured in to America. Greatest demands were for planes, tanks, ammunition, ships, and machine tools. Such ordering could not possibly be filled quickly, so entirely new factories were rushed into construction to raise production capacity. With heavy losses in western Europe, as well as over the high seas due to submarine sinkings, the list of needed materials grew rapidly to encompass foods, clothing, shoes, rubber, steel, wire, timber, crude fuels, and hundreds of other supplies. With Britain's ability to pay cash and to carry its supplies from overseas virtually exhausted, Roosevelt pushed through the Congress with the narrowest margin of votes the famous Lend-Lease bill. FDR had said, "We must be the great arsenal of democracy." The Act was a virtual free order-blank for acquiring any thing needed by England (and later by Russia) to combat Hitler, and for "....any nation whose defense....was vital to the defense of the United States." This meant a vast expansion of the U. S. merchant marines to carry whatever the United States could lend, lease, transfer, or trade. It was the most liberal foreign aid measure in history.

As a result, the jobs situation changed dramatically, and almost overnight. From a still massive number of idle workers, estimated at eight million in 1939, workers were soon in short supply. Women entered the work force by the hundreds of thousands, made popular by publicity given to lady riveters in airplane factories and to lady welders in ship building yards. And the pay was getting better every day. As defense contractors began to compete for workers, the old 40-hour work week soon became a 50-hour work week, with time and one-half for overtime.

Shortly thereafter, with the President's declaration of "an unlimited national emergency," a rapid expansion of the armed forces was undertaken. This further reduced unemployment rolls, as the U. S. army, navy, air force, and marine corps began competing for enlistment volunteers. In a few weeks, the Selective Training and Service Act was passed, requiring the registration of all males 20 to 25 years of age. While memories of World War I horrors were still fresh in the minds of some, the fearsome "draft" in America was now a reality. It was put into force with astonishing rapidity by help from every county courthouse in the country. Soon an army of 1,848,000 men had been "selected." They began taking up residence in the rudimentary facilities of dozens of training camps across the country. Again, more goods and services were needed to operate the camps, more food and clothing, more guns, tents, vehicles, equipment, and fuel. Yes sir, the Great Depression was on its way out.

These several events that so changed the economy and America from a nation in isolation to the arsenal of Democracy did not, of course, occur overnight, and rural America remained mired in poverty. Ironically, the thousands of American heartland towns were not brought off rock bottom with this tidal wave of federal money for the national defense. True, during 1940 the farmer and his family gradually became better off as commodity price support levels were raised, but his production costs rose too. Eventually pressures forced a belated national price and wage control law to dampen inflation. A great many of the small farm-town communities actually declined in population, workers and farmers departing for high-paying jobs in aircraft and ship building yards of the west coast, or closer to homes, building such training camps as the mammoth Camp Dodge in Iowa and Camp Riley across the river in Wisconsin.

Back in those fateful four days in September 1939 for Europe, R. V. had his hands full managing the North Iowa Fair in its first five-day run under his direction. I took a day or two off from bank work to see those prize winning livestock, the farm machinery display, the fruit and vegetable produce displays, and to make a quick sortie through the midway carnival ground. Same old stuff. Much more to my liking than the swarming crowds at the hot, dusty fairgrounds were the peaceful, quiet, sleepy, dog-days of late summer and early autumn in Rock Falls. It was sure to be restful, tranquil days in the little village and particularly after a year in the university. The weather remained warm, but the stormy season had passed. Farmers were busy in the fields, so the town was still, but for an occasional truck or tractor driving through town, a dog or cat in the street, someone digging potatoes or picking sweet corn in his back yard garden, kids throwing rocks at the light poles. I tended to the same banking business, such as it was, while contemplating the years ahead with growing apprehension.

I was ready, willing, and impatient to return to the university, eager for serious study and to get on with my career, now that the jock and playboy phases were over. I was now interested in money and banking as a profession, a pursuit for which I would be taking new courses. It would be good to see companions in the fraternity, where I would be living for another year and where I had my same job as waiter and dishwasher at the SAE house.

Within a week after the fair closed, I was on my way. Another $7.00 ticket on the Rock Island out of Mason City, and in less than two hours, I was in downtown Minneapolis. A short walk through the red-light district, past the fine Nicollet Hotel, and to the curb at Hennepin Avenue, there to hail the trolley. Over the river bridge by the Falls of St. Anthony, a turn to the right, and I soon hopped off at the campus entrance for the three blocks walk down University Avenue to number 1725. I was back.

"SOVIET TROOPS MARCHED INTO POLAND AT 11 P.M.; NAZIS DEMAND WARSAW GIVE UP OR BE SHELLED; FIERCE BATTLE IS RAGING ON WESTERN FRONT." (September 17, 1939)

"HITLER TELLS ALLIES IT IS HIS PEACE OR A FINISH FIGHT; BRITAIN AND FRANCE FOR WAR TILL HITLERISM IS ENDED; RUSSIAN NAVY REPORTED BLOCKADING ESTONIAN COAST." (September 20, 1939)

The autumn and winter terms passed quickly. With new study program and no basketball, my grade average climbed remarkably. It was a curious six months in that there was little talk among my companions about the worsening world situation. I suppose college students felt somewhat sheltered from world affairs, the European war still considered far away. In 1940, the draft had yet to be enacted. A handful of older seniors were 21 years old, hence few were concerned about an imminent call-up. With the politicians assurances of "no foreign entanglements" and that our boys "...would not again fight on foreign soil," not many of my friends seemed concerned about military service.

My social calendar was blank. I was content with the uncomplicated life of a serious student. I had no spending money, and with no social obligations, it was a relief not needing money. Total expense for a three-months term was only $175.00. No movies, no dining out, no dancing, just the great athletic events of the seasons and an occasional symphony concert at Northrop Auditorium, a fitting conclusion to the last months of the Great Depression.

I did have the great pleasure of an unexpected visit from my brother Jerome in late 1939. Still a student at the University of Michigan, he came to Minneapolis for the annual football contest between the rivals for the Little Brown Jug trophy. Jerome was a very enthusiastic Michigan sports fan. He and I had three fine days together, which meant a great deal to me. I was able to provide him a room and meals at our fraternity house, over his objections, of course, as he still imagined the college fraternities and sororities as elitism at its worst. However, we talked of many things, mostly about the international crisis. I believe that he left town feeling somewhat better about "all those damned Greek societies."

R. V. AT HIS BEST

In the spring of 1940, my father wrote to me expressing considerable pride that the North Iowa Fair Board had re-elected him and with a raise in his salary for a second year as the fair's Secretary and General Manager. He was pleased, as he had enjoyed this new job immensely and had worked so hard at it. It was a welcome change of pace after so many years in the quiet little bank. It was a great outlet for his personality, energy, and spirit to meet the hundreds of new people outside the confines of Rock Falls. It had been a great challenge for him, and he had made the fair a resounding success.

His re-election posed a problem, however, in terms of his trying to do two jobs well, at the bank and the fair. I knew that he could not do justice to both and manage his farm as well. Our arrangement of the previous summer had worked well, my filling in at the bank while he was off on fair business. He would not admit that he needed more time soon to manage the fair business, but I made a quick decision. I suspended my formal education after two quarterly terms and returned to Rock Falls in mid-April to resume my banking duties for the next five months, more or less, until the fair ended after the first week in September.

It was a good decision financially, as the family was short of cash, as usual, and I didn't want to ask for more support from home or to borrow more, but from a scholastic point of view, it may have been unwise. Had I remained in college through the spring term, I would have earned three years toward graduation, and I could have finished in the spring of 1941. Still, I wasn't in any hurry, as it seemed certain that the U. S. Army would be a first stop after I had graduated in any case. The over-riding reason for deciding was to enable R. V. to give full attention to another large agricultural fair in Iowa.

Except for one incident in mid-summer, my five months with the bank proved uneventful, especially in contrast to university life and the big city. I had the leisure to do some serious reading of technical books on money, banking, and economic history, and I was able to keep abreast of a worsening world crisis. It was quite clear that American entry into the war was no longer a question of "if" but of "when" that moment would arrive.

"GERMANS OCCUPY DENMARK, ATTACK OSLO; NORWAY THEN JOINS WAR AGAINST HITLER; CAPITAL IS REPORTED BOMBED FROM AIR." (April 9, 1940)

"NAZIS INVADE HOLLAND, BELGIUM, LUXEMBOURG BY LAND AND AIR; DIKES OPENED; ALLIES RUSH AID." (May 10, 1940)

"NAZIS PIERCE FRENCH LINES ON 62-MILE FRONT; TAKE BRUSSELS, LOUVAIN, MALINES AND NAMUR; WASHINGTON SPEEDS ITS BIG DEFENSE PROGRAM." (May 18, 1940)

"NAZIS AT CHANNEL, TRAP ALLIES IN BELGIUM; CROSS AISNE RIVER 60 MILES FROM PARIS; FRANCE CAN'T DIE, REYNAUD TELLS PEOPLE." (May 22, 1940)

"ALLIES ABANDONING FLANDERS, FLOOD YSER AREA;
A RESCUE FLEET AT DUNKERQUE; FOE POUNDS PORT;
ONE FORCE CUT OFF FROM THE SEA AS LILLE FALLS."
(May 30, 1940)

"ITALY AT WAR, READY TO ATTACK; STAB IN BACK, SAYS
ROOSEVELT; GOVERNMENT HAS LEFT PARIS." (June 11, 1940)

"GERMANS OCCUPY PARIS, RUSH ON SOUTH; CAPTURE HAVRE,
ASSAULT MAGINOT LINE; FRENCH ARMY INTACT; SPAIN
SEIZES TANGIER." (June 15, 1940)

"FRENCH SIGN REICH TRUCE, ROME PACT NEXT; BRITISH
BOMB KRUPP WORKS AND BREMEN; HOUSE QUICKLY PASSES
2-OCEAN NAVY BILL." (June 23, 1940)

The Great Depression was no longer in the forefront of our thoughts. The major concern that frightful summer became the survival of Great Britain and the fast approaching involvement of America.

The one incident which provided some local excitement in an otherwise restful summer occurred one morning with a suddenness that I wasn't prepared for. It was one of those hazy, hot, humid, mornings in town when nothing seemed to move. I was behind the counter in the bank, opposite the front door, fiddling with ledgers or something, when the front door opened and a fellow hurried in. He was at the cashier's counter in an instant, poking a small blue-steel pistol over the counter toward my stomach. His dirty cap was pulled well down over his eyebrows, he wore large dark glasses, and his overcoat collar was pulled over his mouth and nose almost to his eyes. I could make out nothing of his face. He said rather quietly, "Give me all the money in your cash drawer."

The robber's hand with the pistol in it shook so that I wasted no time in emptying the cash drawer of all of the greenbacks and tossing them over the counter to him. In no more than a minute, he was on his way with about $1,200 of the bank's till money. I rushed to a side window in time to see a car lurching away in a cloud of dust, a cardboard paper wired over the license plates to preclude identification. I was frustrated and angry, wishing I had grabbed him while he was so close to me, but that might have been a rather foolish thing to do.

Our bookkeeper, Erna Kramer, was on the phone immediately to the County Sheriff's office in Mason City, while I ran next door to the tavern, where I found Lloyd Hansen. We rushed out, jumped into his car, and "gave chase," as they say. I reckoned that the robber was taking the road north out of town, and sure enough, he was. We pulled to within a short distance behind him in a matter of minutes, as he turned eastward on a side road. He apparently did not realize that he was being overtaken, and Lloyd and I decided to hang back just far enough to keep him in sight, but not to arouse his fears of being trailed. I expected (quite erroneously, as it turned out) that the sheriff and his men would be with us in no time and could join in the chase, enabling us to corner and capture our prey. Thus, trailing the robber eastward, we momentarily lost sight of him over a slight rise in the country road. On coming over the rise ourselves, we saw that he had stopped his car for some reason, possibly to change clothes or count his loot.

As Lloyd and I were not armed, we were afraid to confront him directly, so we stayed back and stopped as well. This aroused the robber's suspicions, and he sped away immediately. He traveled over the narrow byways north and east of Rock Falls at terrific speeds, with Lloyd and I in hot pursuit. What a movie scene it would have made! We were going too fast, as we soon learned. Coming to a rise followed by an abrupt decline in the roadbed, we actually took flight for a few feet, bounced back to the road surface, lost control over the car, drove it into the shallow ditch upright, and nearly overturned. In doing this, the car's exhaust pipe beneath the frame was pinched partially shut. We came out of the ditch upright, but a constricted pipe reduced the speed of our car considerably. We watched helplessly as our robber disappeared over the horizon.

Getting back into town and to the bank, we found that the sheriff had still not shown up, so the chase was over. When he finally came, about an hour later, and when R. V. finally got word of it and showed up, there was an endless round of questioning. Some of the questions by the sheriff to me intimated that perhaps I had been an insider in the whole deal, so I forcefully disabused him of that notion. We counted the remaining cash in the vault to find out the extent of the loss (covered by insurance, of course), and that was the end of the episode. Without a description of the man's face or identification of the car, we had nothing to trace. He was never apprehended. It was a quickly done, clean heist. (I should have asked the sheriff if he was an insider, as it took him so long to show up.)

In the vault were the bank's protective means against such incidents. These were two huge rifles, Spanish-American War versions of a very high-powered rifle that could have brought down our robber at 500 yards. And there was a box of ammunition, great four-inch long shells with bullets the size that could have ripped our robber apart. The trouble was that the rifle barrels and their inner firing chambers had long ago been packed with a heavy grease as a preservative against rust. The grease had hardened to a nearly solid mass. It is well that we did not give chase with one of those and try to fire it, for it surely would have back-fired and blown our heads off. So much for the Great Rock Falls Bank Robbery of 1940.

My father was actually amused by the event. The next day, after the questioning, he dressed in the manner that I had described of the robber. He watched me from outside the bank, waiting until I was behind the cashier's counter as the day before and then rushed in with a toy gun in his hand. It startled the hell out of me, until he pulled off the dark glasses and cap and burst out laughing.

Another incident is noteworthy, one that rivaled the bank for high drama. For me, it provided far more amusement than excitement. In late summer, my father received a letter, then a few days later a personal visit from agents of the federal government's Internal Revenue Service. It was to advise my father of a forthcoming audit of his tax returns for the past several years. They felt that he had been underpaying his income tax obligations, and they intended to find out. Maybe someone had ratted on my father just out of spite, hoping to get a percentage of any added payment due, a provision of the law still in effect today. Goodness knows, my father had made enough enemies in that community in his lifetime as banker, lumber dealer, mayor, farmer, school board member, staunch Republican, so often jawboning with somebody about something.

The day was soon arranged to put aside his duties as General Manager of the fair to meet with three auditors of the revenue service at the Farmers Savings Bank. After a friendly discussion in the Board of Director's room in the back area of the bank, he told me (I was working the cage out front) that the men were to have the use of the boardroom for as long as needed. It had a large oak table and chairs. He had brought from the bank vault and placed on the table box after box after cardboard box of old records of his own business affairs, conveniently stored where he so often came in the evening to work on things. Then R. V. returned to his work for the North Iowa Fair.

They must have rubbed their hands with glee, probably figuring that here was some operator who, for ten years or more, had been operating a lumberyard and a farm implement business, plus having purchased, operated, then sold three farms, plus having built, managed, and sold a gas station, plus having been employed by the Farmers Savings Bank for two decades, plus having tried to derive some extra income on the side by clerking sales and selling life, property, auto, and casualty insurance, plus working for the North Iowa Fair Board, and in all of those years he had paid so very little federal income taxes. They must have thought that they were going to strike gold on this audit and punish this outspoken Republican. They were eager to have at those boxes of records.

The bean counters probably were from a district revenue office in Des Moines, thus having to stay in a Mason City hotel (the local Morse Hotel, Todd House, and South

Side Hotel had been closed some 40 years ago). They drove over to Rock Falls every morning to pour over that mass of records that R. V. had saved in connection with his taxes and myriad deals. They dug and dug for three weeks. I was amused to watch this drama unfold. They said hardly a word all day. If so, it was in hushed tones among themselves. Their only words to me were good morning and good evening. There wasn't a place in town where they could buy lunches, so they brought brown bags of food from Mason City and ate in the board room, never outside in the fresh air. Perhaps they felt that it was unfair to R. V. to expose themselves and have the whole town talking about R. V. evading taxes. More likely, it was a matter of dignity. People knew that there were these three guys working over papers in the back room all right (little escaped notice in town) but for all they knew, it was the customary annual banking examination by the State.

Despite what would have been an ordeal for most people whose records were under intense scrutiny by the feds, and despite his demanding work schedule for the fair, R.V. was polite, patient, and the perfect gentleman with the auditors. On two or three occasions during the course of the audit, they met together for discussions. These meetings must have helped the auditors because I could visualize the complexities of some of his deals, as he had described them to me, and I could well imagine the need for explanations and elaborations to the auditors.

R. V. always had several irons in the fire at a time, as my mother would very often characterize his complicated dealings. His explanations, presented with the straightest of faces, must have boggled the minds of those revenue agents, who were probably accustomed to straightforward, systematic transactions and records. They didn't know the CHIEF DEALER. I have often wished that my father had left Rock Falls at a tender age and had settled into a growing, rather than a dying, community and had become established in real estate and commercial development activities. He might well have made a fortune between 1900 and 1940.

Well, one day those fellows finished the job in the boardroom of the bank, handed back to me all of the boxes that my father had turned over to them, walked out quietly, and didn't come back the next day. A few days later, there was this letter from the revenue agents, and I asked my father how he made out. He showed that wonderful smile of his and said, "Well, John, they discovered that I have been overpaying on my income taxes, and that I've got some money coming back to me...by George."

I shook his hand. Because I had come to know my Dad well in a business sense as well as personally, I was not the least bit surprised at the outcome of that tax audit. I almost could have predicted it from the beginning. For one thing, he was as honest as the day is long, clean as a hound's tooth, straight as an arrow. Second, he kept that mass of documented information and detailed records, but he also stored a lot in his head, and he was not the most systematic and fastidious keeper of orderly books and records. In filing tax returns, without a doubt, if there was some question about a claim or a declaration or a deduction, he would not have taken the time or trouble to study the laws and regulations, because he was too busy on other things. He would have chosen to err in favor of the government, rather than himself, and overpay the tax by a few dollars. Third, I must repeat, R. V. was indeed one of the last of the big-time spenders, so much that I can well imagine many of the costs of his operations came close to, equaled, or exceeded gains from the operations, and left him very little if any profits to be taxed. This was particularly true of the expensive herds of purebred Aberdeen Angus cattle, which really were some one hundred and fifty of R. V.'s individual pets, not the tax shelters that the herds were for those well-to-do breeders. Finally, while the lumberyard was a great money-maker in the Twenties, it was a great money-loser in the Thirties, and the same was true of the farms and everything else. R. V. did so many things for the sheer fun of it.

Indeed, my father was in technical bankrupcy for the last 35 years of his life, starting with the Great Depression in 1930. He had borrowed money wherever he could -- from the Farmers Savings Bank, the First National Bank of Mason City, the suppliers of the products that he sold at the lumberyard, and from Aunt Myrtle. He had borrowed to buy cars and trucks. He had mortgaged his farms, his home in Rock Falls, and his herd of cattle. He had enjoyed the generous "line of credit" at Bliem Brothers General Store for many, many years. When it was all over and settled up, he left a net estate of just one hundred sixty-two dollars and eleven cents. But, my how he enjoyed life!

INDIAN SUMMER

The Great Depression left Rock Falls and the American heartland in that autumn of 1940 just as it had arrived 20 years earlier -- quietly. The benevolent government would never again allow farm product prices to collapse. Mammoth machines had taken the drudgery out of plowing, planting, and harvesting. Fast cars over blacktop county roads had brought farm families within minutes of immense supermarkets. Factories, commercial businesses, railroads, and new federal defense plants were putting everyone back to work who wanted to work, and the Army, Navy, Air Force, Marines and Coast Guard had plenty of vacancies. With more money around, deposits were up at the Farmers Savings Bank, and so too were loans on crops, guaranteed by government. Preparations for another world war were sweeping hard times away, propelling the agricultural heartland toward decades of unprecedented prosperity....and sowing the seeds of new and different troubles. But that's another tale.

I too left Rock Falls and the agricultural heartland, in that autumn of 1940, and just as I had arrived 20 years earlier -- quietly. R. V. had managed another successful North Iowa Fair. Now he could return to the bank, the farm and his Aberdeen Angus cattle. I could return for another year of college in the crisp, autumn air of Minnesota. It was good to be back, dishwashing and all. Within about two weeks of returning, I was very astonished to learn that I had been selected to be the Chapter House Manager for the Alpha Delta Phi fraternity for the school year. I was so pleased and so grateful. All of my meals and my room rent were compensation for managing our cook and maid, collecting member dues, paying bills, tending to the maintenance of the house and grounds, keeping financial records, and reporting on those records to university authorities. And it meant that no longer need I work for meals at the other house and eat in its kitchen, pleasant as that experience had been. I could now take meals with fellow Alpha Delts.

The job was not difficult except for the cook and the maid. Our cook, a huge, conscientious woman, insisted on consulting me about menus and about the exact dollars and cents that she should spend per person per meal. The maid, a precious, tiny Irish lady, Mrs. Wyman, sought my advice and permission on the slightest of details of her tasks in keeping clean and tidy a quite large house with large dining and living room, library, and 12 to 15 private rooms occupied by not so tidy young men. I must have given both cook and maid an impression that, as new manager I intended to run a tight ship. Mrs. Wyman mistakenly called me Mr. Wilkins, which I left uncorrected and which soon would become my nickname in the fraternity. And I ran a tight ship, albeit at the expense of occasional complaints about the food. The school year of 1940-1941 passed quickly.

I did not return to Rock Falls in the summer of 1941. My father was not reappointed to the North Iowa Fair work, due to the blatant nepotism on the part of a board member, so R. V. didn't need me at the bank. I worked at the Federal Reserve Bank of Minneapolis for three months, thanks to my friend Kyle Fossum, who had graduated in the spring, soon starting on an illustrious 37-year career in the Federal Reserve System's top ranks. I commuted to the bank by streetcar, lived in the fraternity house, and being the sole occupant, served as caretaker of the property.

> "HITLER BEGINS WAR ON RUSSIA, WITH ARMIES ON MARCH FROM ARCTIC TO THE BLACK SEA; DAMASCUS FALLS; U.S. OUSTS ROME CONSULS." (June 22, 1941)

My senior year at the University of Minnesota started in September 1941, with war clouds rapidly darkening over America. During that autumn, nearly every male student of my acquaintance seemed certain that this would be his last pre-war year of study. For most, it would be so. Events broadcast by radio to all of us on that December 7 morning had ended the nation's irresolution.

"JAPAN WARS ON U.S. AND BRITAIN; MAKES SUDDEN ATTACH ON HAWAII; HEAVY FIGHTING AT SEA REPORTED." (December 8, 1941)

"U.S. DECLARES WAR, PACIFIC BATTLE WIDENS; MANILA AREA BOMBED; 1,500 DEAD IN HAWAII; HOSTILE PLANES SIGHTED AT SAN FRANCISCO." (December 9, 1941)

"U.S. NOW AT WAR WITH GERMANY AND ITALY; JAPANESE CHECKED IN ALL LAND FIGHTING; 3 OF THEIR SHIPS SUNK, 2D BATTLESHIP HIT." (December 12, 1941)

My college year began with good news. I was to get a second year's appointment as fraternity house manager, for which I was again deeply grateful. Then, in mid-year, came a truly stunning surprise. I received advice from a university scholarships committee that I had been selected as one of only twelve out of some 2,000 senior class men as a member of Iron Wedge, the University of Minnesota's Senior Mens Honor Society. This was indeed an honor. Good thing that I gave up basketball three years earlier.

When the second quarterly term ended in late March of 1942, I had the requisite credits and honor points for the Bachelor of Arts degree, economics major. Now faced with the inevitability of military service, for many of us the looming question was: enlist or wait for the draft? To be drafted exposed us to possible mismatch of man to assignment, not uncommon in the military services. Why not enlist in a service of our choice -- Army, Navy, Air Force, Marines, and then try for assignment to some branch within the service -- infantry, quartermaster, artillery, tanks, medical, chemical, transportation, judge advocate general, finance, flight training, etc -- in which each considered himself best qualified to serve?

My friend Kyle and I, with background qualifications in money, banking, and finance, felt that we were tailor-made for the Finance Department, U.S. Army, as paymasters, accountants, and the "servicemens' bankers." What else! But the concern was, how to be recognized as most suitable for the Finance Department by some recruiting sergeants at the induction station after taking the big step of enlisting. That could be very risky indeed.

Kyle suggested what seemed an outrageously presumptuous approach, the direct route to the top. We should each write a letter to the Chief of Finance, U. S. Army, Washington, D. C., stating our qualifications and requesting assignment to that Department upon enlistment. It was a long shot, but worth a try. To our great surprise, within two weeks, we each received a cordial letter from Colonel Danby, Chief of Finance, U. S. Army, authorizing and directing exactly what we had requested, and advising that orders would follow naming a date and place for enlisting. We were to present the Colonel's letter at the enlistment station, and we were to be assigned to the Army's Finance School at Fort Benjamin Harrison, Indiana, for our basic training. Worth a try, all right.

Armed with this potent directive from on high, I finished my final term of studies, and without waiting to be formally graduated, I returned home to get ready for war. What could be finer than to know what you were to be doing during the war, and that it was a fair match of talent to assignment? (The degree, granted "in absentia," reached me in Europe two years later.)

The morning of May 16, 1942, was not a happy one for my parents and me in Rock Falls. I had received the instructions on the place and time to enlist. The time had come. My parents seemed unusually quiet during that long drive to the induction station at Fort Des Moines, but it was some comfort to have the letter from Colonel Danby for presentation to the military authorities.

We arrived at the appointed hour at the old fort, the handsome, historic frontier setting with its graceful parade ground, a fort erected to repell the Indians nearly a century earlier. Our goodbyes were done quickly, with a very few words, and they drove off. I turned and entered into yet another world. During the next two days of processing -- at times traumatic, at times hilarious -- I became Number 17067522. As I expected, those sergeants were displeased about the letter from Colonel Danby. They had it checked out all the way to the top in Washington, D.C., which meant three days of waiting at the fort alone, since other inductees and enlistees of May 16 had shipped out.

Finally, my shipping orders came through: report to the Commandant, Finance School, at Fort Benjamin Harrison, Indiana, for basic finance training; proceed immediately. What a relief! Soon I was in a jeep, then on a train, and heading east out of Des Moines across the rolling prairies of the heartland. It was spring planting time, and everywhere the rich, black loam was being turned over, smoothed and seeded. My thoughts ranged over the past 20 years during that train journey, believe me, but a not-so-lilting refrain as Cole Porter's "Just One of Those Things" would keep intruding:

> You're in the Army now,
> You're not behind the plow,
> You'll never get rich,
> You son-of-a-bitch,
> You're in the Army now.

When the train crossed the long railroad bridge above the Mississippi River from Iowa into Illinois, about where Elijah Wiltfong had ferried the river on his way west into Ioway country 89 years earlier, I felt that it would be a long time before I would see Iowa again, and then only as a visitor and stranger. But for the moment, with the Army life just ahead, I felt blessed with good luck: free food, free clothing, and free shelter, plus $21.00 every month ....by George!

POSTSCRIPT

ONE MORE TIME!

It was a Saturday morning in mid-summer 1989 when another stranger headed for Rock Falls for a look around the town. His L-1011 flight out of Boston was an hour late in bringing its 300 passengers to Gate 45 in St. Louis, so a one-hour connection had become one minute. He ran through Concourse A, caught the shuttle bus to Concourse D, then a quick sprint brought him to Gate 65.

"Your Waterloo flight has departed," said an attendant at Gate 65. "When's the next flight?" said the stranger. "Tomorrow," she said. "You've got to be kidding," he shouted. Mobile phone in hand, the young lady said, "Maybe I can hold it, if it's still on the ground." A pause, and then, "Jump in this van and I'll run you out." Swerving amid taxiing planes of assorted sizes, the van made it to a revved-up little prop-plane, the stranger hopped in, and soon the hedge-hopper was bouncing along over the confluence of those two great rivers, the Mississippi and the Missouri.

It was clear to the stranger that he was back in the heartland when the pilot's voice on the intercom described the flight and the plane's safety features. That midwestern twang was unmistakable evidence. The ride north over the square patterned section, township, and county borders crosshatching the Iowa prairie was a mercifully short hour and 15 minutes. Touchdown at Waterloo airport was on time to the minute at 1:19 p.m. With rental car contract signed, the stranger was out of the airport and on his way.

It was a pleasant drive up old highway 218, following the valley of the Cedar River to Charles City, then across the prairie to the valley of the Shell Rock to Mason City. The stranger had a pre-arranged stop to make in Mason City so he was able to time his arrival in Rock Falls for about five o'clock. This would allow him an hour for a good look around the town before the six o'clock get-together before the seven o'clock dinner in the gymnasium of the old Falls Township school building. The occasion? It was the night of the reunion of Rock Falls high school graduates.

The stranger drove into town from the south, crossed the railroad on Spring Street, and turned west toward the Rock Island Depot and the Wilkinson Brothers lumberyard to park the car and walk on into town. No depot, no station platform, no stockyards by the sidetrack! No lumberyard, no 12-bin coal shed, no elevator, no feed and cement shed! No two-story lumber shed, no hardware room, no office, and no machinery showroom! Gone, all gone, not a trace! The only remaining bit of evidence of the past was the ancient Fairbanks-Morse weighing scales, dwarfed by another, many times its size for the modern, eight-wheel truck-trailers. Surrounding the scales were seven enormous, circular steel "Stormor" grain bins, all connected overhead with a system of pipes and chutes designed to move soybeans into and out of the bins into railcars and trucks. Where once a large sign mounted atop a little office building read "Wilkinson Lumberyard, R. V. Wilkinson, CHIEF DEALER," now displayed a small sign on a mammoth, all-metal, windowless shed, and it read "Rock Falls Grain Co."

Along the sidewalk north toward the town center, the two original houses on Spring Street had been removed, but the former South Side Hotel, south of the bridge where the road from the west of town joins Spring Street, remained to serve as a residence. Walking on to that graceful concrete-arch structure that spanned the Shell Rock, with its numbers 1929 notched in commenorative stone, the stranger paused. Visible upstream of the bridge, to the west was the rock falls that Elijah Wiltfong selected 140 years ago for his mill dam site. Downstream to the bridge were seen the sand bar, fishing hole, swimming pond, and ice-skating pondage areas. Just to the north of the bridge, hidden by weeds, were the foundation walls of the Old Stone Mill but the hitching posts and rails were gone.

Just ahead, a half a block's walk, was Mill Street -- main street, and of special interest to the stranger. He paused before the sign above the door of the brick building on the corner and read, "Town Hall, Rock Falls, Iowa." The stranger seemed to recall over the door the lettering "Farmers Savings Bank." Next door was a sign, "Rock Falls Tavern," then a vacant boarded up auto repair shop, then a gaping hole, like a missing tooth, where it seemed to the stranger there once stood Bliem Brothers General Store.

Across main street was a neglected, weather-beaten DX gas station, now closed and peeling paint. Where the old Morse Hotel, later Oscar's cluttered ruins, had once stood there was now a patch of weeds. The stranger's gaze came to rest on an attractive old bungalow that faced north on Mill Street, just opposite the "Teacherage," formerly the New York Hotel and Livery Stables. The large expanses of surrounding lawn, the stranger seemed to recall, once grew a large flower garden, a fruit orchard, a place where dogs and chickens and rabbits were housed, and ideal place for sledding down the long slope to the ice-bound river in the winter time.

Strolling north past another vacant lot where Charley Calvert's house once stood, to the intersection of Glover and Madison Streets, the stranger came to the Modern Woodman and Royal Neighbors Hall on one corner, listing badly to leeward, windows boarded over. On another corner, the oldest house in town remained, built of native limestone, where Delos Stickney had lived with his wife Sloane, next to their variety store, where one could always buy a piece of licorice, a store later to become the U.S. Post Office. On a third corner was the metal structure called "Varner's Repair." Wasn't this where Bert Olden's fabulous blacksmith shop had stood? What a loss to the town. Like the Rock Island Depot might have become, Bert's shop may well have made a great museum, a place to display the tools of his bygone trade and perhaps to show Toad Sutton's collections of Indian arrow heads and spear points, perhaps even some 19th century farm machinery and implements. On the fourth corner, the once handsome house of Henry and Anna Krug stood vacant, in disrepair.

At the top of Glover Street was the old stone church, calm and sedate, graceful of line, well placed overlooking the town. What a pleasure to see it still standing. The stranger entered and advanced directly to the pulpit where the Reverend Collister once banged out his sermons to the thump of his fists on the Bible, where Bert Morse rambled through his endless extemporaneous benedictions. What a spot for a June wedding, he thought, like the one 43 years ago that June, when the beautiful young English lady with the quiet charm was married to R. V.'s youngest boy.

As I stood in the church, lost in the remembering of that blessed wedding, the young Reverend Harlen Gillespie approached. "So you were married here, " he said. "You bet," I replied. His congregation numbered 135 members, about what it was back then. It was his last week as minister of the Rock Falls and Plymouth Methodist Churches. Yes, as of old, the poor guy had to start the final song of the nine o'clock service in Rock Falls, and then hurry down the aisle, out to his car, up the dusty road to Plymouth, and into the pulpit barely in time to start the ten o'clock service. It so happened that the program for the next Sunday service listed all of the pastors "of the Plymouth - Rock Falls Charge," from 1867 to 1989, 48 pastors in all, average time for each only two and one-half years. Reverend Gillespie said it was a Methodist policy to move its pastor's frequently.

    Leaving the church, I strolled to the cemetery at the high end of Market Street, a quiet field of gravestones on the hill, with a view over the prairie far to the east and the wooded valley of the Shell Rock to the west. What a serene resting place for all of them...John, Jane, Wendell and Ellen, Theodore and Blanche, Jessie, Leonard and Mabel and Elliot, Valentine and his two wives and his children, Roger, Conrad, Henry, Anna, Rufus, Edith, and Jerome, with countless other pioneers from the world over. I lingered to read more than 200 familiar names of the Falls Township farm-town families, friends, and neighbors from 15 foreign countries and four generations, from the Twenties and the Thirties. I could only bring myself to leave when a flock of feisty, quarrelsome blackbirds or starlings began literally to drive me from the cemetery, swooping down toward me as though to say, "Leave this place, leave it in peace and come another time."

> The curfew tolls the knell of parting day,
> The lowing herd winds slowly o'er the lea,
> The ploughman homeward plods his weary way,
> And leaves the world to darkness and to me.

    The shadows warned that it was getting on to sundown. I lingered again before walking back down into main street and turned east to the school building, such a fine structure after more than 65 years. R. V. had lost a lifelong battle to prevent the town's school from inevitable consolidation with and transfer to Nora Springs, so it wasn't a school any more. But the Rock Falls Betterment Association had saved the building and had thoughtfully renovated and converted it into a fine community center for all ages and public purposes.

    The school yard overlooks the Shell Rock River offering an almost bird's-eye view of the rolling pasture lands beyond. They had become a part of R. V.'s Aberdeen Angus cattle ranch. It is no longer a pasture. It alone made my long trip from Boston well worth while. This was, and it will always remain, the Wilkinson Pioneer Park.

    There is a brief story about this park. During World War II, R. V. Wilkinson traded his Prairie Farm, 160 acres of cropland which his father had farmed before him for the Dave Gildner 280-acre riverside stock farm, so that R.V.'s pastures could graze his herd of purebred cattle within a short walk of his Mill Street home. He called it Sundance Farm. To the few who really knew R. V., and few did, some other purpose was in his mind in acquiring that beautiful setting than just to graze his black angus cattle. After all, he had traded a good quarter section of cropland for a less than good mix of pasture and river west of the river road and poorly drained pasture and about 100 acres of decent cropland east of the road. In fact, the land was inadequate to support the large herd of cattle year-around with grass, hay, and grain.

That half completed, then abandonned, rock fill dam, the work of "Rooosevelt's WPA make-work politicians," had messed up the most scenic segment of the Shell Rock River. That dam and everything else about Roosevelt and the democratic party, come to think of it, rankled R. V. as long as he lived. It would be like R. V. to prove to the Town and County just what an individual could do, without government subsidies, in the lasting interest of conservation and scenic preservation. And he did prove it.

In 1960, Rufus and Edith, joint owners of the farm, set aside 22 of the best river pasture acres adjoining the Town of Rock Falls, named it the Wilkinson Pioneer Park, and with legal assurances that it would forever remain as park and playground for campers and picnickers, gave it to the Cerro Gordo County Conservation Commission. Never mind the cost. R. V. was heard to declare more than once, "By George, Edith, we showed 'em, didn't we?"

There is more to the story. Shortly thereafter, the Commission was persuaded by R. V. and Edith to expand the park by purchasing and dedicating about 40 acres more land to the park and playground. Today, the Wilkinson Pioneer Park encompasses some 61 acres of beautifully tended park, picnic and camping areas along two miles of the Shell Rock River, including shelter house, cooking grills, and volley ball courts, walking trails, a small fishing lake, and now a covered bridge (of all things).

What's more, the Conservation Commission, recognizing the river valley's beauty, and at R. V.'s urging, advanced a Green Belt concept to encompass an additional 287-acre tract of woodland bordering the river toward Nora Springs. With this land and further tracts along the river acquired from time to time, the Green Belt now extends for 12 miles from Rock Falls to Nora Springs, with a scenic drive over its entire length -- about 600 acres along the river, including the nucleus of the idea, Wilkinson Pioneer Park. On the mid-summer evening when I viewed it from the school yard, I could count at least 40 camping vehicles occupying spaces reserved for them, a hundred or more picnickers around the shelter area, with campers' children in large numbers at play in the park, all together probably as many using the park as the resident population of Rock Falls.

Now the sun was setting over the trees to the west of

the bridge and park. It was time for the school reunion. It was a fine dinner at tables set in the school gym, followed by a fine program. Thirty-three members of the Mason City River City Chorus came out to Rock Falls that evening all duded out in flat-topped straw hats, wide suspenders, bow ties, and stiff white shirt collars, and they sang all of the songs from Meredith Wilson's great musical, "The Music Man." The Chorus was highly skilled and wonderfully entertaining.

    I sat at dinner with Truman Motland and Leona Sievertsen, the three of us being the only graduates present of the 1937 class of six, 52 years ago. We compared interests and had a good chat. We talked about the midwestern small towns, as farm-town communities, many dying, swept away by overwhelming forces of technological, economic, and social change, ill-conceived national policies and misguided programs. And we agreed that we were powerless to alter the course of events. We talked of a simpler, quieter, friendlier, fairer time, the days of the Music Man, and the dark days of the agricultural depression. People could take the hard times back then. They were more self-sufficient. We were not so sure about the next time.

    The next morning, with a couple of hours to spare before heading back to Waterloo airport for the flight home, I drove across the few miles of rolling prairie for a last look at Rock Falls and its surrounding farm community. I wanted to see a few of the old familiar farmsteads, those lively centers of farm life with their various implements, threshing machines, strong teams of horses, dairy and beef cattle herds, sheep and pigs, chickens, ducks, and geese, dogs and cats, all of the pens and sheds, barns and silos and gardens and orchards, and windmills. They had been so much a part of the town, keeping it from becoming a ghost town before the coming agricultural revolution.

    What I saw were a dozen ghost farms, to north, south, east, and west on the sideroads leading out of Rock Falls. Where once had been the handsome Willard F. Main farmhouse and outbuildings to the east, there was now a smooth, flat field of grain -- not a structure, not a tree or bush, for reminder of the farmstead, but a driveway leading nowhere. Bert Morse's magnificent old farmhouse that overlooked the Shell Rock River to the west of town....gone, and the outbuildings in shambles of disrepair. To the south, Active Acres....no longer an operating farmstead, just the decaying house. To the north, the once beautiful Edgewood Farm, established by John and Jane Wilkinson in 1872, all of its outbuildings now in the last stages of decay....unpainted for 40 years, the house needing repair. Finally, R. V.'s Sundance Farm, the old Gildner place where R. V. had kept his Aberdeen Angus herd....buildings gone without a trace, just the windmill remaining, its blades turning quietly in the breeze. Five ghost farms within shouting distance of the vacant lot that was once the great Bliem Brothers General Store, five examples of a million or more ghost farms in the American heartland.

You could feel it coming in the Twenties as the tractor took the place of working horses, then in the Thirties when the combines roared through the grain fields, with a driver doing the work of seven men at harvest time. Then came amazing improvements in other labor-saving machinery, and in seeds, feeds, fertilizers, pest and weed controls, and that revolutionary way of milking cows with a machine, saving that back-breaking labor twice a day squeezing the milk out of a cow by hand!

It didn't take long for farmers, working 80, 160, and 320 acres, the old family farm idea, to realize that they could not afford the great new machines and the expensive, efficient equipment to use only a few days a year on small acreages, so they either sold out to a neighbor or bought out a neighbor. Where there was at least one farm on each quarter section in the old days, a 640-acre spread became the prevailing farm unit. Before long it became a section and a half, then two sections, 1,280 acres, then larger. That much land was needed for a single operator to justify a quarter of a million dollars in machinery. Where there were once eight or ten small farmsteads, now one large one was more efficient. The rest were bull-dozed away or left to decay.

A young fellow I talked with near Waterloo previously had a yard full of machinery and 1,000 acres of corn. He spends two weeks in the spring planting, fertilizing, and applying pest control chemicals to the soil. In the fall, he devotes two 24-hour days, around the clock to harvesting his corn crop. The rest of the year he devotes to his trendy haberdashery in the city. At least he stuck around. Many farmers in Iowa plant in spring, head for their lake cottage in northern Minnesota for a summer of fishing, return in the autumn to harvest the grain, sell it to Uncle Sam, store it in huge bins on the farm for Uncle Sam, collect a generous storage fee, and head for Florida or Arizona for the winter.

But if times were so bad in the Twenties and Thirties for the farmers, how come they were so good in the next 40 to 50 years? Why were farm commodity prices at rock bottom back then but high enough thereafter by ten-fold, year in and year out, enabling most farmers to buy machinery worth a quarter of a million dollars or more, pay $3,000 an acre to buy out neighboring quarter or half sections, and bull-doze the farmsteads away for a few more acres of cropland? Why could the big farmers then buy a fishing lodge in Minnesota, a boat in Florida, or a condo in Arizona? Finally, how could net cash income (receipts minus expenses) earned from farming in 1988, as reported by the U. S. Department of Agriculture (USDA), total $57.7 billion in comparison to about minus $2.0 billion in 1933, when there were less than one million real farmers in 1988 and about seven million farmers in 1933?

What has happened is clear. For over five decades the federal government has guaranteed to the farmer prices for farm produce at artificially high levels, irrespective of prevailing market prices, has paid farmers not to produce on good cropland, but rather to place it into conservation reserve, has imposed import restrictions on many low cost commodities grown abroad, and has loaned billions of dollars to farmers at low interest rates to purchase more and more land and equipment. All of these programs to prop up farm prices and reduce farm production and borrowing costs have, since the 1930s, transferred over $400 billion from about 35 million taxpaying Americans, primarily living in cities and towns, to about one million farmers, all of the while destroying the vital fabric of rural life, the farm-town community. After 50 years of subsidies, payments to farmers reached a record in 1987 of $16.7 billion, while in 1988 they had to be satisfied with subsidies of roughly $14.5 billion.

What kinds of farmers get this kind of federal money? The answer is: BIG farmers with lots of land. Here is what President Eisenhower said in his farm message way back in 1954 -- 35 years ago:

> "The chief beneficiaries of our price support policies have been the 2 million larger, highly mechanized farming units which produce about 85 percent of our agricultural output. The individual production of the remaining farms numbering about 3.5 million, is so small that the farmer derives little benefit from price supports."

What has happened to the 5,500,000 farmers from 1954? In 1988, there were only 2,158,800 farms left. But that is only a part of the story. In that year, 1,107,600 or 51.3 percent of these remaining "farmers," to use the term loosely, farmed only 117,000,000 acres, only 11.7 percent of all acres farmed. The average size of these subsistence farms was only 105 acres, and most of these "farmers" had full-time employment off the farm, were hobby farmers, or were retired, or were tax-shelter farmers. How could that be? Ridiculous as it may seem, because the USDA defines a farm as one that sells $1,000 or more of agricultural products a year. Thus, if you raised pumpkins on your half-acre back yard, then sold them in a roadside stand at Halloween time for $1,000, you had become one of 2,158,800 hard-working, disadvantaged "farmers." In 1988, one-half of them grossed less than $2,500 on "farms" which averaged 66 acres in size.

And now here this! In that same year 1988, the other 1,051,200 farmers (48.7 percent) farmed 881,692,000 acres, 88.3 percent of all acres farmed. The average size of all of these commercial farms was 840 acres. The biggest 4.3 percent of these farms averaged 2,614 acres with receipts over $250,000 per year each, some reporting gross receipts of several million dollars each.

Why such odd definitions of farms? Because the USDA has successfully perpetuated the myth that we are still a nation of small farmers, that the "family farm" concept of the quarter-section homestead is still the "typical" farm. The reason is that the USDA needs to continue to justify its bureaucratic existence. Ten years ago, when I worked for a time in Washington, D. C., the joke around town was that there were more employees in the USDA than there were farmers. Farm state politicians have done nothing to dispel this myth, and again for obvious reasons. They need to perpetuate themselves in office.

Well, I had viewed enough ghost farms to sadden me on that mid-summer morning in 1989 when I drove through Falls Township and its two hamlets, Plymouth and Rock Falls. I could still picture the bustle of activities on those busy farms and lively towns of long ago, before technology and the misguided farm policies of self-serving bureaucracies and politicians had deadened the atmosphere and spread an eerie silence over the American heartland. It has all been great for the fortunate few aggressive and ambitious farmers who seized the opportunities to expand, and they are all to be congratulated for their successes. But how about the 20,000 heartland towns, villages, and hamlets in which the mostly elderly inhabitants would hardly know a farmer if they saw one any more. Don't mistake me; there isn't a thing inherently wrong about big farms. They are the most efficient producers. But if one farm family replaces five or ten today, then a once thriving farm town of 300 or 400 residents is almost certain to experience a loss of residents similar to the decline in number of farms.

The 1990 Census of Population tells the larger story. The New York Times of August 30, 1990, carried this story, "Census Data Show Sharp Rural Losses." From 1980 to 1990, Iowa's population declined from 2,914,000 to 2,766,658, a 5.1 percent loss and the largest loss of any State, except depression-ridden West Virginia, during that decade. During the same decade, California gained 23.7 percent, Florida 31.1 percent, and Arizona 33.1 percent. The Times of September 11, 1990 carried another story, "Populations Decline in Rural America: A Product of Advances in Technology," saying:

> "The American small town, which has long occupied a revered place in the nation's history and mythology, is becoming something of a museum piece....In 1950 about 44 percent of

Americans lived on farms and in small towns. That number has declined to about 23 percent ....and 77 percent live in cities and suburbs."

So there you are. It had been a nice visit in those soft, waning summer days of 1989. Now it was time to head out. As I drove southward across the rusting rails of the Rock Island crossing, past R. V.'s once Active Acres farm, and on through Nora Springs to Waterloo airport, the question persisted. What is to become of Rock Falls and those 20,000 other midwestern hamlets with fewer than 500 residents? One thing is certain. You can't bring back the railroad, the depot, the stockyards, the lumberyard, the general store, the bank, the gas station, the blacksmith shop and variety store, the pool hall and barber shop, the old creamery, the Old Stone Mill, the Morse, South Side, and New York House hotels and Livery Stables. You can't bring back the Rock Falls schools. In fact, you wouldn't want to bring it all back. The good old days weren't all that great. In fact, they were downright primitive.

But the problem remains that five decades of agricultural policies and programs that help <u>farmers</u> have severed the vital farm-town linkages -- schools, bank, farm store, churches, lodges, and clubs, and have destroyed the vital farm-town <u>community</u>. This has left Rock Falls and 20,000 other towns, villages, and hamlets in the midwest of less than 500 residents on their own, decaying settlements surrounded by ghost farms, formerly the life support systems for these settlements. Still, despite the heavy odds, Rock Falls survives. And it just might not become another Iowa ghost town.

This is because the town still has much in its favor. It has the church, still alive and active. It has the Park and related Greenbelt, 600 acres of recreation amenities. Unlike so many small towns, it is fortunate in being near a small city for shopping, professional services, and some entertainment. Even closer is a new community college out on the prairie east of Mason City just six miles from Rock Falls. It still has the old school building, and it has a natural environment of scenic beauty along the Shell Rock River valley's wooded, low hills, dales, and meadows, very attractive residential settings. (Although in late summer of 1989 the river itself was choked with a green slime, a virtually dead river.) Perhaps most important, the town has the Rock Falls Betterment Association.

This Association came into existence in the mid-1980s to save the handsome old school building from destruction by ball and chain and bull-dozer. It succeeded and, with limited financial resources and volunteer labor, has since converted the building into a civic center, meeting place for functions for all ages. The new roof, heating system, plumbing, windows, doors, paint, and interior furnishings, it has all cost lots of money. The Association has served the community well and has done an outstanding job.

Of course, one might well ask, what's wrong with this peaceful hamlet as it is, why disturb it? Never mind that we have to drive ten miles for a gallon of gas, a loaf of bread, a haircut, doctor, dentist, and job. Who needs the kind of amenities and infrastructure serving larger towns: 12-year school system, fire department, ambulances, police department, snow removal, water and sewer systems, garbage and trash removal, libraries, an outdoor and indoor public swimming pool, adult education classes, an indoor all-year ice skating rink, nursing homes, golf course, field house, tennis courts, bus service, doctors, dentists, and medical clinic? Maybe a better question: who needs such amenities endured by too many urban dwellers as six-lane freeways in your back yards, the deafening roar of jet aircraft, acrid smell of exhaust fumes, roar of highway traffic, drug wars and crime, the scream of police cars, fire trucks, and the house burglar alarm sirens, night and day?

On balance, Rock Falls may indeed be among the lucky, having the best of both worlds, in effect a quiet suburb of Mason City. There are countless other less fortunate small rural settlements where most residents, and particularly the elderly, are denied basic minimum public services that residents of better located, larger towns, and many small cities have come to expect or take for granted. The Town of Lexington, Massachusetts, where I live, with a population of 30,225, offers all of the services and more listed in the above paragraph and it also has a Council On Aging (COA), which offers an almost bewildering assortment of assistance programs for the elderly. (Of course, property taxes to support these generous services are driving the elderly out of town, but the local authorities seldom talk about that!)

Realistically the fact remains that most of America's agricultural communities, so vibrant in the heyday of the Great Westward Movement and the Settlement of the Interior are now in transition from small market towns, to smaller villages, to even smaller hamlets. The trend is irreversible. Resentment toward farmers who prospered from a benevolent government is not justified, but resentment about the neglect of farm-towns left to die is justified. In effect, these original settlements inevitably became little more than retirement communities. Let's face it, our young families are not attracted to small villages without local schools, doctors, dentists, a shopping center, and social services, even though the parents can readily commute some distance to city jobs.

What might such trends suggest as policy for the politicians to support and programs for the bureaucracies to implement? Given the aging of our people, well documented by demographers, is there not some rationale for providing some measure of public assistance for small and declining rural villages, turning to best use the natural conditions of peace, quiet, tranquillity, and serenity offered by the cleaner, healthier rural settings? Would this not be more rational than government offers of tax incentives, loans, and other special favors to developers to overbuild glitzy and very expensive retirement communities, surrounded by lakes, swimming pools, golf courses, ski slopes, shopping malls, and restaurants....all for those more fortunate of our elderly urban citizenry who can pay for such layouts? Could we not persuade our Senators and Representatives in Washington to consider a few policy initiatives based upon where the needs are as much as where the votes for reelection come from?

I submit that the time has come to regard many of today's rural hamlets as "open retirement homes," deserving of some form of public assistance. As such, these "homes" would be clusters of 25 to 50 or even more dwellings, detached from but historically relating to "centers" for the elderly residents. Together, these dwellings and their "center" would constitute a retirement home without walls, so to speak. Typically, such clusters now center around a church, park, post office, tavern, a meeting hall, but not much else, and all are within a short walk of centers. The clusters lack for several public services unique to those needs of an aging residency. This concept is not unlike a successful program in education in Great Britain. There, access to universities has been limited historically. The national Open University (without walls, grounds, or class facilities) was created by law, available to all adults to achieve a higher education degree....and all by mail.

In practice, a federal program could create Open Retirement Homes, offering "residency" as a voluntary choice of each community's inhabitants, perhaps restricting participants to an age group of say 60 years and older. Services might include a small nursing staff, a rotating in-house day care service, the periodic (twice a month?) presence at each center of an examining physician, a dentist, a hygienist, a dietitian; a prescription drug dispenser, reading programs, study and exercise groups and workshops. Other services come to mind: noon hot-lunch counter, meals on wheels delivery service, small library, a reading room, launderette, field trips, periodic (once a week?) trip to a city by bus for shoppers.

The New York Times, which frequently carries items of concern to the nation's elderly, states the basic problem well in an August 17, 1991 editorial:

"THE BEST HOME FOR OLDER ADULTS

"Even when they're well managed, nursing homes are not the destination of choice for most older

Americans. A survey by the American Association of Retired Persons finds that 86 percent of the elderly want to live out their lives just staying put. Society can help relieve them, and social spending, by helping.

"More and more, in fact, are doing so. Tamar Lewin reported recently in the Times that an increasing number of elderly are living in NORC's -- naturally occurring retirement communities, buildings and neighborhoods in which many older adults remain after the young people leave.

"These homebodies seem to have escaped the notice of Congress. Federal aid has traditionally dealt with aging as a health problem: the quality of life has been dealt with only in passing. Little has been spent on the housebound elderly and Congress has devoted little time to the connections between housing, social services and health policies for older adults who stay home.

"Gerontologists call this phenomenon "aging in Place." Most experts agree that aging in place prolongs independence and the quality of life. A draft report by New York City's Office on Aging says that the elderly who stay at home often help keep neighborhoods together. What's in dispute is how generous communities and governments should be in lending a helping hand.

"There are some obvious problems....no bureaucracy in place to determine whether services requested are really needed....once the floodgates open, the stay-at-homes will order everything on the menu... Purists, sympathetic to the idea of aging in place, warn that too much aid will inevitably turn a resiential program into just another institutional nightmare.

"All these dire predictions could come true. What is surely true is that life at home, except for the acutely ill, is sunnier than life in an institution. That surely is help enough.

"Even money may not be an obstacle....Buried deep in a recent National Inst of Medicine report is a startling statistic: If everyone entering a nursing home this year could wait just one more month, the U. S. would save $3 billion. And that's just the dollar gain."

This is a national problem of growing dimensions. In just 13 States which I defined more or less arbitrarily as midwestern America's agricultural heartland, the 1980 U.S.

Census of Population lists 9,483 rural villages, each with less than 250 inhabitants, about 1,450,000 mostly elderly people, and nearly the same number of villages with 250 to 500 inhabitants, another 3,000,000 or more mostly elderly, and about 900 tiny hamlets each with less than 50 inhabitants. The 1990 Census has surely added to this list. The number of such rural settlements is now well over 20,000.

Many of these old farm-town communities have been dying since the Great Depression, but they linger on, terminally ill but kept just alive by social security payments. They lack for even minimal medical services, necessitating travel of 20 to 40 miles or more for doctors, prescription drugs, and other basic services. They all lack for recreational, educational, cultural, and social opportunities. Their inhabitants are truly "the people left behind" about which a report was prepared by President Lyndon Johnson's National Commission on Rural Poverty in 1967. Too bad that the rural poor have no lobby in the U.S. Congress.

Now, with the problems much greater and remedial programs needed more than ever, how could it all be financed? Well, one could say about any federal program that another $100 million won't add appreciably to a federal debt that today exceeds $4,000,000,000,000 (that's right...trillion) or to a projected 1993 deficit of $365,000,000,000 (that's right...billion). Also, in recent years the Congress and the Bush administration have committed almost $500 billion to bail out savings and loan associations, driven to bankrupcy by corrupt and criminal officials, and billions are shovelled into Congressional Districts for "urban renewal" (read "to buy votes"). The U.S. Department of Agriculture has been guaranteeing farmers' incomes for half a century, a program which reached its peak in 1988 when 50,000 Iowa farmers were supported by net incomes of over $57,000.

American taxpayers give -- yes, give, not loan -- $3 billion a year to Israel and $2 billion a year to Egypt, as we have done for the past 40 years, for a "middle-east stability" (what's that again, stability?) We bashed Iraq to stabilize our oil interests at a cost of more billions. Now, President Clinton proposes a "national service" program that provides to some 150,000 students two years (to start with!) of college tuition for every year volunteered for public "service." That is about $60,000 per student, and a total cost of $9.0 billion to taxpapers, not including a few billion to administer the program. It looks like an enormous potential boondoggle in the making.

What's that? No more government give-away programs for the elderly? Well, then, how about loans? It reminds me of a strong historical precedent for solving a problem in the Great Depression that was remarkably similar to today's problem in elderly rural America, and it was remarkably successful over the past 50 years.

During the 1920s and 1930s, as all cities and larger towns throughout America began to enjoy the great benefits and conveniences of central station electric power production and its distribution into every urban home, shop, and office, darkness followed the sunset in all farm-town communities except for the dim glow of the kerosene lamps and candles. Electric utilities refused service outside their cities' borders, unless farmers and villagers paid for the lines, poles and equipment. A low customer density made a service line to rural areas uneconomic. Like today's doctors, utilities simply couldn't be bothered about serving rural America's farms and homes, saying bluntly, "If you want electricity, come and get it."

The Roosevelt administration recognized the problem immediately, appropriating in 1935 $100 million in emergency relief funds to a newly-created Rural Electrification Administration (REA) in the Department of Agriculture. The REA was empowered to make loans to finance the needed power line construction. The loans were required by law repayable within 25 years, with interest rates equal to the average payable on U. S. obligations of ten or more years maturity issued during the preceding year. A Rural Electrification Act of 1936 created a ten-year program of loan assistance, and within six years loans to local REA cooperatives or associations exceeded $374 million. Billions more were loaned to the local coops over the next decades. The 1936 Act enlarged the purposes of the loans to include wiring of members' premises and buying and installing farm and home electric appliances and equipment. Few New Deal programs brought such great and lasting blessings to rural America, and without cost to the taxpayers.

I submit that the time has come for federal policy to recognize the rural elderly problem by legislating a Rural Retirement Act of 1993, creating a Rural Retirement Administration (RRA), in the Department of Agriculture, to loan money to sorely-needed "Rural Retirement Cooperatives." Such a program is long overdue, it would be self-liquidating, and it would save billions of federal tax dollars now wasted on costly retirement services.

Like the REA electric coops of the Depression era, so too with RRA retirement coops as now proposed, the service area need not be confined to a single farm-town community. It could encompass two or three farm-town areas. And like the REA electric coops, the RRA coops would be operated by a Board of Directors, a general manager, full-time staff, and temporary help, in addition to designated professional services available on a periodic basis. The key is that all members of a "cluster" would reside in their own homes while each "Center" of the larger retirement "homes" would house and centralize the facilities and activities. Like the REA coop loans of old, the RRA coop loans, probably in a range of $50,000 to $100,000 for each Center, would pay at the going rates of interest on federal obligations, for amortization in 25 years, and guaranteed by the government if sources of funds were other than the government.

How about member charges? Again, like the REA electric coops, where electric service is billed under a two-part rate structure, one part being the capacity (a readiness to serve) charge, the other an energy (for use of the capacity over time) charge, thus a kilowatt charge as well as a kilowatt-hour charge, the same strucutre is uniquely suitable for RRA coop charges. The capacity charges would be levied on each member, a fixed amount per month regardless of use of Center facilities, for the purpose of paying off (amortizing) fixed costs of the Center; while the use charge would be levied according to each member's use of the Center's facilities, i.e., a variable amount billed monthly for such things as meals, bus trips, pills, dental and doctor fees, lab tests, etc. Clearly, the retirement services and Center facilities could be paid for precisely as electric power services have always been paid for.

One final direct similarity between REA and RRA cooperatives. Just as REA members during the 1930s were able to borrow federal funds to buy electrical appliances for their homes and farming operations, RRA members during the 1990s should be eligible for loans to purchase health care equipment for use in their individual homes.

Sound good? Well, as with everything, there are problems. For one thing, who cares enough about the silent, forgotten, unorganized rural elderly to do anything about their plight? For another, can politicians be expected to redirect their self-interest priorities from the organized urban vote to a broader public interest in issues of fairness and compassion for the elderly rural voter? For another, can the organized opposition of the existing nursing home "industry" and the American Medical Association's lobbyists kill such desirable legislation? It would seem that both would benefit in the long term, just as electric utilities, bitterly opposed to the REA coop movement from the start, profited handsomely from it when they finally came to realize that the coops were among the best of most power companies' customers.

None of these problems is insurmountable. Perhaps I have exaggerated them. There is reason for renewing hope in this atmosphere of change now sweeping the nation after a deadening decade of waste, fraud, and greed. With cooperation replacing conflict and a clearer sense of national priorities, perhaps these and other problems will turn out to be opportunities.

So, on a hopeful note, ends my tale of a town in the American agricultural heartland. It was a time long, long ago, so long that few today can recall or even relate to the severity and intensity of the Great Depression, casting such a pall over the land and so profoundly altering the course of human events. I sincerely hope the readers have enjoyed my tale of life and times in and around Rock Falls, Iowa, as much as I have enjoyed all of the remembering and the writing of those times. Thanks for the memories, Rock Falls. As R. V. would have said, "Those were the days....by George."

NOTES

P. 1   1st paragraph. This was the place. Rock Falls Historical Book Committee, <u>Rock Falls Historical Book</u> (unpublished) 1977, pp. 5-7. Activities of the Wiltfong family described in parts of the first four chapters draw upon that book and the Committee's voluminous background materials and hand-written notes made available to the author by Committee member Ms. Merle White.

P. 6   "slant-eyed, copper-skinned" Federal Writers Project of the Works Project Administration, <u>Iowa, A Guide to the Hawkeye State</u>, New York, Hastings House, 1938, pp. 32-35. See also Silverberg, <u>The Mound Builders of America</u>, Greenwich, New York, Graphic Society, 1968.

P. 6   They spoke 275 languages. National Geographic Society, <u>Indians of North America</u>, Map Supplement to the National Geographic, December 1972, p. 739A, Vol. 142, No. 6.

P. 6   Before they met....and Chickasaw. <u>Ibid</u>.

P. 6   The Ioway, meaning "dustyface"... Federal Writers Project, <u>A Guide</u>... p.36

P. 7   ...shores of a "clear lake." <u>Ibid</u>., pp. 285-286

P. 7   Vast areas...and New Spain. Morrison, Samuel Eliot, <u>The European Discovery of America</u>, the Northern Voyages, A.D. 500-1600, New York, Oxford University Press, 1971

P. 8   ...entire North American Contient. For a detailed account of these three events, see Merk, Frederick, History of the Westward Movement, New York, A. A. Knopf, 1946, pp. 138-140.

P. 8   ...nine-year-old French and Indian War... Encyclopaedia Britannica, Chicago, William Benton, Publisher, 1967, Vol. 22, pp. 608-609.

P. 10   Twenty-five years elapsed... Ibid., Vol 22, pp. 611-629.

P. 10   ...the Land Ordinance Act of 1785... Merck, op. cit., pp. 67-133

P. 10   ...the landscape of the heartland. Ibid., pp. 104-105. See also Kirkland, Edward C., A History of American Economic Life, New York, F. S. Croft, 1946, pp. 138-139.

P. 11   (of many to follow). Ibid., pp. 139-140; see also, Merck, op. cit., pp. 106-115; see also U. S. Department of Agriculture, Land, Yearbook of 1958, pp. 208-209.

P. 13   "with bewildering rapidity," Kirkland, op. cit., p. 149.

P. 13   "passengers of foreign birth" Wright, Chester Whitney, Economic History of the United States, New York, McGraw-Hill, 1949, pp. 214-215, 247-248.

P. 14   ...in 1816 and 1818, respectively. Encyclopaedia Britannica, Vol. 22, "The Rise of the American Nation," pp. 620-629.

P. 14   Arkansas entered...in 1836. Ibid., p 628.

P. 15   ...well-publicized fact. Wright, op. cit., p. 70.

P. 15   ...principle effectively demolished. Kirkland, op, cit., pp. 140-141.

P. 16   The 100-year totals were: Wright, op. cit., pp. 448-454.

P. 16   Robert Fulton proved... Ibid., pp. 277-278

P. 17   ...children of these"marriages." Sage, Leland, A History of Iowa, Ames, The Iowa State University Press, 1974, pp. 44-46

P. 17   and desolate land. Merk, op. cit., pp. 171-172

P. 17   The Black Hawk Purchase....for settlement. Federal Writers' Project, A Guide..., pp. 44-46

P. 18   ...for the rest of the decade. Ibid., pp. 46-47.

P. 18   ...harsh settlement...Indian nations. Ibid., p. 48.

P. 19   ...north-south political balance. Ibid., p. 51.

CHAPTER II

P. 22   The Spirit Lake Massacre...before the good times came. For a scholarly treatment of this subject, see Thorton, Russell, American Indian Holocaust and Survival, Population History Since 1492, Norman, Okla., University of Oklahoma Press, 1987.

P. 22   ...the Grindstone War... Federal Writers' Project, A Guide..., op. cit., pp. 284

P. 22   ...the Spirit Lake Massacre. Ibid., pp. 409-411

P. 23   During the next spring... See first note to Chapter I above re Rock Falls Historical Book.

P. 28   Hundreds, perhaps thousands of such grist mills... Wright, Carl, in Mason City Globe Gazette, "Survey of Old Mills in Iowa...," February 20, 1944. This newspaper story details the histories, locations, and types of water-powered grinding mills operated in norther Iowa in the 19th century.

P. 29   Kirkland, op. cit., p. 300; Wright, op. cit., pp. 314, 585; Merk, op. cit., pp 435-436. Each of these economic histories details the development of large milling centers in the agricultural heartland.

P. 30   Iowa's Governor Samuel Kirkwood... Federal Writers' Project, A Guide..., op. cit., p. 54.

P. 31   Ibid., p. 56. See also Schlesinger, Arthur Meier, Political and Economic History of the United States, 1829-1925, New York, The McMillan Company, 1925. p.180.

P. 33   ...builders of the American Empire. Merck, op. cit. pp. 230-239.

P. 33   ...national Preemption Act in 1830. Ibid., pp. 233-234.

P. 33   ...further inducing the rapidity of settlement. Ibid., p. 235.

P. 33   The Homestead Act of 1862... Ibid., pp. 236, 401, 433.

P. 34   "rapidity of a prairie fire" Kirkland, op. cit., p. 362. See also the excellent account of Iowa's railroad-building period in Sage, op, cit., pp. 108-115, 204-208.

P. 34   ...companies at low interest rates. Ibid., pp. 363-368.

P. 35   ...largesse in the history of any nation. Ibid., pp. 376-381.

P. 35   ...widened to 15 and 20 miles. Ibid., p. 78.

P. 35   ...pressed westward across Iowa. Federal Writers' Project, A Guide..., op. cit., p. 54.

P. 35   ...3,000 miles of trackage... Ibid., pp. 87-88.

P. 36   ...James J. Hill, the master builder..., Martin, Albro, James J. Hill and the Opening of the Northwest, New York, Oxford University Press, 1976, pp. 288-292.

CHAPTER III

P. 48   ...since 1846 but moved in 1859. Encyclopaedia Britannica, Vol 12, p. 508.

P. 48   (Disciples of Christ, 1881), Ibid., pp. 509-511.

P. 48   "Of all the motley crowd..." Rock Falls Historical Book Committee background research notes, source unknown.

P. 55   ...by Professor Leland Gage. Sage, A History of Iowa, op. cit., pp. 92-96.

P. 58   ...old iron and wooden share. Encyclopaedia Britannica, Vol. 9, p. 89.

P. 58   ...through the mid-1930s. Ibid., Vol. 9, p. 91.

P. 59   ...working the prairie soils. Sage, A History of Iowa, op. cit., pp. 69-70.

CHAPTER IV

P. 61   Mark Twain aptly named it the Gilded Age. Josephson, Matthew, The Robber Barons, New York, Harcourt Brace, 1934, Foreword.

P. 62   ...2,232,000 inhabitants. Encyclopaedia Britannica, Vol. 12, p. 504.

P. 62   "astride the crossroads and gateways of commerce," Munn v. Illinois, 94 U.S. 113, 1876, as discussed in Electric Power & Government Policy, The Twentieth

Century Fund, 1948, pp. 94-95.

P. 63 ...manufactured clay products. Federal Writers' Project, A Guide..., op. cit., pp. 94-95.

P. 63 In 1824, Joseph Aspdin patented... Encyclopaedia Britannica, Vol. 5, p. 154.

P. 63 ...hard coherent mass. Ibid., pp. 155-158.

P. 65 Two Germans,... Ibid., Vol. 2, p. 865.

P. 65 ...were sold in 1904. Ibid., p. 867.

P. 65 Mass production per se... Ibid., Vol. 12, p. 505: see also Federal Writers' Project, A Guide... p. 107.

P. 68 "free high school education..." Ibid., pp. 107-110.

P. 78 ...in the front line trenches. Wright, Economic History, op. cit., p. 757.

P. 79 ...to our European allies. Encyclopaedia Britannica, Vol. 15, p. 837. See also Beard, Charles A. and Mary r., America in Midpassage, Vol. II, MacMillan, New York, 1939, p. 407.

P. 79 ...all countries of 7,450,000. Wright, Economic History, op. cit., p. 758.

P. 79 ...from diseases as from battles. Federal Writers' Project, A Guide..., op. cit., p. 59.

P. 79 ...a patriotic duty. Wright, Economic History, op. cit., p. 749.

P. 80 ...to a 272 in May 1920. Wright, op. cit., pp. 759-765.

P. 81 ...the day of reckoning. Sage, A History of Iowa, op. cit., pp. 249-254.

CHAPTER V

(All source material from Rock Falls Historical Book Committee)

CHAPTER VI

P. 94 ...the Nobel Peace Prize... Encyclopaedia Britannica, Vol. 23, p. 554.

P. 94 ...for the 1920 race. Schlesinger, Arthur M., Jr. The Age of Roosevelt, The Crisis of the Old Order, 1919-1933, Houghton Mifflin Company, Boston, 1957 p.49.

E

P. 94   "...a long line of frugal..." Ibid., p. 56.

P. 94   Cox and Roosevelt campaigned... Encyclopaedia Britannica, Vol. 11, p. 94.

P. 95   ...40 percent in the two-year period. Wright, Economic History..., op. cit., pp. 765-766. As a general note, all agricultural grains and livestock prices as noted for several different years throughout this book were taken from Kansas State Board of Agriculture, 62nd Annual Report and Farm Facts, 1978, most prices having been recorded since 1866.

P. 99   "father of wireless telegraphy" Kirkland, A History... pp. 426, 653; Josephson, The Robber Barons, op. cit., pp. 384-385.

P. 120 Sage, A History of Iowa, op. cit., pp. 186-195.

P. 121 ...exceeded 6,000 closings. Ibid, p. 254.

P. 123 ...the last to receive electric service. Encyclopaedia Britannica, Vol. 8, pp. 209-210.

CHAPTER VII

P. 129 "The New Day." Encyclopaedia Britannica, Vol. 20, p. 692.

P. 129 "I do not choose to run..." Schlesinger, The Age of Roosevelt, p. 87

P. 130 ...all nations with the United States. Ibid., p. 84; See also Kirkland, op. cit., pp. 693-694, 701-703.

P. 130 ...income over the same years. Kirkland, op. cit., p. 704.

P. 131 ...sum of $8,440,000,000. Ibid., pp. 704-705.

P. 131 ...nearly $2,000 per year!!! Author's calculations based upon 1990 Census of Population data and the monthly Federal Reserve System Bulletins, 1992, 1993.

P. 131 "..in this dazzling era." Kirkland, op. cit. p. 705.

P. 131 ...declined in June of 1928. Ibid., p. 706; see also Wright, op. cit., pp. 774-779.

P. 132 ...far below production costs. Sage, A History of Iowa, pp. 277-278.

P. 132 "Prosperity...around the corner." Schlesinger, The Age of Roosevelt, op. cit., pl 162.

F

P. 134 Ibid., <u>The Crisis of the Old Order</u>. pp. 162-163.

P. 135 "With no money..." Ibid., p. 171.

P. 135 "If America meant anything..." Ibid., p. 170.

P. 138 ...a sad and disgraceful incident. Sage, <u>A History of Iowa</u>, op. cit., pp. 289-298.

P. 140 Beard, <u>America in Midpassage</u>, op. cit., p. 149

P. 140 Schlesinger, The Age of Roosevelt, <u>The Crisis of the Old Order</u>, op. cit., pp. 440-455.

P. 140 ...refuge in February. Sage, <u>A History of Iowa</u>, p. 301.

P. 145 ...recapitalized and sold. Ibid., p. 293-294

P. 148 ...72 consecutive wringers... <u>Encyclopaedia Britannica</u>, Vol. 11, pp. 726-727.

P. 149 referendum on July 10, 1933. Sage, op. cit., p. 301

CHAPTER VIII

P. 166 ...and raise farm prices! Sage, op. cit., p. 299.

P. 167 ...Golden Age of Agriculture. U.S. Department of Agriculture, <u>The Yearbook of Agriculture,</u> "After A Hundred Years," pp. 543-546; Schlesinger, pp. 27-84.

P. 167 ...Commodity Credit Corporation. Ibid., pp. 557-561. For more detail, see Economics Section, pp. 506-614.

P. 170 ...the young J. Edgar Hoover. <u>The New York Times, Page One</u>, Major Events, 1920-1988, Times Books, 1988, Headline page for July 23, 1934.

P. 171 Massive infusions of cash... Wright, op. cit., p. 792.

CHAPTER IX

P. 188 ...grip of the Great Depression. Garraty, John A., <u>The Great Depression</u>, Garden City, Anchor Books, 1987, Chapter X, "How it Ended," pp. 238-257.

P. 197 Acheson, Dean, <u>Present At The Creation</u>, "My Years in the State Department," W. W. Norton, 1969, pp. 21-26. See also Sherwood, Robert E., <u>The White House Papers of Harry Hopkins,</u> Eyre & Spottiswoode, 1948, p. 273.

P. 197 Acheson, op. cit., pp. 27-30.

P. 197 Sherwood, op. cit., pp. 275-276; Wright, pp. 796-810. ...the Great Depression was on its way out.

SELECTED BIBLIOGRAPHY

    Those who, over the past 60 years, have been fascinated by American history generally and the history of midwestern America specifically, as I have been, know of the vast literature about events of the last two hundred years 1790 to 1990. There are many volumes on such major epics as The Opening of the West, The Great Westward Movement, Settling the Interior, Frontier America, the Agricultural Empire, The Railroad Building Era, and others.

    Two volumes remain, in my view, unexcelled in the excellence of their coverage and interpretation of some considerable economic aspects of those major growth periods in the American heartland. They are: Kirkland's <u>A History of American Economic Life</u>, and Wright's <u>Economic History of the United States</u>. These great works, assigned to me as textbooks in economic history at the University of Minnesota, Graduate School of Economics, in 1949, have found a place "between the lines" of many pages of <u>Rock Bottom</u>. Other source material too voluminous to cite <u>meticulously</u>, but very helpful to me, have been the several publications of the U.S. Department of Agriculture <u>Yearbooks</u>.

    In writing my small history of a small part of America"s heartland, it seemed unnecessary to footnote virtually every page with citations to so many scholars merely to assure deserved attributions, particular as Kirkland's and Wright's works so thoroughly distill those of no less than 900 others whom they cite. Therefore, the following is a partial list on which I could draw from my library, keep-footnotes to a minimum. My own addition to the historical

a

literature, focussing as it does on one small town and one family in that town, needs no footnoting, as it has relied upon personal observations and experiences.

* * * * * * * *

Acheson, Dean, <u>Present at the Creation</u>, My Years in the State Department, (New York, W. W. Norton & Co., 1969)

Adams, James Truslow, <u>The Epic of America</u>, (New York, Blue Ribbon Books, 1931)

Adams, James R., <u>The Big Fix</u>, The Inside Story of the Great American Bank Crisis, (New York, John Wiley & Sons 1989)

Beard, Charles A. and Mary R., <u>America in Midpassage</u>, Vol. III, The Rise of American Civilization, (New York, MacMillan, 1939)

Billington, Ray Allen, <u>Westward Expansion</u>, A History of the American Frontier, (New York, MacMillan, 2d Edition 1949)

Blakeless, John, Ed., <u>The Journals of Lewis and Clark</u>, A New Selection, (New York, Mentor, 1964)

Board of Governors, <u>The Federal Reserve System</u>, Purposes and Functions, (Washington, D.C., The Federal Reserve System, 1963)

Bovard, James, <u>The Farm Fiasco</u>, How Federal Agriculture Policy Squanders Billions of Dollars a Year, Sacrifices the Poor to the Rich, and Gives Congressmen and Bureaucrats Vast Arbitrary Power Over American Citizens, (New York, Kampmann, 1989)

Broehl, Wayne, <u>John Deere's Company</u>, A History of Deere & Company and Its Times, (Moline, Il., Ferguson Publ., 987)

Carpenter, Allan, <u>Between Two Rivers</u>, Iowa, Year by Year, 1846-1940, (Mason City, Iowa, Klipto Loose Leaf, 1940)

Chase, Stuart, <u>Idle Money, Idle Men</u>, (New York, Harcourt Brace, 1938)

Clark, Evan, Et. al., <u>Electric Power and Government Policy</u>, (The Twentieth Century Fund, New York, 1948)

Congdon, Don, Editor, <u>The Thirties</u>, A Time to Remember, (New York, Simon and Schuster, 1962)

De Voto, Bernard, <u>Across the Wide Missouri</u>, (New York, Bonanza Books, 1946)

_____ <u>Year of Decision, 1846</u>, (Boston, Little Brown Company, 1943)

_____ <u>The Course of Empire,</u> (Cambridge, Riverside Press, 1952)

Encyclopaedia Britannica, Inc., *Encyclopaedia Britannica*, (Chicago, William Benton Publishers, 1967)

Federal Writers' Project of the Works Project Administration Iowa, *A Guide to The Hawkeye State*, (New York, Hastings House, 1938)

Friedman, Benjamin, *Day of Reckoning*, The Consequences of American Economic Policy Under Reagan and After, (New York, Random House, 1988)

Garraty, John A., *The Great Depression*, (Garden City, Anchor Books, 1987)

Heilman, Grant, Ed., *Farm Town*, A Memoir of the 1930s, (Lexington, MA, Stephen Greene, Penguin, 1974)

Ickes, Harold L., *The Secret Diary of Harold L. Ickes*, (New York, Simon and Schuster, 1953)

Iowa Department of *Agriculture, Iowa Agricultural Statistics*, 1985 and 1989, (Des Moines, Iowa Crop and Livestock Reporting Service, 1985 and 1989)

James, Marquis, *The Life of Andrew Jackson*, Part One, The Border Captain, Part Two, Portrait of a President, (The Bobb-Merrill Company, New York, 1938)

Josephson, Matthew, *The Robber Barons*, The Great American Capitalists, (New York, Harcourt Brace, 1934)

Kantor, MacKinlay, *Spirit Lake*, (New York, World Publishing, 1961)

Kennedy, Paul, *The Rise and Fall of the Great Powers*, (New York, Random House, 1987)

Keylin, Arleen, Editor, *The Depression Years* as reported by The New York Times (New York, Arno Press, 1976)

Key, V. O., Jr., *Politics, Parties, and Pressure Groups*, 3d Edition, (New York, Thomas Y. Crowell Company, 1952)

Kingman, William K., *1929, The Year of the Great Crash*, (New York, Harper & Row, 1989)

Kirkland, Edward C., *A History of American Economic Life*, (New York, F. S. Croft, Revised Edition, 1946)

Leech, Margaret, *In the Days of McKinley*, (New York, Harpers, 1959)

Martin, Albro, *James J. Hill & The Opening of the Northwest*, (New York, Oxford University Press, 1976)

Merk, Frederic, *Manifest Destiny and Mission in American History*, A Reinterpretation, (New York, Knopf, 1963)

Merk, Frederic, *History of the Westward Movement*, (New York, Knopf, 1978)

Morrison, Samuel Eliot, *The European Discovery of America*, The Northern Voyages, A.D. 500-1600, (New York, Oxford University Press, 1971)

Parkman, Francis, *The Oregon Trail*, (New York, Farrar & Rinehard, 1931)

Pilzer, Paul Zane, *Other People's Money*, The Inside Story of the S&L Mess, (New York, Simon and Shuster, 1989)

Rock Falls Historical Book Committee, *Rock Falls Historical Book* (unpublished) 1977

Sage, Leland, *A History of Iowa*, (Cedar Falls, University of Northern Iowa Press, 1971)

Schlesinger, Arthur Meier, *Political and Social History of the United States, 1829-1925*, (New York, The MacMillan Company, 1925)

Schlesinger, Arthur M., Jr, *The Age of Roosevelt*,
The Crisis of the Old Order
The Politics of Upheaval
The Coming of the New Deal
(Boston, Riverside Press, 1957, 1959, and 1960)

Sellers, Charles, and May, Henry, *A Synopsis of American History*, University of California at Berkeley Series, (Rand McNally and Company, Chicago, 1963)

Sherwood, Robert E., *The White House Papers of Harry L. Hopkins*, Vol I, September 1939 - January 1942, (Eyre & Spottiswoode, 1948)

Silverberg, Robert, *The Mound Builders of America*, (Greenwich, New York Graphic Society Ltd, 1968)

The *Cannon Falls Beacon*, Silas Shelton Lewis, Ed., Cannon Falls, MN, May 24, 1929.

The *Cerro Gordo Press*, Mason City, Iowa, January 8, 1858.

The *Chicago Herald*, Chicago, Il. December 8, 1915.

The *Chicago Herald Examiner*, Chicago, Il, May 8, 1919.

The *City Express*, Mason City, Iowa, 1871-1874 (some issues)

The *Des Moines Register & Tribune*, Des Moines, Iowa, 1920-1977 (some issues)

The <u>Mason City Globe Gazette and Times</u>, Mason City, Iowa, May 8, 1919.

The <u>Mason City Globe Gazette</u>, Mason City, Iowa, 1920-1936, (some issues)

<u>The New York Times, Page One, Major Events, 1920-1988</u> as Presented in The New York Times, (Times Books, 1988)

<u>The New York Times, The Depression Years</u>, Arleen Keylin, Editor.(Arno Press, New York, 1976)

Thornton, Russell, <u>American Indian Holocaust and Survival</u>, A Population History Since 1492, (Norman, Okla, and London, England, University of Oklahoma Press, 1987)

de Tocqueville, Alexis, <u>Democracy in America</u>, Volume 2, The Henry Reeve Text as Revised by Francis Bowen, (New York, Vintage Books, 1945)

Tuchman, Barbara W., <u>The Proud Tower</u>, A Portrait of The World Before the War, 1890-1914 (New York, MacMillan, 1962)

U. S. Department of Agriculture <u>Yearbook</u>
  <u>After 100 Years</u>, 1962
  <u>Crops in Peace and War</u>, 1950-1951
  <u>Land</u>, 1958
  <u>Insects</u>, 1952
  <u>Grass</u>, 1948
  <u>Science in Farming</u>, 1943-1947
  <u>Keeping Livestock Healthy</u>, 1942
  <u>Climate and Man</u>, 1941
  <u>Farmers World</u>, 1964

Waller, Robert James, <u>Just Beyond the Firelight</u>, Stories and Essays, (Ames, Iowa State University Press, 1988)

Wilkinson, Herbert E., <u>Sun Over Cerro Gordo</u>, (Iowa City, University of Iowa Press, 1952)

Will, George, <u>The Morning After</u>, American Successes and Excesses, 1981-1986 (New York, The Free Press, 1986)

Wright, Chester Whitney, <u>Economic History of the United States</u> (New York, McGraw-Hill, 1949, 2d edition)

<u>Wall Street Journal</u>, New York, 1980-1993 (various issues)